W9-CPY-895

Books of Merit

Breaking the Silence

ALSO BY TED BARRIS

MILITARY HISTORY

Victory at Vimy: Canada Comes of Age, April 9–12, 1917

Days of Victory: Canadians Remember, 1939–1945
(with Alex Barris, 1st edition, 1995)

Deadlock in Korea: Canadians at War, 1950–1953

Canada and Korea: Perspectives 2000 (contributor)

Juno: Canadians at D-Day, June 6, 1944

Days of Victory: Canadians Remember, 1939–1945
(Sixtieth Anniversary edition, 2005)

Behind the Glory: Canada's Role in the Allied Air War

OTHER NON-FICTION

Fire Canoe: Prairie Steamboat Days Revisited

Rodeo Cowboys: The Last Heroes

Positive Power: The Story of the Edmonton Oilers Hockey Club

Spirit of the West: The Beginnings, the Land, the Life

Playing Overtime: A Celebration of Oldtimers' Hockey

Carved in Granite: 125 Years of Granite Club History

Making Music: Profiles from a Century of Canadian Music
(with Alex Barris)

101 Things Canadians Should Know About Canada (contributor)

BREAKING THE SILENCE

VETERANS' UNTOLD STORIES

FROM THE GREAT WAR TO AFGHANISTAN

TED BARRIS

THOMAS ALLEN PUBLISHERS

TORONTO

Library and Archives Canada Cataloguing in Publication

Barris, Ted
Breaking the silence : veterans' untold stories from the Great War to Afghanistan / Ted Barris.

ISBN 978-0-88762-465-0

1. Canada—Armed Forces—Biography.
2. Veterans—Canada—Biography.
3. Canada—History, Military—20th century.
4. Canada—History, Military—21st century.
I. Title.

U54.C2B372 2009 355.0092'271 C2009-902632-5

Editor: Janice Zawerbny
Jacket image: Stefano Rellandini

Published by Thomas Allen Publishers,
a division of Thomas Allen & Son Limited,
145 Front Street East, Suite 209,
Toronto, Ontario M5A 1E3 Canada

www.thomas-allen.com

Canada Council for the Arts

The publisher gratefully acknowledges the support of the Ontario Arts Council for its publishing program.

We acknowledge the support of the Canada Council for the Arts, which last year invested $20.1 million in writing and publishing throughout Canada.

We acknowledge the Government of Ontario through the Ontario Media Development Corporation's Ontario Book Initiative.

We acknowledge the financial support of the Government of Canada through the Book Publishing Industry Development Program (BPIDP) for our publishing activities.

13 12 11 10 09 5 4 3 2 1

Printed and bound in Canada

For Charley Fox . . . the torch bearer who served his country, never forgot his comrades, and helped break the silence.

CONTENTS

Acknowledgments

The process of acknowledging veterans began the first time I attended a Remembrance Day observance and realized I didn't know what I was supposed to remember. It's taken a good part of my life as a journalist, broadcaster, author, educator, and Canadian citizen to solve that dilemma. The assembly of this book has helped me recognize the gaps in my knowledge of veterans' experiences. It's dispelled some myths. It's introduced many truths. It's given me an array of personalities and stories that I can recall whenever I'm asked to explain who veterans are, what they went through, and why their time in uniformed service deserves our attention. It's also allowed me the privilege of sharing my revelations.

I first offer thanks to each man and woman veteran I've ever encountered. They number in the thousands. I won't list them here because you will meet many of them in the pages that follow. But I do wish to acknowledge that for them sometimes giving the gift of memory was painful and seemingly unrewarding. Often it took telling and retelling for me to understand. On occasion it led us into uncharted emotional territory. I just hope this book begins to compensate that unexpected pain, that repetition, and all those hours spent on the porch, at the kitchen table, or in the downstairs den with that guy holding a microphone and notepad. The blessings of my association with veterans are the close friendships I've found among them. The curse is that their age has often cut short our time as friends. Too many have passed during the creation of this book.

For many years, the fraternity that has drawn veterans together—inside and outside the military—has likewise invited me into its confidence. Legions, institutes, societies, publications, and commemorative associations have delivered contacts, provided much-needed context, and have always encouraged my work. Similarly, the traditional information sources—museums, archives, libraries, government records departments—have dutifully provided ample data whenever I've requested it. As well, the not so traditional sources—militaria collectors and war history clubs—have always stepped forward too. Most have asked for nothing in return, but to keep veterans' stories in print, on the air, and online. Perhaps all these organizations have come to realize—if a little late—that veterans deserve a higher public profile.

Though it may sound odd, I would also like to acknowledge my good fortune. It's not a spiritual thing, but sometimes the reason I picked up the phone and called that day, followed a gut feeling or instinct, saved that odd news clipping from the paper, or sometimes in frustration relied on simple guesswork, was serendipitous. My wife, Jayne MacAulay, has often insisted that my encounters with so many of these people and these wartime events were "meant to be." Neither she nor I is a fatalist, but neither do we want these delicious coincidences to stop. Nor would I want the attitude of my family through such enterprises to change. Like my parents always did, Jayne, our daughters Quenby and Whitney, and their husbands (John David Massey and Ian Ross respectively), as well as my sister Kate Barris, have sometimes wondered about my preoccupation with veterans and their recollections. They have never doubted my conviction to write this personal account of what I found.

Acknowledging one's publishers may seem self-serving, but in part this journey began at their invitation. Because he has always been as eager to know about his veteran father as I was about mine, Patrick Crean, my publisher, has spurred my curiosity from the beginning of this project. I thank my editors, Janice Zawerbny and Wendy

Thomas, for their guidance and encouragement throughout, and David Glover for his input above and beyond the job of marketing manager. My gratitude, as well, to designer Gordon Robertson and image specialist Beth Crane, for their vision—literally and figuratively—as we assembled this book. Thomas Allen Publishers is a publishing team that answers its own telephones . . . and listens.

Despite all I've learned about life and death in the time and place of war—from those who survived it—I still don't claim to know all of what I am supposed to remember during two minutes of silence on November 11. I believe, however, that I have learned to look past the cenotaph and beer parlour, beyond the service ribbons and berets, and sometimes through the tears or laughter of memory. My quest to replace veterans' silence with the revelations of their experience continues.

— Ted Barris, 2009

1

BEYOND REMEMBRANCE

ON THE SECOND-LAST DAY of 2008, I spoke at the funeral of an air force veteran remembering his contribution as a Second World War flying instructor. John Stene had fled his homeland—Norway—as the Nazis invaded, taught expatriate countrymen to fly military aircraft at the Toronto Island "Little Norway" training school, then in 1943–44 piloted Halifax bombers over Europe through twenty-nine missions, and earned two Distinguished Flying Cross (DFC) medals. After the war, he emigrated to Canada, where he spent the rest of his life. After Stene's funeral reception in Toronto that December day, I joined rush-hour traffic exiting the city. A thought occurred. I would make one stop on my way home.

I drove my car toward one of Toronto's north-south commuter highways, the Don Valley Parkway, and parked near one of its prominent overpasses. I left the car and walked onto the Wynford Drive bridge. In a biting north wind, I decided to wait for the hearses carrying the bodies of the three latest Canadian soldiers killed in Afghanistan to pass by.

"I suddenly felt the urge," I told a fellow who arrived shortly after I did with a Canadian flag tucked under his arm.

"I live nearby," the flag-bearer told me. "I try to be here each time they go by."

At first, we two were the only ones on the bridge. Soon after, a brigade of four or five firefighters and two ambulance crews stopped their vehicles on the bridge and turned on all their emergency flashers. Over the next hour, many more adults arrived in their cars, came by as they walked their dogs, or, like my acquaintance with the flag, came from nearby apartment buildings. One man appeared carrying his two young children. For a while, the little ones seemed more interested in the firefighters and their vehicles' flashing lights than anything else. Then their father calmed them and focused them on the Don Valley Parkway beneath the bridge on which we were all gathering.

"I don't even know the men's names," said a teacher standing next to me.

"Michael Freeman, last Friday," I mentioned to her. "Then Gregory Kruse and Gaetan Roberge on Saturday, I think."

I thought about the significance of these spontaneous bridge vigils that had gone on for several years. I wasn't certain how or exactly when they began, but because the bodies of fallen Canadian soldiers had to travel from Canadian Forces Base Trenton (in eastern Ontario) to the Toronto coroner's office before being released officially to their families, people began paying their respects by assembling silently on overpasses along Highway 401 and the Don Valley Parkway. A groundswell of civilian sentiment and media coverage led to a petition and eventually to the official renaming of that section of the 401 running from Trenton to Toronto as the "Highway of Heroes."

As the number of mourners on the bridge appeared to grow to forty or fifty, what occurred to me about these impromptu tributes was that they brought the deaths of these servicemen and servicewomen closer to Canadian civilians than at any time in our history. In both World Wars and the Korean War, Canadian war dead were eulogized and buried in cemeteries nearest where they fell—at Beny-sur-Mer in France, Groesbeek in Holland, or Pusan in South Korea, for example. Besides peacekeepers killed on duty in recent years, to my knowledge, only during NATO military operations in

Afghanistan had those killed in action been physically returned to their families in Canada. And consequently in front of fellow citizens' eyes too.

It was almost 5 o'clock now. An air force vet suddenly appeared among those assembling along the sidewalk on the bridge over the Don Valley Parkway. He wore his blazer, beret, and medals. He didn't know Freeman, Kruse, or Roberge either, but I suspect he understood their families' pain. Like the men he'd known and lost overseas a generation ago, he felt the three men deserved his presence, "because Canada needs to respect what they've done," he told me.

Within minutes of his arrival, the traffic on the southbound parkway suddenly thinned to nothing. Police cruisers, working ahead of the military entourage from Trenton, had blocked traffic from entering the DVP or held back vehicles to allow the convoy unencumbered access to the parkway. The late afternoon sky and empty roadway seemed to blend together in a continuous dark backdrop. Then, from the bridge, we could see the flashing lights of the escort vehicles in the distance and close behind three stretch limousines and three smoke-glassed hearses. As the convoy approached the overpass, the assembly on the bridge and even the flags strung along its railing fell silent. Hats came off. The veterans and firefighters present saluted. In the instant that one of the limousines passed beneath us, we could see someone in the passenger seat waved back in gratitude. The half-dozen vehicles of the entourage disappeared beneath us.

Most of us stood quietly for a few more seconds, a half-minute maybe, in the wake of the convoy. Then, almost as quickly as the hearses had passed, the southbound traffic on the parkway resumed its rush-hour density. A young radio news reporter who'd been standing with us on the bridge recorded comments. She spoke to my acquaintance with the flag. She talked to the dad with the kids. Then she asked me why I'd come.

"It's something I've never done before," I admitted to her. "I've written books based on soldiers' stories. I've delivered eulogies for veterans who've passed on in old age. But I've never personally paid my respects to young Canadian servicemen so soon after their deaths."

That's not to say my first bridge vigil was my first tribute to either war dead or veterans. Since the 1980s, when I became aware that this country's wartime story was disappearing because, as everybody told me, "they never talked about it," I've felt drawn to veterans both professionally and personally. Whether the accounts of volunteers who became the Allies' shock troops in the Great War beginning at Vimy Ridge, or those who gave a fledgling air force its wings serving in the British Commonwealth Air Training Plan, during the Second World War, or those who signed up for service in Korea in Canada's so-called forgotten war, or more recently veterans from the NATO mission in Afghanistan, I have searched for, recorded, and chronicled war stories. Not to glorify the battles, but to know (and share the knowledge of) men and women in the middle of those battles. And either by accident or design, en route to learning more about them, I have befriended veterans—hundreds of them—in every part of Canada.

Still—as a writer—I have kept my distance, tried to remain neutral, and let veterans' voices, diaries, letters, service logs, memoirs, and photographs tell their stories. Through a half-dozen books, scores of documentaries, and numerous periodical features published, I have remained a witness to their accounts. I have faithfully quoted and paraphrased what they told me to then stitch into a retelling of events. I have sometimes played father confessor. But, I believe, I have always maintained my role as a correspondent only.

In 1999, I stepped slightly outside that role as a part-time instructor at Centennial College in Toronto. That year, a member of the school's journalism faculty took a year-long sabbatical and I attempted to fill his shoes through the fall and winter semesters. Once I had begun to feel comfortable as an instructor and with my teaching colleagues at the college, I asked a rather innocent question about the autumn timetable.

"What does the college do on Remembrance Day?"

Even the man who had invited me to apply for the part-time position at the college, Professor Steve Cogan, was caught a little off guard. As patriotic as I later discovered he was, even Steve admitted that as a rule the college had no events planned for November 11. Nor had it ever. He said that except for a few words of explanation and an ad lib silence in those lecture rooms where instructors felt it necessary, November 11 was just another day. Besides, he pointed out, for the young people at the college—some graduate students, but mostly those fresh out of high school—the idea of acknowledging the original Armistice, at the eleventh hour of the eleventh day of the eleventh month, was pretty much a meaningless exercise. Few if any of our students, particularly those from the Caribbean, Africa, the Middle East, Asia, and Latin America, would understand what it was about anyway. It would be as relevant as the history of the Roman Empire, he suggested. Well, the gauntlet had been thrown. It was a challenge I sensed I had to meet.

"That's going to change," I said. "I'd like to see this campus come to a complete stop during our own Remembrance Day observance."

It took a year to orchestrate it, and fortunately I was invited back to teach another full year at the college. But during the fall of 2000, Nate Horowitz, the dean of the communications school, agreed to have all classes on campus cease for about an hour on the morning of November 11, so that students, faculty, and staff could attend a ceremony I had prepared. Meantime, I had contacted a member of the Royal Canadian Legion in that part of Toronto. Howard Walker had served as an aero-engine mechanic in Coastal Command of the RCAF during the Second World War. I asked if he could encourage members of his Branch No. 617, also known as the Dambusters Branch, to speak about their connection to the famous 1943 bombing raid to destroy industrial dams in Germany's Ruhr River basin. Howard obliged and offered to supply a colour party as well—Legion members who would parade in the appropriate flags as a backdrop to our ceremony. We would read "They shall not grow old" from the remembrance poem "For the Fallen." In addition, instead of recorded music to begin and end our two-minute silence around 11 o'clock, I found a trumpeter at a local high school band to perform "The Last Post" and "Reveille."

Our first Remembrance Day observance that year succeeded because the veterans, in particular Len Read, told his personal story of growing up in London, England, during the war. The uniformed, ninety-year-old veteran described how two of his older brothers had enlisted in the Royal Air Force (one killed in 1941) and a third in the British Army. He told riveted students, most of whom had never seen a man in an RAF uniform, that he'd aspired to become an air gunner, but instead trained as an aero-mechanic, servicing the very Lancasters (with 617 Squadron) that had carried out the Dambusters raid. Then, to seal the connection between the Legion veterans and our students, I encouraged them all to meet casually in the campus cafeteria for coffee and conversation. For an hour, our students surrounded Len Read, Howard Walker, and the other veterans for interviews and photographs.

"It's like living history," one student commented. "It's inspirational to hear about the sacrifices of another generation."

Because the year 2000 marked the fiftieth anniversary of the start of the Korean War, the following November 11, I invited members of the Korea Veterans Association of Canada to speak before the two-minute silence. In 2002, our Remembrance Day ceremony paid tribute to three women veterans. Leading up to the sixtieth anniversary of D-Day, I brought in three veterans of the Normandy invasion to describe their experiences. During the sixtieth anniversary year of the liberation of Holland, I found two paratroopers who participated in Operation Market-Garden and two Dutch-born Canadians who recalled for our students their communities being liberated by Canadian troops in 1944–45. In 2006, I invited a Holocaust survivor. And in 2007, we observed the ninetieth anniversary of the battle at Vimy through the eyes of a merchant navy veteran whose father had served with the Canadian Corps at the historic battle.

As rewarding as having veterans tell some of their wartime stories in front of hundreds of college students each year proved to be, however, over time I sensed I needed to do more. I had successfully brought veterans out of the closet—to divulge some of their tougher memories of fear, shock, and loss—on November 11. I had engaged students whose only concept of war was "the war on terror" in Iraq and Afghanistan after 9/11. I had even convinced the college that all instruction on our campus should stop, as an act of remembrance. But it was still in a traditional Remembrance Day context.

I realized that in some ways I was reinforcing the stereotype of the veteran in our midst. We were still parading the colours, the flashbacks, and the veterans in their blazers, berets, and medals through a short ceremony and two minutes of silence in front of an attentive congregation. As well intentioned and moving as our tributes were to these servicemen and servicewomen, I was still employing a cliché—aging veterans, bowing their heads in deference to national emblems, to their fallen comrades, and to a long-ago-and-far-away war. I sensed I needed to go beyond remembrance.

I recognized that gathering veterans' stories and then reconstructing wartime events as they reported them to me wasn't enough. That was the history part. I realized that analyzing and researching the context of their experiences did not necessarily shed any new light on who they are, what their perceptions of combat are, what made them respond the way they did, and why the events of war changed them. That was a different story. That was the human part. And getting that, I concluded, required setting aside the veteran stereotype, exploring research methods other than those I'd learned as a broadcast interviewer or print journalist, and occasionally throwing myself into the deep end to see what happened. Sometimes I had to set aside customary sources of war history—regimental diaries, commanding officers' memoirs, and official war records—in favour of more tangible grassroots sources. Sometimes I had to push and probe veterans to reveal their emotions when they would rather not. Often I had to allow my own emotions to show. Along the way I had to get closer to my subject than I ever had before, and to report that too. In order to break the silence of veterans' memory, I had to break with the traditional ways of reporting it. In order to change our perceptions of veterans, I had to look beyond November 11, beyond the local cenotaph, and beyond the blazers and berets.

And so, several years ago—even as I researched and wrote about D-Day, Vimy, and other wartime events as a historian—I began to take a more subjective view of my encounters with veterans. I set about creating a journal of my journey with them. Like those choosing to grieve the deaths of Canadian troops in Afghanistan at public vigils on bridges over the Highway of Heroes, I had decided to pay my respects to veterans by publishing the stories behind their stories.

2

"TORCH BEARER"

School kept the secret very well. With the exception of the War of 1812–1814—including readings about General Brock's heroic death in the defence of Niagara and the British burning of the White House—neither my elementary school nor my high school teachers devoted much classroom time to Canada's military history. By edict or accident, when I was in school in the 1950s and 60s, the school curriculum virtually eliminated war as a subject worth studying. With the exception of one grade school teacher, Mike Malott, who often deviated from the prescribed course to introduce us to such wartime figures as John McCrae, Billy Bishop, John Gillespie Magee, and Padre John Foote, I never heard or saw the words "war hero" and "Canada" in the same sentence. It just wasn't done. Those weren't names or facts worth acknowledging, much less celebrating.

I don't think I can prove it as Ontario Ministry of Education policy either, but the notion that Canadians had willingly participated in warfare, sacrificed enormously, and come home with victory or at least with heads held high, never made it into school curriculum in my day. Certainly, when it came to twentieth-century wartime history, we were taught that Canada had dutifully followed Mother England into the Great War in 1914, had declared war against Nazi Germany in September 1939, and as a signatory to the UN peace charter had joined other nations to fight the Korean War from 1950 to 1953. But learn about the courage and sacrifice at Vimy, Ypres,

Passchendaele, Hong Kong, Dieppe, Ortona, Falaise, or Kap'yong? No. Recognize that blood shed in battle could have even the remotest connection to Canada's nation-building? No. Feel some sort of pride in Canada's military heritage? Never. Not when I was in school anyway.

Nor was the military ever acknowledged in a positive way at my parents' home. Born in New York City in 1922, my father, Alex Barris, was raised in a household that held pacifism in highest regard. Compelled by the events of December 7, 1941, at Pearl Harbor, to volunteer for U.S. Army service, Dad nevertheless detested weapons and violence of any kind. That may explain why recruiters streamed him into the army medical corps. Medics weren't required to carry firearms, and I guess that seemed a reasonable compromise in an unreasonable time. Perhaps my father's sense that U.S. foreign policy after 1945 seemed untenable contributed to his decision to leave his native country too. At the first opportunity to write for a living and in a national culture known more for its accommodation than its militarism, my father took a reporting job with the *Globe and Mail* in 1948. I was born in Toronto the next year. Like many sons of fathers who've served in uniform, I discovered the fact in adolescence and wondered what he'd experienced. The opportunity to find out presented itself as the school year was ending in 1964. It was literally and figuratively an accident.

On the final day of classes that year, my Grade 9 phys-ed instructor had no curriculum left to teach, so he gave us a bat and a ball and told us to play some pick-up baseball. I loved playing shortstop, the position my dad always liked most. Not long into the game, however, the catcher and I chased the same infield fly and collided head-on. The collision broke my nose, knocked out some front teeth, and put me out cold for a couple of minutes. I spent several weeks recuperating in bed at home. My father happened to be working in his office at the house at the time, so he spent many hours trying to distract me from my pain by telling me stories. It wasn't long before I popped the big one.

"What did you do in the war, Dad?" I asked.

I didn't realize it then, but my father employed the same defence mechanism many veterans of the Great War, the Second World War, and the Korean War have used. Never tell the rough stories, the remembrances of destruction close by. Don't revisit the moments of death and dying that bring back the horror of the experience. Under no circumstances let loved ones see you break down and cry. Instead, protect them from the truth. Always recall the antics, the quirky tales, and maybe the odd near miss. Never let them know the hell of your war.

That's what my father did. For several afternoons in a row, as I lay in bed recovering from my schoolyard wounds, my father regaled me with just the war stories he knew would leave me laughing. For a year during the war, Dad explained, he endured U.S. Army training camps from Kansas to Mississippi and rose to the rank of sergeant. During one stint in the winter of 1942 he recalled being assigned the job of waking the battalion commander well before dawn so that the officer would be the first on the parade ground conducting daily roll call. One morning, fearing he might sleep through his alarm, my father accidentally woke the commander an hour early. Dad still winces at the recollection of his senior officer shouting into the freezing Kansas pre-dawn, "'A' Company, report! . . . 'B' Company, report!" Nobody answered because nobody was up yet.

My father told me about army food—C rations, or "shit on a shingle," and coffee that tasted like mud. Everybody in the army hated the food and the cooks hated everybody back, he told me. No troops ever got any food they liked. So, from the moment he received his baloney sandwich ration each morning until noon when he sat down to eat, my father searched for anybody who hated the peanut butter sandwich ration as much as Dad hated his baloney sandwich ration. Only then could he eat lunch—two peanut butter sandwiches.

"Then there was the time we stole a jeep," began another story and my father recounted his most bizarre story of all. It was at the end of the war, following VE Day, when his U.S. Army unit—302nd Regiment Battalion Medical Section—was stationed in Czechoslovakia. He had always wanted to see Prague, but at the time U.S. Army officials had declared the Czech capital city off-limits. No matter. On a Friday night, he and several army buddies "borrowed" the jeep, travelled hundreds of kilometres around military checkpoints, sneaked into Prague for a Saturday night, and then spent the rest of the weekend finding inconspicuous ways of retracing their steps to barracks in time for reveille Monday morning. Making it back just before dawn, my father and his co-conspirators were informed of a change in U.S. Army policy. The next weekend, the brass would issue furloughs for everybody to, you guessed it, Prague.

Dad's repatriation story probably topped them all. Finally given orders to return home in December 1945, my father's medical unit arrived at Marseilles, France, to board a Liberty ship. In his haste to embark, Dad explained, he leapt from a troop truck, caught his foot on the tailgate, and tumbled to the ground. The resulting impact gashed his forehead and bruised his elbow (requiring an arm sling), although he admitted he still managed to join the twenty-four-hour crap games on board the ship en route home. Eleven days later, when the vessel docked in New York City, the wounded were escorted down the gangplank first, including Dad (looking every inch the conquering hero in his forehead bandage and arm sling) and two of his buddies from sick bay (a guy who'd picked up a case of the clap in Marseilles and another who'd gotten drunk one turbulent night on the ship and sustained cuts and bruises getting into his bunk). He recalled the pier receiving party—a band playing "When Johnny Comes Marching Home" and three Red Cross women, serving coffee and doughnuts. He remembered their pitying looks "as if we'd just been flown home from the blood-drenched beaches of Normandy."

Toward the end of those days of my convalescence at home that June of 1964, I asked my father one last question about his war. "Were you awarded anything? A medal? Something?"

Presently, my father retrieved a medal with five points on it, hanging from a short red and blue striped piece of ribbon. He made no fuss over it. He shrugged off any mention I made of his wartime bravery. He simply suggested, if I really cared about it, that I should put it in safekeeping. So I tucked the medal into a dresser drawer jewellery box with my cufflinks and tie clips and promptly forgot about it. Although I had managed to get an answer to "What did you do in the war, Dad?" it was, after all, the answer *he* had chosen to give. He had gone only as far as he felt comfortable. The rest, I deduced, would have to be left to my imagination.

Dad had successfully kept the silence—a kind of unwritten code among veterans not to reveal the reality of wartime memory.

About the same time—1964—my father became a Canadian citizen. By this time, not only had he elevated his profile as a newspaperman, writing his daily "Barris Beat" column in the *Globe and Mail* and then the *Toronto Telegram*, but he had also developed the column into a CBC TV late-night talk and variety show that he hosted. And although critics and reviewers began referring to him as a TV personality, he went to great pains to downplay his notoriety. In print and on TV, my father much preferred to shed light on other show business performers, particularly Canadian ones. Nobody expressed more pride in Canada's new maple leaf flag, its multicultural and multilingual mosaic, or even its growing penchant for peacekeeping roles in the world more than my U.S. expatriate father. In fact, during the mid-1960s, he readily accepted an invitation to MC a tour of United Nations sites in Cyprus, where Canadian troops tried to keep the peace along the green line between feuding Turks and Greeks. His only souvenir of the trip was a turquoise-coloured baseball cap with the UN global insignia on the front. In summers, when the family escaped the city to a hobby farm for holidays, he wore that hat incessantly. He couldn't say enough about the Canadian peacekeepers he'd met on that entertainment tour.

My father was equally verbal about international politics as he saw them. And when the American branches of the family came to visit us in Canada—at Christmas or for summer holidays—Dad never hesitated to talk politics or reveal his anti-war sentiment with my aunts and uncles. They rarely agreed on such issues, and though the resulting household debates embarrassed some members of the family, I was fascinated by them. From as early as I can recall, he challenged American involvement in Vietnam.

"Who gave the U.S. the right to police the world?" I remember him asking.

Detesting American foreign policy did not stop my father from studying it. He still craved U.S. news reporting. So, over supper, we would first watch CBC TV news and then the *CBS Evening News with Walter Cronkite*. At our household, Vietnam truly became "the living room war," and its nightly images and sounds disturbed my parents, my younger sister Kate, and me. Not surprisingly, my father's deeply felt pacifism and outspoken objection to the war and American involvement in it rubbed off on me. My father never insisted I agree with his views. But his passion and his reasoned arguments against military intervention in Southeast Asia seemed hard to refute.

Ironically, my father's freelance career drew him back to his native home. In 1969, at the height of the war in Vietnam and with Hollywood seemingly crying out for writers with my father's calibre of TV experience, he decided to take a crack at writing TV situation comedies and variety shows back in the States. The whole family moved to California . . . except for me, that is. Since I had already begun my own career in broadcasting and writing at (then) Ryerson Polytechnical Institute in Toronto, it seemed pointless to transplant me to Hollywood too. Besides, my own anti-Vietnam War feelings and misgivings about U.S. military policy had bubbled to the surface by that time. And with the very real risk, even as a foreign student at a California university, that I could become eligible for the draft, my father and I agreed that I didn't "look particularly good in an American military uniform."

I stayed behind in Toronto at a time when colleges, universities, and post-secondary institutes, even those in Canada, had become hotbeds of anti-war, anti-military sentiment. As students we accused our governments, our corporations, our military of conspiring in what Dwight Eisenhower had described as "the military industrial complex." I attended Toronto meetings organized by members of the (eventually outlawed) Students for a Democratic Society. I felt right at home writing criticism of the war in the Ryerson student press. I quoted classmates, who were draft dodgers and resisters themselves, about what they called "the corruption of U.S. military training and service."

I joined demonstrations in front of the U.S. consulate in Toronto. I even tempted fate, travelling to U.S. university campuses to be closer to the action of the major protests. To my family's horror, when I crossed the border by bus I was given a thorough going-over by U.S. immigration authorities and drew sneers from some fellow travellers for my long afro. It happened to be the same week in May that U.S. National Guardsmen fired into student protestors—killing four of them—at Kent State University in Ohio. All this, rightly or wrongly, fuelled my distrust of anything to do with the military. I was very much my father's son.

It took a number of years—and a veteran of my father's war—to change my attitude. It didn't happen entirely overnight. Nor was my father prepared to accept my change of heart right away. However, one of the watershed moments that forced me to review my long-standing distrust of military thinking, my suspicion of military activity, and my refusal to accept that the military had contributed in any way to the fabric of Canada occurred in 1990. As a writer and broadcaster, particularly as a freelancer whose survival was directly proportional to his creative output, I was always searching for stories that had never been told. Carrying on the tradition of my father, I had begun a weekly newspaper column and a regular commentary on CBC Radio—both called "The Barris Beat."

This particular fall day—just a week before Remembrance Day—my search for stories for "The Barris Beat" took me to Tillsonburg, a small farming community outside London, Ontario. There, I learned, some aviation buffs had recently begun seeking and acquiring former Second World War training aircraft called Harvards and Yales. Since 1985, their group, the Canadian Harvard Aircraft Association (CHAA), had raised funds in the area, enough money to purchase some of these derelict aircraft. Then they had mustered sufficient volunteer know-how to refurbish these former war birds from scratch to be flown much the way they were half a century before. I chose November 4 because it was one of the last CHAA fly-days of the year. Members, families, and visitors could watch the group's prized, rebuilt Harvards take to the air one last time before they were mothballed for the season.

As air shows go, this CHAA fly-day was small potatoes. No Snowbird aerobatic flights, no national corporate sponsors, not even visiting military aircraft from nearby Canadian Forces or U.S. Air Force bases. No. When I arrived at the Tillsonburg airport that Saturday morning, I noticed a couple of small hangars open, a relatively small tarmac with grass runways beyond, and a couple of CHAA banners hanging from jury-rigged wooden frames. Neatly arranged in front of the modest hangars, however, four bright yellow Harvards were lined up in perfect symmetry, each with dual cockpits and controls because—just like during the war—today some rookie pilots would get some time in the air under the watchful eye of the more experienced pilots in the second cockpit. The same way they had at hundreds of military flying schools across Canada between 1940 and 1945, on this November day forty-five years later, these Harvards' noisy Pratt and Whitney engines would shortly roar to life for the first training flights of the day. As seductive as these vintage aircraft and their roaring engines seemed, I was drawn initially to some of the volunteers hovering about the tarmac—pilots doing flight checks, ground crew monitoring the Harvards' engines, and one or two older men offering explanations for first-time visitors.

"Anybody got loonies for twos and fives for the cash box?" asked a heavy-set gentleman wearing a CHAA ball cap and a broad smile. "Nothing like the sound of a Harvard in all the world." And he got some coins from onlookers to ensure there'd be change at the canteen for the sale of coffee and sandwiches throughout the day.

The man making change and offering admiring remarks about the deafening roar of the Harvards was seventy-year-old Charley Fox. A founding member of CHAA and eventually the chair of the publicity and promotion committee (not to mention the day's cashier at the CHAA canteen), Charley Fox probably knew more about flying the aircraft lined up on the Tillsonburg airport tarmac than anyone there. Maybe anyone in Canada. I soon learned that was because he had flown Harvards as a sprog student pilot in 1940 and then taught on them as an instructor in the British Commonwealth Air Training Plan (BCATP) from October 1941 until May 1943. Having become one of the country's top military flight instructors, Charley Fox earned a transfer from Training Command to combat operations on Spitfires during the air war over Europe—from D-Day to VE Day. As a member of Fighter Command overseas, he became so skilled in the air war against the German Luftwaffe bombers and fighters as well as hostile ground targets that he was twice decorated with the Distinguished Flying Cross (DFC) for his service.

Of course, it took me a while to discover all that. Several years in fact. Former Flight Lieutenant Charley Fox—much like my father—was not one to brag about his wartime record. All I learned, as I interviewed him that CHAA fly-day in November 1990, was that for nearly two years he had taught military aviation students on Harvards fifty years ago how to take off and land in adverse conditions, carry out night flying exercises, use aerobatics in mock dogfights with enemy fighter aircraft, and (he hoped) how to survive an operational tour during the Second World War overseas.

I also learned that afternoon, as I accompanied him to town for more coffee and cream for the CHAA canteen, that he'd arranged a "second seat" for me. That was training jargon for a trip in the second cockpit during one of the afternoon's formation flights. I would fly as a passenger in a vintage military training aircraft that very day. About an hour later, decked out in a fleece-lined flying jacket, parachute, and leather helmet, I suddenly found myself—for all the world—feeling like a wartime student getting his first orientation flight in a Harvard circa 1940. I also found myself thinking not about "the U.S. military industrial complex" I had protested as a university student in 1968, but about Winston Churchill, who, according to Charley, had described the training of BCATP pilots in Canada as "the decisive factor" in winning the Second World War.

Something had happened that day at the Tillsonburg airport. I had always been fascinated by flying and aircraft. I had never felt compelled to learn to fly, but I had always enjoyed the experience as a passenger on turboprop and jet flights across Canada or abroad. But flying in the seat of a cockpit with needle, ball, and airspeed indicators in front of me, aileron pedals at my feet, and a steering column between my hands—that made flying a more immediate experience. I sensed a kinship with the thousands of young men who'd come from across the Commonwealth a generation ago to learn military flying technique. Anything I'd read about their ordeal—leaving homes in New Zealand, Australia, South Africa, and the U.K. to train for months and graduate (or be washed out if they couldn't make the grade) in faraway Canadian training schools—suddenly had pictures attached. I could now visualize the young student pilots—intent on flying Hurricanes and Spitfires for the destruction of an Axis enemy—graduating or failing in this very cockpit. That's how close I'd come to their experiences, to their life stories that November day.

It really was a turning point as a writer of history, indeed, a chronicler of Canada in wartime. Before I left the fly-day in Tillsonburg, I had signed up for CHAA membership to support the relaunching of those half-century-old Canadian war birds, the Harvard aircraft. What's more, Charley Fox had begun to alter my thinking about the role of the military in Canada's past, about wartime service involving thousands of instructors and the more than 200,000 students they trained, and about the untold stories that could (and should) be gathered and recorded about them. In addition, he had also given me the idea for something more than a "Barris Beat" column in the newspaper and/or item on the air, but rather a full-length manuscript. And he had initiated something else I hadn't expected: a close and enduring friendship.

In the months immediately following my trip to Tillsonburg, Charley began sending a steady flow of information—my first CHAA newsletter, notification of the monthly meetings, specs (engine size, weight, wingspan, cruise speed, stall speed, diving speed, fuel capacity, and fuel consumption) about the more than 20,000 Harvards employed in the BCATP during the Second World War. As much as I sensed I had to digest all this technical data on these training aircraft, I was more drawn to the sentiment Charley Fox attached to one of his beautifully handwritten notes:

"There is so much interesting information about the [Harvard] people that has to be talked about," he wrote finally. "And none of it is on paper yet."

My aviator acquaintance kept issuing challenges in my direction. To join him and his Harvard aficionados. To listen to his and their BCATP stories. To probe a little deeper than a ninety-second news bite or short radio documentary. To invest the time the stories demanded. And after every challenge Charley Fox offered his usual helping hand. The following year, he strongly recommended that I attend one of the oldest, continuously running reunions of Second World War veterans in existence, the annual gathering of former BCATP instructors at No. 6 Service Flying Training School at Dunnville, Ontario (where Charley had been stationed during the early days of the war). Their first reunion had taken place in 1945, at the end of the war; he insisted that I come to meet some of "the best instructors Canada ever produced" during the forty-sixth reunion at a hotel in Hamilton, Ontario. He would introduce me to each former pilot instructor, help me with my line of questions, and, if I thought it might help, sit in on the interviews to spur the stories he knew were tucked away in their memories. I never worked so hard at a series of interviews in my life, interviewing former Dunnville instructors hour after hour for two days straight.

In the weeks and months that followed the Dunnville instructors' reunion, Charley took a lot of time out of his own busy schedule to chauffeur me around. Every weekend, it seemed, he called, suggesting a new trip we should take to meet yet another of his former instructor colleagues somewhere around Ontario—Jack Harris in Mississauga, Livingston "Cap" Foster in Smiths Falls, Charlie Krause in Toronto, Art Harrison from Owen Sound, and Larry Walker in Chatham. I was amazed at the man's stamina. Then over seventy, he was officially retired and receiving some pension, but he seemed compelled to supplement his income by working at odd jobs, not to mention his newfound occupation of ensuring that I reach, meet, and interview every instructor he knew. My military aviation mentor had apparently chosen me as the official Canadian historian of the British Commonwealth Air Training Plan. That was that.

By Christmas I had accumulated scores of interviews; by the following spring, hundreds of them. Charley's leads and those I'd found through air force associations, aviation historians, flying clubs, cadet leagues, and veterans groups, and via broadcast appeals and classified ads in newspapers, took me from one end of Canada to the other. One of my requests for information was spotted by the editor of a national publisher and that brought a book contract. I had a deadline and plenty to do, so, as my father often said, it was time to "apply the seat of the pants to the seat of the chair" and get it done. The following year, I completed the full manuscript and asked the man who'd sparked the project in the first place to read the first draft for errors and omissions. Charley had it back to me almost overnight.

Behind the Glory was published in the fall of 1992. The publication prompted a national tour, appearances, and speeches. Reviewers and broadcasters began referring to me as a military historian. Given my revulsion from things military not too many years before, it caught me off guard. What put my mind at ease, I guess, was the blurb the publisher had printed on the dust jacket. "Ted Barris has assembled a fascinating collection of facts and anecdotes adding to our Canadian flying heritage. The size and scope of the plan was not readily apparent or really understood by those who made it work. Now its tremendous achievement in supplying the Commonwealth air crew requirements during the Second World War has been recorded for posterity." The credit followed: "Charley Fox, past president, Canadian Harvard Aircraft Association." I was certainly prepared to accept that endorsement. By November that year, the book was on the best-seller list, almost exactly two years from the day I'd met my military mentor.

Whether I was prepared to acknowledge it or not, over the time I had come to know Charley Fox, my writing of wartime history began to preoccupy much of my professional work. Periodical editors approached me to write features based on wartime anniversaries and themes. Suddenly, publishers seemed interested in what content I could offer from the Second World War and the Korean War. As well, my attitude about those veterans who had given me their stories had shifted dramatically. While I continued to research and deliver the facts of their experiences in war, I had been moved by the dedication of their volunteer service, their respect for authority as citizen soldiers, their loyalty to cause and comrades, their fears both real and imagined, and often the system's betrayal of their sacrifice. Whenever I read at writers' festivals, delivered keynotes on special occasions, or spoke to students, veterans groups, indeed, whenever I was asked to speak to the general public, I found myself gravitating to the stories of veterans to make a point.

Inevitably, on Canada Day, Thanksgiving, and certainly leading up to Remembrance Day each year, I accompanied my wartime storytelling with personal comments about veterans' rights being violated. I generally concluded remarks by insisting that veterans' recollections be gathered, preserved, acknowledged, and celebrated. I was becoming an advocate for veterans with no authority to do so except for the platform given to me by my research and writing. Often I would arrive at publicized events and find Charley Fox there in the audience listening again to stories he'd heard me tell numerous times before. He said he was just offering moral support. Frequently, if I knew he was present, I would invite him to join me in front of audiences to relate his own experiences and those of his former comrades-in-arms to punctuate the advocacy. With his usual modesty, Charley would deflect praise for himself or his wartime record. On one occasion, I wondered out loud about all the time and energy he was investing in everybody else's wartime stories.

"Where does this advocacy for other veterans come from?" I asked him.

He explained that he had been honourably discharged on July 25, 1945. He had then immediately booked passage aboard the troopship *Louis Pasteur* to Montreal, reunited with his wife, Helen, in

Toronto, where they spent a night at the Royal York Hotel, and awoke on August 14 to hear that the Japanese had surrendered. The war was over on paper and in fact. So, Charley said, he got reacquainted with his young son. He returned to the retail job his Walker Store employers had held for him. And he seemed prepared to leave the war in the past. Not long after resettling in Guelph, Ontario, however, he received a visit from the mother of one of his childhood chums, Andy Howden, who'd been killed in the air war overseas. The distraught woman grabbed Charley by the shoulders and shook him right there in the store.

"Why my Andy," she cried, "and not you!"

"Mrs. Howden, I don't know why not me," he replied, trying to console the woman. So deep was the effect of the apparent contradiction that *he* should survive the war and not his chum, that Charley said he eventually committed himself—quietly at first and then later as a retired businessman and honorary colonel of 412 Squadron—to recounting the stories of fellow Canadian veterans and paying them lifelong tribute with every waking breath. Eventually, his crusade to inform schoolchildren, historical societies, service clubs, and even serving troops about the legacy of veterans became known as Torch Bearers Canada. His sporty red Saab, with a flaming torch emblem on its bumpers, zigzagged across the province constantly delivering him to more speaking engagements than he'd flown sorties. At every venue he arrived and spoke from the heart, without fanfare, and without a speaking fee. He never stopped answering Mrs. Howden.

Meanwhile, through the 1990s, my father and I had begun to collaborate in our writing—on radio and television scripting and on several books. During our work together writing manuscripts, we eventually turned to wartime stories. Dad sensed that I had gained some credibility writing stories about Canada in wartime. Despite his continued philosophical opposition to war and violence, he began to feel that perhaps gathering, researching, writing, and publishing the stories of veterans—like himself—had relevance and value, particularly as the country approached the fiftieth anniversary of VE Day. So we began to plan such a book. I travelled to western Canada interviewing veterans, while he went east doing the same. We listened to each other's tapes. We invited even more personal anecdotes on radio and TV talk shows and through veterans' publications. We transcribed the stories and assembled the manuscript. We didn't always agree about the way to present the stories, but inevitably the intensity of the veterans' memories themselves shone through the writing.

Coincidentally, a few more stories about my father's wartime experiences cropped up in our co-authorship of the next book. I learned that his medical unit—part of Gen. George S. Patton's Third U.S. Army in Europe—had spent its last days of training near Devizes, in southern England, and that he'd landed in France a month after D-Day, in July 1944. His unit immediately began responding to needs of the wounded, giving them first aid and bearing stretcher after stretcher behind the lines—from central France all the way to western Germany. His tour of duty had included service during the Battle of the Bulge just before Christmas in 1944. He admitted to me that his days in the Ardennes forest had been awful.

Our collaboration, *Days of Victory: Canadians Remember 1939–1945*, was published in time for May 8—VE Day—1995. The book brought great satisfaction to the hundreds of veterans whose reminiscences appeared in it. It gave us a feeling of accomplishment to know we had preserved such remarkable experiences too. Equally rewarding were the upbeat reviews; in fact, within a few weeks of the VE Day half-century observances, our book reached number one on most national best-seller lists. The exhilaration I felt gaining that response and recognition as co-author with my father was difficult to top. A few years later, the original publishers of the book disappeared, but not the appetite for the book. We contemplated another way of packaging it in time for the sixtieth VE Day anniversary. Dad didn't make it that far.

Years of smoking and insufficient physical exercise caught up with my father in 2002, and he suffered a series of strokes, the last of which on February 26, 2003, stole various of his faculties. The greatest loss of all, however, was my father's encyclopedic memory and his facility for telling and retelling all those wonderful stories in his inimitable fashion. The family soon learned that Dad's aphasia was permanent. He and I would never again be able to communicate with spoken words. His battle with aphasia and my mother's quiet assurance that he might one day recover lasted eleven months (he died January 16, 2004). As often happens at times such as these, we began sifting through my father's papers. One day, my mother, Kay, discovered among Dad's files a document left over from his short-lived career as a medic in the U.S. Army during the Second World War. None of us had ever seen it, not even my mother. It was a rolled-up citation, with official-looking trim and a typewritten narrative. In part, it read:

> Tec 4 Barris is liaison sergeant for this organization whose normal duties are those of maintaining the chain of evacuation from Battalion Aid Stations. . . . In this capacity Tec 4 Barris expresses an unselfish devotion to duty. . . .
>
> On 12 February 1945, one litter squad failed to return after an operation by the 1st Battalion 302nd Regiment in Campholz Woods, Germany. Tec 4 Barris personally entered these woods, which were heavily sown with mines and booby traps, and located the members of his squad. Two . . . were wounded and the remaining two were disoriented. He managed to extricate [them]. . . .
>
> His total disregard for personal safety and his continual service . . . above the call of his particular duties are in keeping with the highest of army traditions.

A few lines into the citation, I suddenly remembered the days I had convalesced at home in 1964. I recalled my father regaling me with stories, including some from his wartime experiences. I remembered the medal he'd modestly given me, the one I'd stowed away in my jewellery box. And when I retrieved it, I realized what it was. My father's medal was the Bronze Star. When I researched the medal's criteria, I discovered that although the medal was the fourth-highest combat award the U.S. Armed Forces can bestow upon its serving soldiers, it was usually awarded for meritorious achievement, that is, "doing one's job well." Somehow that suited my father's disposition and attitude about military service during the war. I guess he had surveyed the situation that horrible winter day, recognized a responsibility, perhaps asked himself "Why not me?" and pulled those men out of the minefield. He'd never aspired to be in a war zone and yet he never considered what he did in uniform heroic. He just did what he thought was right.

That's where my father's distrust of things military intersected with Charley Fox's respect for them. Like so many citizen soldiers in the World Wars and Korea, they had both signed up, sure they were doing what had to be done, but uncertain as to the outcome. They had fulfilled the commitment of their enlistment and a full tour of duty overseas. Then, when the shooting stopped, they had returned to civilian life content to leave the war and all its memories behind. And pretty much forgotten. With the exception of Mrs. Howden's outburst in the Walker Store, Charley had managed to leave his war behind until he chose to remember it. My father, on the other hand, had managed to leave his war behind because he left the army behind, left his home country behind, and, despite his anti-war debates with family and friends, kept his war out of sight and out of mind.

Despite their silence, what my father hadn't counted on and what Charley Fox was surprised to find in me was an unstoppable curiosity to know more about their wartime experiences and a genuine passion to write about them. To write about them as thoroughly and as honestly as possible. I was learning that veterans never talked about what they had seen and lost, but like taking up the gauntlet, I was determined to break that silence. I recognized that if I didn't take the time to sit and listen, question and record, transcribe and retell, their valuable stories would go unnoticed to the grave. I also sensed that journalists, historians, and moviemakers often got it wrong and I had a chance to help veterans set the record straight. My own experience of not having their stories taught to me, of learning American and British military history by rote, and of educators dropping an important thread of Canada's past, told me I had to put a human face on the legacy closest to where I lived. I was discovering that where some insisted there was no uniquely Canadian story—on the Western Front in 1917, at D-Day, in Korea, or at hundreds of airfields on the home front—I could prove otherwise. And would.

Charley Fox had become a torch bearer to pay homage to his comrades who had never come home. My father had become a war storyteller as a professional challenge. Each man's journey to tell veterans' stories had included me, influenced me, and inspired me. This book reflects on the men and women my journey encountered and the discoveries I believe others need to know.

On the day my family and I paid tribute to Dad with a celebration of his life at the Arts and Letters Club in Toronto—February 2, 2004—my sister and I expected perhaps 100 or 150 people. Nearly 300 jammed into the club's auditorium to hear producer Bob Jarvis, dancer Joey Hollingsworth, comedian Roger Abbott, journalist Barbara Klich, broadcaster Dale Goldhawk, musician Rob McConnell, and broadcaster Peter Jennings offer testimony to a life well lived. My daughter Whitney Barris and accompanist B.J. Byers performed one of my dad's favourite Broadway show tunes, and my sister Kate and I reflected on Dad's love of his family, his profession, and telling a story with a good punch line. None of those who spoke or performed to honour Dad's memory had travelled to the celebration to recognize my father's status as a decorated veteran, except perhaps symbolically.

Unannounced, after the presentations, Charley Fox emerged from the throng of people in the Arts and Letters auditorium. When I saw him, I cried and hugged him as if he were a life preserver. He suddenly felt like a member of my immediate family. This veteran who had come into my life more than a decade before realized how important this tribute was to my mother, my sister, and to me. Charley was there out of respect for the man, the father, the journalist and broadcaster, and, he told me, the fellow veteran. Charley knew my father's wartime record would be the last thing Dad would care to remember, but Charley had given my dad's wartime years new meaning in my life. He knew it would drive me to search further, write more, and join him in sharing that legacy with other Canadians.

3

"THEY JUST FADE AWAY"

THE MEETING comes to order as the Officer Commanding stands and pounds the handle of what had once been a German hand grenade atop what had once been a German military helmet. The smack of the O.C.'s Knob Kerry gavel—steel on steel—pierces the din of chatter like a gunshot and brings all the hubbub in the room to a sudden halt. At once, the twenty-one Canadian army veterans seated around a U-shaped dining table face and acknowledge the O.C. And as he begins to recite the club's salutary poem, everybody joins in:

> We don't give a damn for Kaiser Bill
> For Kaiser Bill is balmy.
> And we don't give a fuck for old Von Kluck*
> And all his bloody army.

The recitation is punctuated finally by a shout of "Hurray!" Then peels of laughter follow. Tonight, the men present have taken

---

* Employing elements of the "Schlieffen Plan" of intended quick victory in a short war, Gen. Alexander von Kluck led the German First Army and its fourteen divisions during the first German offensives into northern France in 1914.

particular delight reciting their signature poem with its foul language and bravado. Extra emphasis has been placed on the four-letter words for the benefit of wives, family members, and others who are not normally in attendance at these meetings. The men seated at this dining table at the Union Club of Saint John, New Brunswick, are all veterans—most from the Second World War, some from the Korean War. For eighty-eight years now they or their predecessors have gathered like this as the surviving members of the Byng Boys Club, perhaps the oldest surviving veterans' organization.

In 1919, a year after the original Armistice that brought an end to "the war to end all wars," some hardy veterans of the Great War in that Maritime city decided to recognize their survival with a club that commemorated their former commander. Beginning at the battle of Vimy Ridge, in April 1917, Lt. Gen. Julian Byng had led the members of the Canadian Corps in combat along the Western Front. So much had the rank and file Canadian troops adored their British commander that in battle they began referring to themselves as "the Byng Boys."

In fact, late on the first day of the four-day battle at Vimy against the Germans in occupied France, the first of nearly 100,000 Canadians reached the top of the ridge and began digging in for an expected enemy counterattack. Some of the army engineers preparing the way for following infantrymen erected a sign on a newly captured enemy position. "Do-Drop Inn. Working Parties a Specialty. Daylight Parties Preferred. Picks and Shovels are Not Provided Here," the sign read. "(Signed) Proprietors, The Byng Boys."

"You had to have been brought out of battle on a stretcher in order to be eligible for the Byng Boys Club," the O.C. told me.

Years later, when the last of the Great War vets from Saint John passed on, continuation of the club fell to veterans of the Second World War and later Korean War veterans. Since 1919, the Byng Boys Club has enjoyed scores of different members. But tonight—May 22, 2007—is different. After nearly nine decades of assembling, pounding the Knob Kerry gavel on the helmet, and dining on the memories of past victories and defeats, the remaining members feel they are too old and feeble to carry on the tradition any longer. Tonight is the final meeting and farewell dinner of this unique organization. And I was in attendance because I had been invited to provide the keynote speech at this the very last meeting of the club's existence. It was a command performance I would never forget.

Seated at the head of the table, I scanned the faces of the veterans in front of me. Most, as the membership criteria stipulated, had indeed been wounded in wartime. Gathered in that one room were nearly 2,000 years of life lived. Out there were twenty-one walking war diaries that included battle honours from Dieppe and Hong Kong to Ortona, Juno Beach, the Scheldt, and even at Kap'yong. Out there sat a dozen colonels, a host of other officers and men who'd received the Military Cross, the Distinguished Flying Cross (DFC), and enough volunteer ribbons and medals to fill the display cases at the Canadian War Museum in Ottawa. Although I had spoken to hundreds of groups—from elementary school students to veterans of the two World Wars and the Korean War, and peacekeepers—I had never been asked to officiate at the dissolution of a historic organization. In addition, when I thought about the military careers of the men I faced that evening, I wondered what possible keynote message I could deliver. What could I tell them that they had not heard at a Byng Boys Club banquet before? I decided to begin the evening's journey closest to their hearts. At Vimy.

"Days ago, I stood and watched Canada's most precious and meaningful war monument rededicated in front of more than 20,000 visiting Canadians," I began. "In the afternoon sunshine on the anniversary, April 9, the gleaming stone of the newly refurbished memorial nearly knocked your eye out. It was so beautiful."

Knowing that none of the current Byng Boys members—for health reasons—could have made the trek to Vimy for the recent ninetieth anniversary ceremony, I decided to take them there in words and images. I described the recent elaborate efforts to restore the monument to its original condition in 1936 when sculptor Walter Allward first completed his masterpiece. I recounted some of the highlights of the late afternoon ceremony in 2007. At the base of the monument, the Wall of Defence, with its 11,000 names of Canadians with no known graves, was slipping into the shadow of the afternoon light. The lone figure of Mother Canada mourning her dead sons seemed more real than ever. I tried to explain what scores of bagpipes, bugle fanfares, and the voices of a large children's choir sounded like echoing off the face of the stone out over the Douai Plain. And I highlighted what wisdom some of the dignitaries had offered in honour of the occasion; Queen Elizabeth's words seemed most appropriate when she said, "Among those fixed points around which history turns, Vimy for Canadians is perhaps the greatest."

Yet even the Queen could not have known the most moving and memorable aspect of a day full of tributes. Throughout the day, as many of the 20,000 tourists explored the grounds around the monument—250 acres of land that France had bequeathed to Canada as sovereign territory in 1923—they met Canadian high school students. More than 3,000 of those young people wore green khaki army shirts, with brass buttons, epaulettes, and a white patch sewn above the left breast pocket. On each patch: the name of one of the 10,000 Canadian casualties at Vimy in 1917.

What's more, I told the Byng Boys, each of the students knew the history of the name written on his or her white patch. From Uxbridge, Ontario, I met Rebecca MacDonald, wearing the name of her great-grandfather, Walter James MacDonald, who'd lost an arm after Vimy. From Port Perry, Ontario, I met Robb Phillips, wearing his great-grandfather's name, Joseph Kennedy, a corporal wounded by machine-gun bullets at Vimy. Walking next to him was student Cotter Allen, who said the man on his patch, Cpl. Arthur Barnard, had died at age thirty-five on the first day of the Vimy battle; student Michael Riseley, wearing the name Pte. Ralph E. Bowen, said that his alter ego had been a plumber in Canada but had died a volunteer in the CEF (Canadian Expeditionary Force) at age twenty-one on the first day of the battle at Vimy Ridge. The names of the casualties, I suggested to my audience at the Union Club, had been lost in life but were alive again "like walking ghosts" on the breast pockets and in short biographies offered by each of the student visitors. And the students, not the dignitaries, might well have been the stars of the ceremony.

"Those young Canadians have done the Byng Boys proud," I told my Saint John audience. "In that one day at Vimy, those students did as much to advance the cause of remembrance and to raise the profile of Canada's nationhood as the ninety Armistice Days since 1918. They are to be congratulated for putting the achievement of Vimy back in our hearts and our classrooms."

At five minutes to 11 a.m. on the original Armistice Day, a Canadian private named George Price advanced with a patrol of the 28th Northwest Battalion toward a German strongpoint near Mons in Belgium; across the front line a German sniper spotted him and shot him in the chest; he was the only Canadian killed on November 11, 1918. That evening, Ella Mae Bongard, a Canadian army nurse who'd attended wounded for thirteen months at Etretat, France, heard news of peace and celebrated by "carrying lighted torches [through the streets] and with our army capes turned inside out to show the scarlet lining." When he wrote home to family in Lethbridge, Alberta, about the Armistice, artillery gunner George Rennison couldn't help thinking about the banking life he'd left behind and would soon rejoin; "what will be the attitude of the bank regarding the granting of credit to Germans and Austrians in the future?" he mused. Charlie Venning's first taste of the peace got delayed. Captured during a bungled gas attack at Vimy in March 1917, he'd spent the duration tending pigs in German POW camps at Munster and Sennelager; when he learned of the Armistice he refused to work, but that angered his captors and they put him in prison for fourteen more days. Such stories of the first Armistice survive in diaries, letters, and archived newspaper clippings.

The closest I ever got to an eyewitness account of the first Armistice, however, happened very much by accident. In the spring of 2004, while touring my book *Juno: Canadians at D-Day* through western Canada, a local bookseller in Saskatchewan staged a reading and autographing session. Partway through the evening, Jean

Gordon, the publicist for the Saskatoon event, handed me an unmarked brown manila envelope.

"When you get some time, have a look at this," she said.

I thanked her, but never got the chance that night to ask about what the envelope contained. We didn't make contact again until a year or so later when I began to assemble first-hand accounts of Canadian soldiers at Vimy Ridge. I suddenly rediscovered Jean's unlabelled envelope and read its contents, nearly fifty pages of an infantryman's diary from the Great War. But without any ID, I had no idea whose memoirs they were. There were several references in quoted conversations to "Mac," but that was all. Fortunately, Jean had enclosed her business card so I called for an explanation. These were the wartime recollections of her great-uncle Gavin McDonald. In them, the volunteer from Craik, Saskatchewan, recounted his entire wartime experience—from the moment he enlisted at age twenty-three in 1915, through all his first-hand experiences overseas fighting at the Somme in 1916, at Vimy and Passchendaele in 1917, and finally during the capture of Mons in the fall of 1918.

"When I got to the main road, I got a ride in the back of a truck going in the direction of Mons," McDonald wrote in one of his last entries about the war. "I must have been on the truck over two hours and I knew we must be getting close, so I was standing at the back fully loaded—pack on my back, haversack on my right side, on my left my gas mask and water bottle and my rifle in my hand. . . .

"I dropped to the road, but the pack on my back spoiled my balance and I fell back on the road. When I hit the ground, my ears started to ring. As I had not hit my head on anything I wondered what made them ring. I sat up and looked around. All the doors on the street had flown open and people were running, dancing, singing and laughing. Then I realized what had happened. I had fallen on my back on the road at 11 a.m. on the eleventh day of the eleventh month. My ears were not ringing, but the church bells sure were. The war was over!"

What proved most extraordinary about McDonald's recollections was that they almost did not get written or consequently published here. When I phoned Jean Gordon in Saskatoon for an explanation of the unmarked memoirs, she told me about the Gavin McDonald she and her sister Judy Wood had known when they were young women. Their uncle was an original. In 1905, at age thirteen, he and his family—father, mother, and three sisters—homesteaded on 160 acres near Craik, northwest of Regina. Salt of the earth, the McDonalds farmed there for more than half a century, when Gavin and his sister Katie retired to Victoria, B.C. When Katie died, Gavin wrote his memoirs. The first draft of Gavin McDonald's "Narratives"—nearly 30,000 words—was rich with anecdotes and insights of life on the land. Conspicuously absent from his chronological telling of his life story, however, were the years 1915 to 1919, during which he'd served overseas with the Canadian Expeditionary Force.

"I didn't think anyone would be interested," he told his nieces Judy Wood and Jean Gordon. "It's tougher to recall the experiences from the war."

For many reasons, I discovered, survivors of the Great War did not talk about their experiences. Men who had volunteered for service in the Canadian Expeditionary Force (and were therefore not career soldiers) considered the war a matter of fulfilling an obligation of citizenship or duty to the King, much like jury duty or casting a ballot. Therefore, veterans perhaps looked beyond the entire wartime episode as if it were simply a necessary evil, a relatively short interruption in a working life, while building a business or raising a family. A further reason veterans, such as Gavin McDonald, avoided reflecting on the war, was perhaps a sense of guilt; why had he survived while 60,661 of his CEF comrades-in-arms had not? In his mind, at least, it might have seemed an insult to the memory of those who had been killed to talk about defying death in the war and enjoying life beyond it in peacetime. It was clear to Jean Gordon and her sister Judy Wood, however, that their uncle Gavin felt blessed to have returned alive and at least outwardly unscarred by the ordeal. Instinct compelled them to ask for an explanation of that four-year gap in his memoirs.

"Write about your wartime experiences, Uncle Gavin," the two great-nieces apparently entreated. "Please do it for us."

Some time later, McDonald completed a forty-eight-page amendment to the original memoir. A copy of McDonald's additional narrative of his experiences in the Great War was what Jean Gordon had passed to me in that brown envelope in 2004. What first struck me about McDonald's wartime memoir initially was his rather casual enlistment in the army in the first place. In the fall of 1915, he noted, "we had a good crop . . . good prices, over a dollar a bushel, a good time to try and get the well closer to the buildings. . . . After I had got most of the drilling done, I enlisted and joined the army on December 3, 1915."

After training and transport to Britain, Lance Corporal Gavin McDonald became a member of Princess Patricia's Canadian Light Infantry (PPCLI) in the 3rd Canadian Infantry Division. At Ypres a shell casing grazed his chin. Outside the city of Albert, France, his company sergeant major had both legs blown off. In the early days at the Somme, his best friend was paralyzed by shrapnel. And at Vimy he assisted in tunnel construction, each day filling sandbags with the chalk subsoil the miners were digging from saps under no man's land, each night dumping the contents into nearby shell holes to camouflage the excavation going on right under the noses of their German enemy.

Though not a historian, nor even a trained writer, the young prairie farmer managed to capture the essence of wartime moments. Even as much of Western Europe and North America prepared to celebrate a long-awaited armistice and soldiers anticipated repatriation, L/Cpl. McDonald saw more than the obvious. On November 11, 1918, the big story at Mons, Belgium, appeared to be the political infighting between Allied commanders. In fact, as McDonald made his way by truck to rejoin his battalion for what was clearly a final engagement or two of the war, the officers commanding the Canadian and British troops were jockeying for victorious recognition. With most of Mons in Allied hands, that November day, McDonald's sister battalion—the Royal Highlanders from Montreal—sent its pipe band into the streets of Mons to lead Maj. Gen. Arthur Currie and the Canadian Corps' triumphant arrival. This because, the previous week when the Canadians planned a victory march into Valenciennes, the British commander, Gen. Henry Horne, had upstaged Currie and insisted that British troops lead the way. The histrionics of the army brass aside, Gavin McDonald's account of the pipers' parade into Mons proved far more telling.

"I was marching along in the second platoon from the front [when] I noticed all the townspeople staring at something behind me," McDonald wrote. "It was the pipers. They had all thrown their pipes over their shoulders and all the ribbons were flying in the breeze [and] they started to play. I think it was 'Bonnie Dundee.'

"The people went wild. One man got out on the street and [did] a clog dance, wooden shoes and all. They were a big hit. That night, I was in a café and got talking to an old lady. . . . She said she could never see how the Allies could win the war with all the men and guns and everything the Germans had. With all the materiel the Germans had, they did not have any of those men in short skirts, carrying those things that squalled. That was what won the war, the kilties and the bagpipes."

It took another four months for Gavin McDonald to get home to Craik from the war. It took another fifty years before he wrote about it. It took an unlabelled envelope, passed to me partly out of frustration, for his stories to see the light of day. His two great-nieces—Judy Wood and Jean Gordon—said they had previously approached official archives and museums about saving and/or publishing Gavin McDonald's "Narratives," but none seemed interested. The good fortune of their gift to me meant that, while I was preparing my new book, *Victory at Vimy*, I would gain a better understanding of the average soldier's lot in the Great War. Veteran McDonald had painted the clearest depictions of primitive existence in the trenches, murderous offensives, relentless loss of life, and in that simple Armistice Day memory, how he and his comrades-in-arms had prevailed.

The actual Armistice signing on November 11 took place in the forest of Compiègne, northeast of Paris, aboard the private railway coach of Allied Supreme Commander Ferdinand Foch. Though the document brought hostilities to an end until the Treaty of Versailles could be drafted and signed the next year, even Marshal Foch recognized, "this is not peace; it is an armistice for twenty years."

Armistice at the end of the Second World War in Europe, twenty-seven years after deliberations in Foch's railway coach, took place on the second floor of Supreme Forward Headquarters at Rheims, France, on May 7, 1945. Victory-in-Europe (VE) Day was celebrated the next day. Three months later, the Americans dropped atomic bombs on Japan forcing their surrender (VJ Day) on August 15, 1945. Nevertheless, in Canada, November 11 has remained the annual day of wartime remembrance.

As a journalist and someone whose freedom always seemed a given, each Remembrance Day I try to find an untapped veteran's story to illustrate the experience of life without that birthright. In 1994, as co-host of a TVOntario current affairs program about Ontario's education system, I found one.

The story had its roots in Canada's connection with the Netherlands during the Second World War. When the Nazis invaded Holland, members of the Dutch royal family fled the country and were eventually welcomed to Ottawa, where they stayed throughout the war. In 1945 when Crown Princess Juliana returned to a liberated Holland, she hadn't forgotten the hospitality of Canadians or their capital city. She sent a gift of 100,000 tulip bulbs, not only as a symbol of her gratitude for wartime sanctuary in Ottawa but also to recognize those Canadians who had served and sacrificed in the liberation of Holland in 1944 and 1945.

It was not a one-time gift. The bulbs kept coming, a million of them every year, followed by an annual explosion of primary colours each springtime when the tulips bloomed at public sites around Ottawa. During the fall of 1994, in an attempt to raise awareness of the unique relationship between Holland and Canada, the ministry of Veterans Affairs, through a division called Canada Remembers, decided to send some of that annual shipment of bulbs to elementary and high schools across the country. That way students could plant commemorative gardens to honour those same Second World War veterans.

It occurred to me the plan had a fatal flaw. Students in Canadian schools didn't know what they were supposed to remember. For teenagers or younger children, any discussion of war and veterans would have been restricted to the 1991 Persian Gulf War or some other hot spot within their lifetimes. Anything prior would have seemed like ancient history. It took a while, but I finally found a school—Pickering College in Newmarket, Ontario—that planned to take delivery of some imported Dutch tulip bulbs with the idea of planting them in a large flowerbed outside the entrance to the school that autumn. I approached the school administration for permission to bring two veterans into a Grade 8 classroom to help illustrate the connection between Canada and the liberation of Holland fifty years before. I asked if I could videotape the interaction between the veterans and the students. They agreed.

Inside the Pickering College classroom, the students had set up two stools for their guests and then arranged themselves—some seated on chairs, others on desks—to be as close as they could to the veterans in front of them. At sixty-eight, Anne Pompili sat very erect. She was dressed in a skirt and jacket. She spoke directly to her audience of twelve- and thirteen-year-olds, never hesitating or holding back any of the details or the emotions she felt. When she smiled, her entire face smiled, even though her story was anything but a happy one.

"My first experience of war was the night of the ninth of May, 1940. I listened to the radio with my father and Hitler promised never to invade Holland," Anne said. "Next morning, the tenth of May, the German planes flew into Holland to bomb Rotterdam. I was thirteen years old."

She was Annie Keijzer then. She explained to the students that her father ran a small hotel in the eastern Dutch town of Enschede, just a few kilometres from the German border. Initially, despite the German invasion, Annie was allowed to continue school, although

German language instruction became a priority. Curfews soon followed and identification certificates became mandatory. Then German troops began conducting *razzias* (raids); they cordoned off blocks in the town and systematically confiscated radios, food, precious household possessions, and eventually young Dutch men to work in German factories or labour camps. Before long, the Keijzer family, like most, needed coupons for basic food items and stood in bread lines to survive.

"My mother and I went to the farmers [outside Enschede] and traded my mother's beautiful linen for food," she told the Pickering College students. "One day when we went to the farmers and had a lot of food, we were stopped by the Germans. I was wearing the food. They asked if we had food and [hoping to bribe the Germans] I said, 'Yes. All sorts of things.' I offered them some cherries that we had picked. They said, 'Go on. We can see that you have nothing.' We got on our bikes and my mother was making a wet trail. She had wet her pants, that's how scared she was."

Anne shook her head and laughed out loud at the thought. Some of the students laughed too, but when she added that she wondered how she could have been so bold when the Germans shot civilians for smuggling food, the laughter stopped. Then it was time for the students' second visitor to introduce himself. Bruce Evans was born in 1923, four years before Anne, on a farm north of Toronto. Wearing his formal veteran's blazer with its ribbons and medals, Bruce recounted his enlistment and early military training experiences to the students.

"I joined the Canadian army on September 9, 1942. I'll never forget that date," he began. He described coping with the challenges of basic training—learning to hold and fire a rifle. But it turned out the toughest bullet to dodge at Camp Borden, Ontario, was the illness that ran rampant—influenza, measles, and chicken pox. Next came a rough ocean crossing and getting oriented in Britain. Eventually, he found his way into the First Hussars Regiment, as a gunner-operator, training in Duplex Drive tanks that would make amphibious landings in Normandy on June 6, 1944. He was wounded on Juno Beach on D-Day but rejoined his regiment as it finished clearing

German armoured units from ports along the English Channel en route to Belgium and eventually Holland. The liberation experience was as much an eye-opener for Bruce Evans as it was for the Dutch people being liberated.

"As we moved through Dutch villages and towns, we began to realize how grateful this country would be for its liberation," he told the students. "Even at night the Dutch people came out of their homes to wave and call out. Some began writing chalk messages on our tanks, telling their friends they had been liberated. The reception they gave us was overwhelming.

"During the liberation of Apeldoorn, the tank battles caused a lot of destruction. [At one point] to protect ourselves from snipers, we moved our tank between two damaged houses. Suddenly, I noticed this tapping sound on the outside of the tank. We peered outside. Lo and behold there was a Dutch family handing up a bowl of fruit to us, taking a great risk doing it. It was all they had."

Bruce became caught up in the story. Anne and the students could see his eyes welling up at the thought of lost tank comrades and innocent Dutch civilians dying during the liberation. Instinctively, Anne touched Bruce's arm with reassurance. That helped him through the emotional moment. Their initial nervousness was gone now. They were not just reciting tired old war stories. They were triggering each other's memories. Despite some of the disquieting mind's-eye images unearthed, they didn't feel the need any more to sanitize the frightening sights and sounds they remembered. Because they were suddenly supporting each other in front of the students, perhaps they felt they could go anywhere they needed to get the points across. They became particularly candid when they began answering the students' questions. A young girl asked Anne whether friends were imprisoned by the Germans during the war.

"A lot of my friends who were Jewish were taken away," she said. "And my father." Anne explained that without her knowledge, her father had hidden thirty Jewish friends and their families in the attic of his hotel in Enschede. He managed to gather enough food and clothing to keep them alive, but he was eventually betrayed and "my father was sent to a German work camp, we didn't know where. They confiscated the hotel. But I went there to speak with the [German officer] who was in charge of the whole town. It took four weeks before I was able to have a talk with him. He was rude, twice slapped me in the face because I said I didn't know what was in the attic."

The classroom fell silent. All eyes were on this elderly woman as she shed fifty years to describe the fear she felt for her father's life and her own. She explained that these events drove her to join the Dutch Underground. Since she had earlier studied at a beautician school, Anne first took on the job of bleaching Jewish women's hair blond to make them appear more Aryan. After that, she served as a courier delivering copies of the Underground newspaper, secret packages, identification documents, and clothing that was channelled to Allied airmen who'd been shot down and needed civilian disguises to evade the Germans and make their way back to England. She received a special armband, with the insignia of the Inner Country Resistance on it; when the Allies arrived, she was to wear her armband and guide the liberators through Enschede to known German installations.

Another student asked what happened when the Allied troops arrived.

"The first liberator I saw was a Canadian soldier with two guns in his hands," she said. "I kissed him I was so happy. We took out the tricolour [flag]. We ran in the streets and were singing. The next day, I got my first ride on top of a tank . . . to show the Canadians how to get out of the town and on to the highway to Germany. People came out of hiding and danced in the street. My father's hotel was a mess. My father [freed from the labour camp] was too ill, but his beloved country was free. We had been occupied for five years. Now we were liberated."

The students asked questions for another half-hour. The boys wanted Bruce to tell them more about tank warfare and they wanted a closer look at his medals—the 1939–45 Star, the France and Germany Star, the Canada Defence Medal, the Canadian Volunteer Medal, the Defence of Britain Medal, and the Normandy Medal (presented to him that year). The girls were curious about Anne's work with the Dutch Underground. To help illustrate some of their stories, the two veterans brought out some photographs. The students particularly enjoyed the pictures of Bruce as a young army recruit and Anne when she was a teenager at school in Enschede. Finally, the students wondered what Bruce and Anne would be thinking about and doing on the upcoming Remembrance Day. The veteran tank commander admitted he would be recalling lost friends and his good fortune of getting through the war alive. "We were there to liberate Holland. We had a job to do and we got it done."

"Fifty years later, we have not forgotten," Anne quickly added. "The Canadians were our liberators, so every year Dutch children are brought to the cemeteries. They each adopt a grave. They tend them and lay flowers at each one."

That seemed the appropriate moment to leave the classroom for the flowerbeds in front of the school. Out came the bulbs and the trowels and the digging began in the afternoon sun. Anne seemed to be the expert on planting tulips so the students followed her lead. But everybody pitched in until the last of the bulbs was gingerly buried in the remembrance garden in front of Pickering College. Thanks to a Canadian who had participated in the liberation of Holland and a former member of the Dutch Underground, a group of Grade 8 students had come to understand the significance of Dutch tulips in Canadian gardens. Suddenly, Remembrance Day wasn't so intangible or just a piece of ancient history.

However, one question remained in my mind: Had the students made the connection between a young Bruce Evans making the commitment to go to Europe to fight and a young Annie Keijzer risking her life for her family and her country? As the last of the bulbs was planted I asked several of the students for their thoughts.

"Anne was just thirteen years old during the war. We're just thirteen," student Danielle Trueman said. "I can't picture myself going through that. I don't think I could have made the decisions they did."

In that instant, a small group of modern teenagers had made the connection between themselves and the generation of young people that had faced a world war and the life and death decisions it threw at them every day. Suddenly, the elderly veterans in front of the high school students weren't ancient history any more. They were mirrors of ordinary youths who had faced a crisis, risked everything, done extraordinary things, and miraculously survived. They had given the contemporary students—and me—something to visualize when they were soon called upon to remember at 11 a.m. on November 11.

Unlike the First and Second World Wars, the Korean War never officially ended. On the morning of July 27, 1953—two years, two weeks, and three days after peace negotiations had begun at Panmunjom near the 38th parallel—the United Nations and communist delegates filed into a so-called Peace Pagoda to complete a truce. At 10 o'clock, Maj. Gen. William Harrison, the senior UN delegate, sat at a plain table across from the chief of staff of the Korean People's Army, Nam Il. Each man signed his name eighteen times on the truce documents. Not a word was exchanged between them. A ceasefire would go into effect twelve hours later. Even as the ink dried on the two representatives' signatures, however, journalists reported "the boom-boom-boom" of distant artillery fire. Between mid-June and mid-July United Nations gunners had fired 4.5 million shells at their Chinese enemies; the Communists had answered with 1.5 million shells. During the very day the truce was signed, American Thunderjet fighters took advantage of UN air supremacy above most of the peninsula and pummelled what North Korean airfields remained in service. Then, just twenty minutes before the official ceasefire, an American bomber dumped its payload north of the 38th parallel for good measure. Finally, at 10 p.m. the fighting—but not the war—ended.

For thirty-three Canadians captured and imprisoned in POW camps during three years of the Korean War, the end of hostilities did not come for at least another few days; for some it was a number of weeks; and in the case of RCAF jet pilot Andy Mackenzie, repatriation did not occur until December 5, 1954, a year and a half after the truce and two years from the day he was shot down over the North. In fact, so extraordinary were the Canadian prisoners' first steps to freedom and away from war, that for fifty years afterward a number of them gathered on the occasion of their capture to reconvene and recall their experiences. Traditionally, for members of the 3rd Battalion of the Royal Canadian Regiment (RCR), their reunion took place at the outfit's barracks in Petawawa, near the Ottawa River in Ontario. It became known as the Hill 187 Reunion and included several pub socials and a church parade, as well as a Saturday night banquet and dance. I attended the Hill 187 Reunion in the spring of 1997 and met, among others, two former Korean War POWs—Jim Gunn and Len Badowich.

Among the first men to accept my invitation for an interview that weekend was Badowich. We sat in a liquor lounge adjacent to the main RCR meeting hall and with the noise of a meet-and-greet session going on around us, Len began to tell me how his life intersected with the military. Born in Poland in 1932, he grew up on stories of his father's experiences fighting for the Polish cavalry against the Prussians during the Great War and against the Bolsheviks in the 1920s. But before the Second World War broke out, five-year-old Len emigrated with his family from Poland to a farm near Brandon, Manitoba. Even on the prairies, however, warfare and military service had an impact on him and his community. There were 3,000 Poles living in one end of Brandon, a city of 20,000, and in 1939 when Hitler invaded Poland most eligible Polish men immediately joined up and disappeared into overseas service.

"Most joined the South Saskatchewan Regiment. Two of my uncles were killed at Dieppe," he said. "There were air force bases of the [British] Commonwealth Air Training Plan all around us, and the army camp at Shilo, Manitoba. . . . In 1943, when I was eleven, you automatically had to belong to the cadet corps. I got an army cadet uniform from school, and put it on for my mother. 'Look Mama,' I said in Polish. 'I'm a soldier.' And she said, 'What kind of a country is this? Eleven years old and they draft him into the army!'"

Len's mother didn't have to worry about his serving at the front in the Second World War, but he did use his cadet uniform (and an accompanying wooden rifle) to march in Victory Bond parades and when he carried returning soldiers' bags home for a quarter per trip. Given his inbred hatred of communism, it was no surprise to his family in 1950 when Len decided to join Prime Minister Louis St. Laurent's "Special Force" of Canadian troops being recruited to drive the communists out of the Republic of South Korea. When he joined up that summer, Len heard the recruiter mention something about the "Royal Canadians." Len interpreted that to mean a tank regiment, but the Royal Canadians turned out to be the Royal Canadian Regiment, one of three army outfits supplying infantrymen for the Korean War. Badowich had second thoughts momentarily, but for him Korea was going to be "an adventure." Except that on the train following embarkation leave, en route to Korea, Badowich sat next to a member of Princess Patricia's Canadian Light Infantry, a soldier already decorated in Korea.

"He started telling me about Korea," Badowich said. "About the Chinese and how they attacked in swarms and hordes and what fighting was like. I just couldn't believe it. [He said], 'With our Bren guns and our machine guns we just mowed them down, but they'd still keep coming and overrun you.'" The way Badowich quoted the vet on the train, he made the irony clear. In other words, little did he realize how close he would come to experiencing exactly that kind of Chinese attack in Korea, nor did Len realize how much the events in the trenches of Hill 187 that last spring of the war would change his life.

Now I needed some indication of the topography of Hill 187. Badowich took a pen from his pocket and began sketching it on the back of a paper placemat. Unlike the more notorious positions along the stalemated Jamestown Line in Korea—Hill 355, Hill 227, and the Hook—the complex of three finger ridges radiating into the Sami-ch'on valley, known as Hill 187, was hardly strategic. Lower in altitude than the other hills (hills in Korea were numbered based on their altitude in metres above sea level) and spread over a kilometre of the front line, the terrain of the steep-sided Hill 187 would prove difficult to defend while its brush and long grass would offer hostile patrols a great deal of concealment. All these factors would play against the Canadian defenders, members of "C" Company of the Royal Canadian Regiment, after dark on May 2, 1953.

Staring at his sketch of Hill 187 on the placemat, I asked where Badowich was situated that night. He pointed to the northwesternmost point of the Canadian position. He emphasized that his section (about eight men) was forward of the No. 7 Platoon position, forward of the "C" Company position, indeed forward of the entire battalion, or as he described it "at the sharp end."

What was worse, he said, when the Chinese artillery began shelling their hillside that night, Badowich's corporal got scared and abandoned the section. That left L/Cpl. Badowich in charge of the section. Though the night was moonless and completely dark, when the Chinese shells exploded—two or three per second—Badowich's group noticed movement in no man's land and deduced that enemy troops were trying to break through the defensive barbed wire. A standby patrol from the adjacent RCR No. 8 Platoon area went out to investigate. Badowich shook his head, as he described the patrol being decimated by the Chinese, as was a second patrol from "A" Company. Badowich figured it was only a matter of time before the Chinese troops that had overcome the two patrols entered his forward position. When he reported the situation to Lt. Ed Hollyer, who was in charge of the No. 7 Platoon area, the two men could see Chinese troops pouring into the forward Canadian trenches. Hollyer told Badowich to warn as many of the platoon areas as possible that he was going to order a DFSOS, which meant Defensive Fire and SOS, bringing friendly artillery fire down on their own position. As Badowich passed the word, the barrage began with horrifying intensity. Four thousand of their own shells crashed into Hill 187 that night.

"I remember thinking, 'The Chinese are going to come as soon as this ends. They're going to come.' And they sure as hell did," Badowich explained. "I could see dozens of them in front of me. I jumped into a trench and all of a sudden there was a [Chinese] guy standing in front of me. And he fired. Another guy with me, Keating, he got it right across the chest. The bullets went through my sleeve. Then they threw a potato masher [concussion grenade] and I was knocked out. When I came to I was bleeding from my ears and my nose from the concussion and there was a bayonet levelled at me. That's when I was captured. They took me to the No. 8 Platoon area where I met another prisoner, Pelletier, who was hit in both legs. They made us carry Keating, but there was no sense. He was dead."

Badowich punctuated the memory by pointing and tapping on the No. 7 Platoon area of his placemat map. The images of the capture sank in for a few moments. Then he continued by saying, "When I was a prisoner, though, I came closer to death than this." Len then recounted his POW experience. Though it had occurred nearly half a century before, he could remember many individual days, every physical aspect of his prison camp in North Korea, and each encounter with his captors as explicitly as if the imprisonment had ended yesterday. He said every detail had stayed with him. These were memories he could never shake. From his forced march trip away from the battlefield that first night, to his confinement and interrogation, to his final release at Freedom Village near Panmunjom over four months later, he seemed to have photo recall of everything. What's more, Badowich appeared fearless in his recollections, as if he had dealt with the horrors of the experience and reached some form of closure.

Jim Gunn appeared equally at ease with his capture that same night, although his job description with the Royal Canadian Regiment could well have meant summary execution on the battlefield, no questions asked. Gunn and I sat in the same liquor lounge at Petawawa later that same afternoon as he recounted his memories of the May 2 Chinese attack. Two years younger than Badowich (and therefore underage), Jim Gunn had used his brother's name and papers to enlist at Sunnybrook Personnel Depot in Toronto in 1951. His job in the 3rd Battalion of the RCR was in the sniper section. He denied being a natural marksman because, he said, the scopes on the .303 rifles pretty much made everybody a good shot.

In fact, on the night of the Chinese attack on Hill 187, Gunn had attached an infrared scope to his American carbine rifle because he knew his shift in the forward trenches would require night vision. En route to the "C" Company trenches, however, he and his sniper partner decided the incoming shells and mortars would sufficiently light up the landscape so they wrapped their scopes in a poncho and hid them in the back of their trench. Since the Communist Chinese were notorious for executing snipers, Gunn admitted that disposing of the scopes on their rifles likely saved their lives;* they were captured by the same Chinese troops that overran Badowich's position.

"When the Chinese hit the hill, they just ran up and down the trenches," Gunn said. "Every slit they passed they just threw in concussion grenades. They made two or three passes like that and then went into each trench, just firing their burp-guns. The trench O'Connell and I were in had caved in. When they came, the guy fired and hit O'Connell all up on side of the leg. He was bleeding like hell. When I came to, I was up on my knees and there were eight or nine Chinese with burp-guns and ammo grabbing me. They pushed me out of the trench and down the hill, dragging us through the minefield."

Like Len Badowich, Jim Gunn described the months of his captivity under Chinese guards and interrogators in North Korea with extraordinary clarity and detail. Contrary to the experience of his Second World War brothers in German stalags or Japanese jungle compounds, Jim Gunn said the North Korean POW camps seemed more ad hoc arrangements, little more than Korean villages taken over by Chinese authorities. Generally, the camps were guarded, but not fortified or bristling with gun turrets or barbed wire. They didn't have to be.

It was the environment of the camps and their immediate vicinity that made them inescapable. Most camps consisted of mud and straw huts with ten-by-ten rooms that had a wooden-framed door and windows with paper over them, each containing about ten men. The huts had no lights, tables, chairs, beds, or other furnishings. In summer,

---

* According to some interpretations of the Geneva Convention of 1949, snipers were not entitled to the same rights and protections as prisoners of war.

breezes were the only relief from the heat, and in winter, an adjoining kitchen hut pumped smoke through a flue system into the floors and walls, providing some heat. Solitary confinement, sometimes referred to as "the hole," might be a latrine pit or a sweat box but most often a gap between two village buildings, perhaps thirty metres long by a metre wide. The hole had no toilet or roof. The occupant was forced to defecate at the entrance to the passageway (the same place through which his daily ration of food and water would be passed). Then he would retreat to the opposite end to eat or find what little shelter a blanket and the building walls might provide. And if the environment inside the camp wasn't enough of a deterrent against an attempted escape, the environment outside made success highly unlikely. The country's terrain was inhospitable and the population generally hostile. It would have been nearly impossible for any Caucasian prisoner to escape and remain unnoticed among the North Korean population.

And yet what proved most threatening to the Canadian POWs in those North Korean camps was neither the barriers nor the deprivation. The trouble began, as Jim Gunn recalled, on the long trek north away from the front line at the 38th parallel. En route to Camp 2, beyond the Chinese-held hills, the POW columns suddenly faced the wrath of UN aircrews. Searching for what were described as targets of opportunity, the jet fighter and bomber crews regularly unloaded any excess bombs or cannon shells on enemy convoys; most UN pilots had no idea the trucks or columns of troops included POWs.

"The Chinese claimed that the camp was properly identified as per the Geneva Convention," Gunn explained. "The bombing raids were exploited by the Chinese in their quest to have us sign petitions . . . addressed to such personages as the secretary-general of the United Nations, the president of the International Red Cross, and the presidents or prime ministers of the various NATO countries to stop the bombing of a neutral site. And on a couple of occasions the gates were closed as the planes swept down, so that prisoners couldn't get into the tunnel shelters. A few prisoners were hit. This brought more petitions for us to sign, claiming that our planes were trying to kill us. [The Chinese] suggested if we signed, it would put an end to the bombing."

This was psychological warfare, not the hand-to-hand variety for which troops of the Royal Canadian Regiment had been trained. China was not a signatory to the Geneva Convention, which guaranteed standards of hygiene, medical care, food, accommodation, and supervision for prisoners (standards that would have meant preferential treatment over Chinese soldiers). In addition, China's view was that United Nations prisoners taking part in this unjust war were war criminals and that if they were captured their captors had the right to kill them. However, the Chinese applied a so-called lenient treatment policy, which defined the POWs as "victims of the ruling classes, students who were to be educated and pointed towards the truth." As such, POWs were to be fed, given medical treatment where possible, and neither robbed nor abused. For the Chinese communists, prisoners of war had a distinct propaganda value when kept alive.

Pointing the POWs toward the truth, as they saw it, involved a regular diet of social studies. Chinese interrogators took on the roles of in-class lecturers and discussion leaders. Len Badowich remembered receiving notebooks in which he was expected to record the history lessons delivered each day. Among other "facts" delivered in these settings, Badowich was told that there was a cholera epidemic running rampant in Korea and northern China. The lecturers further blamed the United Nations for dropping germ bombs on unsuspecting Korean villages and troops. But as eagerly as his interrogators wanted Badowich to endorse the lectures and sign the germ warfare declarations, it became clear they were after something more valuable than that. They began one-on-one interviews with him.

"The first interrogation was quite simple," Badowich said. "They just covered military matters. But then it got more severe. All of a sudden the rest of the boys were taken away to a mining camp and I was put in this room. In came the interrogator and he says, 'When is the South Korean Army going to take over from the Canadian

Army?' How the hell would I know? I'm a lance corporal and they're asking political questions. I'm a section leader with eight men under me if I'm lucky. I'm interested in wine, women, and song, not when the South Korean Army is going to take over."

Badowich said he later discovered the Chinese had learned from other prisoners that he had trained Katcom (Korean Augmentation to Commonwealth) or South Korean soldiers for the Canadian Army. As a consequence of the leaked information, Badowich suddenly found himself on a daily firing line to reveal all Katcom activity on the United Nations side of the front line. The interrogators had decided to make an example of him and the brainwashing escalated from there.

"'What rank do you hold?' the interrogator said. 'I'm a lance corporal,' I said. They knew American ranks, but Americans didn't have lance corporals in their army. So he says, 'What's that?' And I said, 'I'm a squad leader.' 'No, no. You're higher than that. You trained Koreans!' It went on and on like this for three days."

I had met and interviewed many prisoners of war before, but never one who'd undergone this kind of psychological abuse. Unlike other vets who'd endured years of beatings, starvation, and solitary confinement in Europe or Japan in the 1939–45 war, Badowich's time in captivity, I knew, came when peace talks were well underway and when it seemed only a matter of weeks or months before some kind of agreement might end hostilities and hasten his release. Still, the images of Laurence Harvey's brainwashed character executing his buddies in *The Manchurian Candidate* and the Robert De Niro character in *The Deer Hunter* forced to play Russian roulette in a North Vietnam POW camp kept crossing my mind.

Badowich hadn't been forced to kill fellow prisoners, but these incessant brainwashing sessions could not have been easy to endure. Not surprisingly, perhaps, I began to wonder what I would have done under such circumstances. I couldn't imagine lasting a few days, let alone months. I sensed, however, there was more than Badowich's Polish dedication to duty that had pulled him through. I asked him if he was religious. He said he wasn't. I asked if he'd thought of his family or a girlfriend as a distraction. No, he said, in Korea there was no room for any feelings. But then I suddenly stumbled on what perhaps saved him when I asked about his interrogators.

"We had nicknames for the interrogators," Badowich recalled. "We called the camp commander 'Blood-On-Your-Hands' because he was this great big six-foot-tall Chinese man. One time the Americans bombed and hit a hospital. They were all civilian casualties. They laid all the bodies out and just as it was getting dark they had us parade one by one past these bodies. And Blood-On-Your-Hands was standing up on the slope telling us, 'You have Chinese and Korean blood on your hands. You bomb and kill innocent civilians.' We were prisoners. We were out of the war."

Badowich, Gunn, and the others had no tangible defence against their interrogators. By the time they reached the work camps well back in the North Korean countryside, the Chinese had stripped their army uniforms away and replaced them with sky-blue work pants, bloused shirts, peaked caps, and running shoes. They were covered in lice and crabs. Without proper food, with insufficient sleep, and with no medical supplies, they were prone to any number of diseases. Their camp commanders forced them to listen, report, and repeat lessons in lectures, and they were forced to work in mines and fields or suffer the consequences. They couldn't resist or escape. So they turned to their own resources as a means of defence. They used what little humour they could muster as their only weapon for fighting back. As a response to one of the propaganda lectures, in which the Chinese displayed alleged proof of UN bacteriological weaponry, one group of Canadian prisoners decided to "help" deliver the evidence. A mouse was caught, fitted with a miniature harness and parachute, and placed in a tree. When guards discovered the "para-mouse," Chinese camp commandants, photographers, and lecturers swarmed over the area to record the latest episode of germ warfare. The prisoners fed on the uproarious spectacle for weeks.

Jim Gunn said he had a copy of the New Testament that a padre had given him before he was captured, and though he wasn't particularly religious, the reading helped to distract him. And what the biblical readings couldn't deliver, his friend Ernie Taylor did. Whenever new prisoners arrived, Gunn said Taylor was at the gate in a flash, picking up the latest news from outside. Most inmates dubbed him "Scoop" Taylor and several times a day as he and Gunn wandered in the compound, Taylor would ask, "How long do you think, Gunner?" (meaning how long until their release). To which Gunn would reply, "Maybe two to three months." Taylor would always respond, "Nah. More like two or three years," and move on.

"Even when we knew damn well the war was over," Gunn said, "we knew the Chinese were just playing with us. One day they'd say, 'Get ready to pack. Tomorrow you go home.' Next day came and nothing. . . . Even the Americans, the Marines that were there, kept saying, 'Trim the tree in '53,' meaning we'll probably be home for Christmas. Ernie would say to them 'Uh-uh. See the Golden Gate in '58.' . . . I don't know whether Ernie was an optimist or a pessimist, but he sure made the time pass easier for me. I was fortunate to spend this time with good guys who were steady but could joke when the occasion presented itself."

Nobody's limericks or satire could have prepared the Canadians, however, for their release and return to freedom in August 1953. Much propagandizing, unrelenting bureaucracy, and the minutiae of the Armistice document delayed Gunn's and Badowich's release from the camps in North Korea. When the trucks transporting the POWs finally crossed the 38th parallel and arrived at Freedom Village, all returning prisoners were immediately told to strip down so that their clothes could be destroyed and their bodies deloused with disinfectant. When they were re-kitted with new army-issue uniforms, they sat down to an immense meal of steak and eggs, beer and cola and ice cream or chocolate for dessert. Most of the men kept the food down only momentarily; their systems were not used to such rich foods, so most vomited the contents back up within the hour. In contrast, Jim Gunn said he got the greatest pleasure from drinking one glass of ice-cold milk (and keeping it down). Following the meal, Len Badowich remembered, all the returning ex-POWs had to go through yet another interrogation, this time by UN intelligence officers.

"The first thing they did was have us swear allegiance to the Queen [Elizabeth II], because the King [George VI] had died while we were in prison. Then they asked, 'Why didn't you escape?' How the hell do you escape in Korea, where the place is full of Orientals? You're white. Where do you go? Nobody could have escaped. These assholes made us feel like we had committed a crime. Or deserted!"

When I later checked on the record of the thirty-three Canadian POWs, I discovered that several had attempted to escape and then paid dearly for it in solitary confinement. Two Canadian prisoners acknowledged they had signed a communist petition, but none of the Canadians wrote declarations against the United Nations Command. No evidence emerged from my research to suggest Canadians in North Korean prison camps had collaborated with their captors. In fact, there was every reason to believe all thirty-three resisted interrogation and indoctrination and that they had sabotaged Chinese brainwashing attempts. Ironically, after debriefing the POWs, Canadian intelligence officials issued the men grades for their internment performance in North Korea. A "white grade" meant undistinguished performance. A "light grey grade" meant low resistance. And a "black grade" indicated suspicion of collaboration with the enemy. Canadian officials graded the majority of men between satisfactory and undistinguished performance. Not one received a better-than-average assessment in the service of his country while in military prison.

Both Jim Gunn and Len Badowich did get VIP treatment returning home. A Canadian Pacific Airlines passenger plane complete with an entertainment troupe and open bar delivered them to Vancouver in late August 1953. Len recalled that he drank too much during the in-flight party and arrived in Canada with a massive hangover. The reporters surrounded the half-dozen or so ex-POWs on the stairs of the passenger liner. The vets looked bleary-eyed and the next day when the *Vancouver Sun* published the photograph, the caption read "POWs returning to Canada still suffering from the effects of their captivity." Their high profile both in the media and among the public faded quickly, however. Not only because the war never really came to a conclusion, but also because of the nature of the veterans' return to Canada, the Korean War rightly earned the moniker "the forgotten war," and its participants did indeed fade back into civilian life almost unnoticed. Gunn said he was released from Shaughnessy Veterans Hospital and made his own way home to Toronto. Badowich told me he got back to Brandon, Manitoba, to a hero's welcome from his family and the Polish parish. After that, he considered that saga of his life over.

"They made a big fuss over me at the beginning," Badowich said, when all he wanted was to sit alone in a beer parlour, go to a movie, read a book, or go out with a girlfriend. Eventually, even the radio stations and newspapers stopped calling and Badowich was just as happy about that. "I wasn't a hero. I was a survivor. I did my duty and was lucky to survive."

When the Hill 187 Reunion wrapped up with a church parade and a light lunch that Sunday, May 2, 1997, I packed up my hours of tape recordings and steno pads of notes and left Petawawa behind. As always, I offered sincere thanks to Badowich and Gunn and other veterans for the privilege of taking away their wartime memories. And I said goodbye, not knowing if I would ever see them or hear from any of them again. Coincidentally, as I drove away, a quotation crossed my mind—a phrase that had risen to prominence during that same Korean War period the Canadian vets were commemorating that weekend. I recalled Douglas MacArthur's peroration to the U.S. Congress in April 1951, when the general rebuffed his firing by President Harry Truman, defended his military strategy in the Korean War, and attempted to preserve his legacy. MacArthur's thirty-seven minutes of oratory to an estimated audience of twenty million television viewers concluded with those historic and often-quoted lines:

"The world has turned over many times since I took the oath on the plain at West Point, and the hopes and dreams have long since vanished, but I still remember the refrain of one of the most popular barrack ballads of that day which proclaimed most proudly that old soldiers never die; they just fade away. . . ."

Generally, the veterans I met that weekend during the RCR reunion in Petawawa (and the thousand or so before and since) had not given me interviews about their wartime experiences in defiance, obligation, or with any agenda in mind. Unlike Gen. MacArthur patching up his legacy with rhetoric, Badowich, Gunn, and others had no need to rebuff authority, defend actions, or preserve reputations. Perhaps to them—former rank and file soldiers—it just seemed the right time to gather around my microphone and remember for the record.

Indeed, my attempts to seek out and interview veterans generally during the 1980s and 90s had yielded a great deal of content for my freelance writing and broadcasting career—newspaper columns, periodical features, radio and television documentaries, and a handful of books. Perhaps sensing their dwindling numbers (by 2000, statistics indicated as many as 500 Canadian veterans were dying each week), veterans collectively recognized the need to speak out, to set the record straight, and to get their stories told while they could. Unlike the 1960s and 70s when the public appeared uninterested, if not repulsed by talk of combat experience, suddenly it welcomed, even invited the opportunity to hear it. Between 1999 and 2008 during the annual Remembrance Day period, for example, and thanks to such programs as the Dominion Institute's Memory Project, more than 1,500 veterans had presented their personal reflections on war in front of an estimated audience of 500,000 young people. It was time. It was appropriate. It was perhaps overdue and necessary to see veterans—clad in berets, blazers, and medals—leading discussions, presenting artifacts, identifying awards, and recounting close calls in classrooms, during town council meetings, at business banquets, and as part of civic ceremonies marking Remembrance Day. Yes, the veterans, at least of the Second World War and the Korean War, were growing older and fading ever more quickly. But not without having their say.

That, ultimately, became my message to the members of Byng Boys Club on the May night of their final gathering in 2007. I had finished my reflections about the exuberance of the young students attending the ninetieth anniversary ceremony at Vimy a month before. I had retold some of the individual soldiers' stories of the Great War that had made that moment in 1917, in my view and the view of many who'd come through the battle at Vimy Ridge, a coming of age for Canada. I had shown the final image from the cover of my book *Victory at Vimy*, illustrating those original Byng Boys aboard trucks leaving Vimy and buoyed by that first taste of victory and that sudden sense of nationhood. And I concluded my talk with one rather bold suggestion.

"The Byng Boys, I believe, have one final duty," I said. "You must ensure that you've passed the torch of memory to that new generation."

And I suggested whatever they felt their message was—"Canada owes much to its veterans" or "Never such holocaust again" or "Make peace not war"—they should ensure that a new generation of Canadians understands what a theatre of war did to them. Whether in classrooms, on streets, at Remembrance Day, or any other time of the year, I said, "you must keep alive the memory of your experience in the memories of those who care to know it."

Late that night, the O.C.'s Knob Kerry gavel came down one last time at the Union Club of Saint John, New Brunswick. The Byng Boys were dismissed. I shook the O.C.'s hand.

"Thank you," I said. "We'll not see your kind again."

4

WHY THEY DON'T TALK

Warriors of my grandfather's generation had no concept of instant, wireless transmission by cell phone from a war in Iraq, nor perhaps even a premonition of top-secret encryption the likes of Enigma in the Second World War. Soldiers of the 1914–1918 war did, however, write things down, in letters to family, illegal war diaries kept in personal notebooks, and memoirs written sometime after their return home. Consequently, the scribblings of average soldiers in the Great War offer those who find them a tangible, simply described, insightful glimpse into the darkness of their experience. The wartime reminiscences of Lewis Buck caught my attention during research at McMaster University in the spring of 2006. Fellow history author and friend Pierre Berton had bequeathed many of his original research documents of the Great War to the archives there, among them reflections from the former farm boy from Wyman, Quebec.

Lewis Buck enlisted with the 4th Battalion of the Canadian Expeditionary Force during a snowstorm in March 1916. The twenty-one-year-old served as a runner and stretcher bearer with his younger brother Billy at the front lines in France through 1917 and 1918. Together the Bucks endured German whizzbang shells, polluted water running through their trenches, and rats crawling around their heads as they tried to sleep. They did their best to suppress fear as they witnessed countless wounded put aboard trains bound for hospitals in Etaples on the English Channel. At Vimy Ridge, the brothers went over the top in the first wave in the pre-dawn behind a creeping barrage. Amid the chaos and noise of the battlefield, April 9, 1917, Lewis and Billy Buck were ordered to seek out rifles stuck in the mud, retrieve the wounded men next to each one, and carry them on stretchers to medical aid stations behind the lines. After the Canadians won the battle, the Buck brothers joined burial details preparing communal graves at the top of the ridge. Nearly 4,000 Canadians had been killed.

"There were twenty to twenty-five men per grave," Lewis Buck said. "We got bottles from the village and wrote the names of each man down, put it in a bottle upside down beside the man's head at the gravesite."

Only one Buck brother came home. Lewis had to bury his brother Billy, killed in action at the Drocourt-Quéant Line in September 1918, two months before the Armistice. Back home in Canada, Lewis Buck tried to resume work on the family farm in the Ottawa Valley. One day, working in an open field with a four-horse team, he heard a noise that sounded like an incoming shell.

"I threw myself on the ground," he said. "And I thought to myself, 'Boy, I may never get over this.' I used to dream horrible dreams. My dad had to come and wake me up at nights. I was dreaming I was back in the war."

Buck's contemporaries called his delayed reaction on the farm shell shock or battle fatigue. He said his way of coping with it was merely to wait for it to "fade away." Although Canadian army psychiatrists claimed they could "scientifically screen [and] categorize" soldiers for battle exhaustion by the time Canada entered the Second World War, when Canadian troops entered battle in Europe in 1943 the army was still unprepared for the psychiatric setbacks brought on by combat. Post-traumatic stress disorder (PTSD) had not entered the Canadian army medical lexicon. Nor had it by the time 27,000 Canadians went to Korea.

I discovered the impact of their trauma midway through the summer of 1997, when I met Jim McKinny. He was days away from his sixty-fifth birthday. We sat on the backyard patio of his suburban Saskatoon home. As his wife, Lee, served us iced lemonade, Jim and I talked about his homecoming from the Korean War. In 1953, when his outfit, the Royal Canadian Horse Artillery, disembarked the train at Winnipeg, the entire unit was formed up at the railway station and marched downtown to the city cenotaph. The twenty-one-year-old gunnery veteran felt genuine excitement, knowing that his parents and girlfriend Lee had come in from western Manitoba to welcome him home.

"But I couldn't face [Lee] for nearly a month," McKinny said. "We only lived twenty-three miles apart, but I just couldn't handle people any more. I had written to her every day I was away, but I just couldn't put my feelings into words. I was literally bushed. Korea had made me a social misfit."

As with Lewis Buck, Jim McKinny was never treated for his shell shock. He eventually broke the ice with Lee and they were married. But he admitted he never talked to anybody about what he'd seen and heard during his tour of duty at the front lines in Korea. It was a chapter of his life he preferred not to talk about. Years later, in 1991, at a Royal Canadian Legion dance in Saskatoon, he told me, McKinny discovered that a new veterans' group was meeting in the Legion basement every month. The Korea Veterans Association chapter had just organized. That's when he first began talking about his Korean tour. I suggested that it sounded like group therapy. Then he pointed to his RV in the driveway. Every summer, he and his KVA pals travelled to Prairie communities that had agreed to rededicate their cenotaphs to include "Korean War, 1950–1953." It took a lot of arm twisting and campaigning, but in half a dozen years, McKinny and his KVA buddies had managed to convince about a dozen Saskatchewan towns, including Lac la Biche, Macklin, and Dundurn, to update their cenotaphs. It was Jim McKinny's way of dealing with the demons of his war.

For the better part of fifty-nine years, Don Kerr managed to keep his D-Day demons at bay. When I interviewed him in 2003, he readily admitted they were never far from his memory. Initially, he detailed his background—born in Montreal, educated at University of Toronto Schools, employed as a repairman at Bell Telephone, and an army enlistee in 1939 at age eighteen. Although he then trained for the invasion as a signaller (communications) with the 2nd Canadian Corps in England, at the last minute he was seconded by the British and landed—June 6, 1944—on Gold Beach at the town of Arromanches, France. He remembered the airspace full of planes, landing craft clogging the shoreline, shells falling from the sky, and machine-gun fire coming at him from German shore positions.

"You're twenty-one years old," he told me. "You're scared stiff. Your life is flashing in front of you. You hit the beach and just scramble for cover."

I asked him if he remembered anything more specific about hitting the beach.

"We're going up the beach and a guy—a British captain—in a jeep took a bullet right through the head," he recalled. Though the years since must have made telling this story less difficult, the image still seemed vivid. "I just gently lifted him out of the jeep and laid him on the beach. I put my Norton [motorcycle] in the back and drove off."

In the lengthy interview that followed his D-Day descriptions, the former signals lieutenant retraced his steps from June 6, 1944, to May 8, 1945. He described numerous close calls. Among his worst experiences was burying twenty-two fellow soldiers following one day's action. And, by the way, he said he managed to hang onto that British officer's jeep all the way from Normandy to Holland by having Canadian insignia painted on its side. After VE Day, he volunteered for service in the Pacific and was promptly shipped home. Then, while on training manoeuvres in the southern United States, he learned the Japanese had surrendered. When I quizzed him about the war's aftermath, he casually acknowledged his Mentioned in Dispatches medal, but added he got out of the army as quickly as he could. In particular, he called the D-Day experience traumatic, "like walking into your death."

No doubt that's why he never looked back, why he never considered revisiting the D-Day beaches, not even figuratively when Steven

Spielberg's *Saving Private Ryan* first came to movie theatres. He recalled having coffee on an apartment balcony one Sunday morning when his daughter arrived. She had just seen the movie and was effusive in praising it. As she recounted the opening scenes, Don said he began shaking and started to cry. "Bullets flying, bombs landing. Just utter, utter chaos. That's why guys don't talk about it," he said.

For the record, Don Kerr did go back, several times. Partly because he joined the Juno Beach Centre organizing committee and then helped raise hundreds of thousands of corporate and government dollars for its creation, he had to return to the invasion beaches for the opening. When I spoke to him just before the trip in 2003, he worried that he wouldn't be able to control his emotions. He feared he would cry openly again. And when—at the end of the inaugural ceremonies at the centre—a helicopter scattered 43,000 poppies from the sky over the beaches, he admitted to tears welling up in his eyes over that. In 2009, he joined my battlefield tour and returned to Juno for the sixty-fifth anniversary observance too. That year, while attending the Menin Gate Last Post ceremony in Ypres, Belgium, officials invited him to recite from "For the Fallen" in front of hundreds of spectators. For a man who had witnessed such extraordinary things in war and peace, his comment following his participation in the Menin ceremony made me cry.

"Ted," he said, "this is *the* highlight of my life."

I learned during an interview with Roméo Dallaire that circumstances creating PTSD among Canadian troops serving in Rwanda in 1994 were remarkably different from those affecting Lewis Buck on the farm in 1918, or Jim McKinny marching to the Winnipeg cenotaph in 1953, or Don Kerr on his balcony in the 90s. In 1994, Lieutenant General Dallaire commanded a force of some 3,000 United Nations soldiers in Rwanda. Suddenly faced with the threat of extremist Hutus massacring both their own and Tutsi tribesmen in that landlocked east African country, Dallaire pleaded with UN officials to expand his peacekeeping force by 2,000 troops. Instead, when ten Belgian peacekeepers assigned to protect the president were killed, UN authorities cut back Dallaire's force to 500 men. During the genocide that ensued, the mission commander and his troops were forced to stand by helplessly as nearly a million men, women, and children died in a hundred days of civil war. Dallaire described for me the kind of dilemma his mission soldiers faced.

"All of a sudden [a corporal] with five guys (you know, he's just twenty or twenty-one years old) arrives at a village. He's held at the gate of the village by a bunch of militiamen (sometimes just kids of fourteen or fifteen). Inside the gate there's a gathering of 200 to 300 people. They're egging on a fourteen-year-old girl with a child on her back and a machete, to kill another fourteen-year-old girl with a child on her back.

"So, does [the corporal] shoot his way through the gate and therefore shoot up part of the crowd in order to save the girl? Does the corporal tell his sniper to shoot the girl with the machete and probably kill her and her child? Or does the corporal simply leave? What does he do? And, in the end, what is the lasting impact of those difficult, traumatic, moral, and ethical problems on him?"

His proximity to the genocide left Dallaire scarred as well. Back in Canada, he busied himself partly as an antidote to the atrocities he'd witnessed. He told me that he began researching, writing, and speaking out about the failure of the Rwandan mission and the need to address the root causes. He blamed outdated methods of peacekeeping. From 1956, when the Canadian Secretary of State for External Affairs, Lester Pearson, recommended a peacekeeping force to ease tensions along the Suez Canal, until the end of the Cold War, Dallaire told me, Canadian troops were trained to be prepared for classic warfare but conditioned to use force only in self-defence. From his own experience, however, he warned that adapting 1950s Cold War warrior skills to meet complex social, political, military, economic, and religious situations was not enough in twenty-first-century peacekeeping challenges. I asked the general if Canadian military schools had responded to teach incoming soldiers how to cope with the chaotic village scenario.

"No. We teach them skills of negotiation, but the content is missing," he said. "As an example, when the [UN intervened in Cyprus in the 1960s and] Turks and Greeks sat down around a table to discuss events . . . essentially we were there as referees helping the communication in a very civilized, structured way. They tried to use all those Cyprus methods in Yugoslavia and found out the first thing is that before you can talk, you've got to get half-pissed, because these guys drink. Then you don't know the language. And then what does that corporal know about the Muslim religion? He hasn't got a clue."

Dallaire's experience in Rwanda drove him to try to change things. He declared the era of the "blue collar soldier" over and called for a new conflict resolution regimen for Canadian soldiers. He testified before a parliamentary committee and, as assistant deputy minister of human resources for the military in 1998, he introduced the "Enhanced Leadership Model," recommending that officers study philosophy, sociology, and anthropology, and that an expanded definition of peacekeeping include conflict resolution. He explained to me that where there's a crisis in a nation-state, peacekeeping nations and armies have to understand—whether it's caused by lack of power sharing (Bosnia), a humanitarian catastrophe from drought and rebels toppling government (Somalia), or long-festering religious or ethnic difference (Rwanda)—knowing the source of the conflict is only half the solution. Responding effectively is the other half. He called for "a whole new generation of leadership" that had a greater understanding "of what the political world is, what the humanitarian world is, and what the nation-building world is."

As Dallaire and I talked, I sensed the man's diligence to correct the mistakes of Rwanda was his own attempt to deal with personal PTSD. I asked him what his last days as military commander in 2000 had been like. He said he was relieved of his duties in April for medical reasons, on grounds that the stress and strain meant he could not command troops in operations any more. That didn't mean Dallaire had been entirely removed from assisting soldiers in future operations. In addition to his training models, the general set out to find ways to "change the culture within the military regarding casualties of the mind." He insisted the military not just try to get rid of them, hide them, or ridicule them, but to address head on the up to fifteen per cent of Canadian troops who were casualties of trauma. In addition, Dallaire told me he'd been putting his Rwandan experience into his book *Shake Hands With the Devil.* He admitted the book writing process was slow and painful.

"You saved many people in Rwanda," I suggested.

"Yes, we saved 30,000," he said, "but we failed in the mission."

One veteran I met probably never intended to tell me or anybody else that the air force nearly court-martialled him in the middle of the Second World War. The story emerged, however, in the course of a series of interviews I requested as research for my book *Behind the Glory* about wartime air training in Canada. The day after Remembrance Day 1990, former Toronto Transit Commission systems supervisor Charlie Konvalinka sat down and wrote a letter in response to a voice he'd heard on radio. He had caught my short on-air request for personal information about flying instructors in the British Commonwealth Air Training Plan. He began the letter without specifically addressing me but sent the correspondence care of *Fresh Air*, the CBC Radio program on which I'd made my plea.

"Regrettably," he wrote on RCAF letterhead, "I think the role of the [BCATP] instructor has never been given the recognition it merited. At a time when the desperate need for aircrews was most urgently felt, it was the instructors who answered the call."

A month later I arrived at a modest bungalow in west-end Toronto. A silver-haired, erect, and fit-looking man met me at the door. Perhaps to offset his short physical stature, the seventy-three-year-old Charlie Konvalinka gave me an unexpectedly vigorous handshake. He told me later he admitted to an innate desire to prove that he could do anything anybody else could, no matter how young or old, no matter how short or tall. His welcoming smile compensated for the Vise-Grip handshake. And no sooner had I removed my coat and shoes when Charlie and his wife, Lorraine, invited me into their small but comfortable kitchen for sandwiches and fresh coffee. I'm sure they felt no one should enter their house without first receiving nourishment and a general get-to-know-you querying. I answered more questions in the first hour of my visit than vice versa.

When it came time for my interview with Charlie, he led me downstairs into the basement, through an unmarked door and into a tiny, plain wood-panelled room beneath the stairs. This was clearly the man's domain of yesteryear. The shelves contained his favourite books about flying, binders with some of his own writing, and a prized mug commemorating his association with airplane manufacturers Noorduyn, for whom Charlie had test-flown his favourite aircraft, the Harvard trainer. The office walls displayed a few air force plaques, certificates, and photographs, including one of his beloved Harvards.

Arguably, between 1941 and 1944, during his time as a BCATP instructor, Charlie had spent more time in the air in Harvards than he had on the ground. Solo or with a cadet in the second cockpit, in frigid prairie air, through maritime fog, upside down or right side up, daytime or at night, and sometimes under the hood (flying only by instruments), Flight Lieutenant Konvalinka had taught and graduated hundreds of airmen destined for overseas combat. When finally his turn came to serve in an RCAF fighter squadron, he had accumulated nearly 2,000 hours of flying time, probably ten times as many hours as the young men flying for Fighter and Bomber Command in the air war against the powerful German Luftwaffe.

It was during our first meeting that Charlie Konvalinka alluded to the confrontation that nearly ended his military career. He described his overseas arrival in the U.K. at Bournemouth, the RCAF aircrew reception centre on the south coast of England in 1944. Among his first memories was that of a mandatory assembly at a town theatre, one of the few indoor facilities able to accommodate such a large aggregation of airmen, in this case, pilots who had until very recently instructed at the Canadian stations of the BCATP. The session was ostensibly a pep talk from an RCAF orientation officer acknowledging the airmen's recent arrival by sea from Canada, acclimatizing them to rules and regulations of life in a British coastal town under rationing and curfew, and spurring these former instructors to the challenges of presently being assigned to combat units around Britain.

"What did he say to you?" I asked Konvalinka.

Charlie hesitated, then said, "He called us a bunch of cowards. He said to us, 'If you'd had any guts at all you'd have been over here fighting.'"

The statement stopped both of us momentarily.

A common myth perpetuated by many combat-hardened pilots was that the BCATP graduates with the highest grades had gone on to become the best operational pilots in the service. Some also believed that they had learned most of their airborne skills by the seat of their pants, on the job as it were, and that their instructors had provided little of the right stuff to keep them alive in real combat. In most cases, exactly the opposite was true. The top ten per cent of BCATP graduates went on (often against their will) to become the plan's next generation of instructors. They were in the eyes of air force planners too valuable to lose in dogfights over Britain or bombing missions into Germany. Still, the stereotype of instructors as second-class flyers with little or no moral fibre persisted.

"You mean that guy in Bournemouth assumed because you were all former flying instructors that you had shirked overseas duty?" I asked.

In that moment I saw in Konvalinka's face the look of a man torn by current and former emotions. Upset having to recount to a stranger one of the darker moments of his career, but now feeling again the sense of injustice and anger he had experienced then, Charlie was suddenly back in that Bournemouth theatre again. I seized the moment.

"What did you do?"

"I shouted out, 'And who, for Christ's sake, taught you to fly? God?' 'Who said that?' this guy stormed. 'I did. I said it.'"

In most air force circles, Konvalinka's outburst at an officer in command would have drawn severe punishment, perhaps even a court-martial. In any case, the two men went before the station commander. Charlie didn't back down at all, describing the altercation exactly as it happened. But since the orientation officer was also a flight lieutenant, the recently arrived BCATP instructor characterized the incident as simply "an argument between officers of equal rank." Fortunately for Charlie that's the way the station commander saw it. The officer on the theatre stage, a veteran who probably needed a posting home, was relieved of his hands-on duties. Meanwhile, Konvalinka went on to complete his overseas tour of duty, fulfilling a lifelong dream—flying Spitfires on operations.

But the orientation officer's implication persisted. At least it did in my mind. Did wartime flying instructors have what could never be found in a flight manual, a syllabus book, or even the King's Rules and Regulations? Could they possibly exhibit what some airmen did under the stress of combat? Did they have what commanders and correspondents searched for in all men at war—courage?

At a point in our first of many interviews, I asked Konvalinka if the BCATP flying instructors were in any way heroes. Perhaps because nobody this side of the ocean, not even the instructors themselves, considered wartime training as particularly distinguished, he chafed at the thought. The only people who got medals, he said, were those probably in a place they wouldn't really want to be and somebody noticed their response under fire and gave them a medal for it. In fact, it was only when Charlie got his overseas posting that his wife, Lorraine, advised him: "Don't get yourself into a situation where you're likely to win an important medal."

Rightly or wrongly, the air force had always considered piloting a Lancaster or Halifax bomber more dangerous than an Anson trainer, and throwing a Spitfire or Hurricane around the sky more life-threatening than doing it with a Harvard. Heroism seemed restricted to the skies over the battlefield. The air force reserved its Distinguished Flying Cross (DFC) for meritorious acts of bravery in the air over enemy lines. At the end of the war, RCAF commanders did award a few Air Force Crosses (AFC) for outstanding service in Training Command at home, but an AFC was not generally equated with heroism or service above and beyond the call.

"If you weren't heroes, what were you?" I asked.

"Competent professionals," Konvalinka said. "When I look at my log books at the number of wings tests [final exams] I administered, each one of those successful wings tests meant that I sent a calling card to Hitler on my behalf. And my wings tests go into the hundreds of pilots that I took up on their last ride to prove that they could fly and wear those wings on their chests."

Charlie Konvalinka's flight log provided numerous examples of competent professionalism. One that nearly killed him occurred early in his instructing career at the RCAF Central Flying School in Trenton, Ontario, during the summer of 1941. His air force superiors had assigned Konvalinka the job of certifying the next crop of instructors for the BCATP, training the trainers as it were. Ft. Sgt. Charlton was his first student. That morning Konvalinka jumped into the forward seat of a Harvard, while Charlton strapped himself into the aft seat. Each had a set of controls. The exercise for the day was spins and recoveries. According to the small red syllabus (or patter) book, the procedure called for the pilot to climb to 6,000 or 7,000 feet, throttle back on the Harvard's 600-horsepower engine, pull its nose up until the aircraft was about to stall, then apply full rudder to the left or to the right and let the Harvard fall into a downward spin. Then he would pull the Harvard out of the spin and resume normal flight.

At the planned altitude Charlton came on the intercom and asked for sole control of the steering column. Konvalinka gave him control and then listened and watched his student instructor run through the exercise.

"I will now do a spin to the right and the recovery," Charlton spoke into the intercom, reciting correctly from the syllabus book.

The Harvard responded exactly as expected. When he throttled back and nosed up, the craft began to stall or stop in mid-air. Charlton gave it full right rudder and the aircraft fell into the spin perfectly. Situation normal. Except for one thing. The bouncing and vibrating that normally accompanied a spinning Harvard was oddly absent. The Harvard was spinning through the air smoothly, as

Charlie recalled, "like a knife through butter." Three thousand feet later, Konvalinka came on the intercom tube to Charlton.

"Okay, that's good," he said. "Take her out now."

Konvalinka heard a shaky, straining voice return, "I'm trying."

"I have control," Charlie said, and the more experienced pilot grabbed the Harvard's forward control column. Standard spin recovery is just as precise as initiating the spin. The procedure requires the pilot to kick on the rudder in the opposite direction of the spin, push down on the control column with the column centred laterally. The Harvard will then kick in that opposite direction, and when it does, the pilot centralizes the rudder pedals and holds them straight (standing on them if necessary) as the airplane finds its way out of the spin.

Charlton had been attempting to do just that. But the Harvard continued to spin and descend without power. The secondary procedure called for powering the engine back up (since it had stopped during the stall at the top of the spin). Charlie throttled up the engine. He then put wing flaps fully down. Then up. Nothing. Finally, ever so gradually, through the combination of adjusting the flaps up and down and using the plane's engine, Konvalinka managed to pull the Harvard out of its death descent. By the time he had levelled off, the aircraft was below a thousand feet. The two men could not have bailed out safely, even as a last-ditch reaction.

Back at the Trenton station, a shaken Konvalinka described the Harvard's abnormal spin behaviour to an engineering officer. Ground crew riggers (those responsible for the aerodynamics of the aircraft's performance) removed the wing fairings, or covers, where the wings met the wing roots on the fuselage. They discovered the bolts holding the wings in place had popped off, leaving the wing fractionally out of rig, or improperly aligned. The result was aerodynamic instability and the nearly uncorrectable spin. In other words, the Harvard's wings could easily have separated from the fuselage and if that had happened, the Harvard would have spun straight into the ground, taking the two flying instructors to their deaths.

At the end of the account, Charlie closed his eyes and shook his head with that brush-with-death amazement. When I pressed him to explain how he had physically and psychologically managed to overcome the Harvard's plunge to earth, he chalked it up to training and reflex.

"In that emergency," he said, "I had gone cold. The emotions were entirely deadened. The brain took over."

The night of the near miss, Charlie Konvalinka sat down to write a letter to a fellow instructor at another BCATP station. He remembered that as he began to recount the spin incident on paper his hand started to shake. A delayed reaction perhaps. He didn't think it was shock. In explaining things to his colleague he remembered he hadn't panicked. He hadn't called out to God or some other greater power to save him. He had grown cold. He had stopped being an instructor imparting his knowledge to a student and had turned into a machine counteracting a mechanical failure. Calling on every possible technique and trick of his young career, he had blocked out his fear of failure and death and relied on his skills. He said finally, "I guess we were the first of the cool professionals."

No wonder the man felt so proud of the training he was doing in Canada during the war. Not surprising, either, that he would react to the hostile remarks of that orientation officer in the Bournemouth movie theatre. At that moment in the summer of 1944, F/L Konvalinka wasn't just another sprog airman taking a dressing down from a seasoned combat pilot. Charlie was a trained and experienced military pilot and the other man's accusations of cowardice and shirked responsibility made Konvalinka bristle. In challenging the Bournemouth officer to his face, the former BCATP flying instructor reacted as directly as he had in the cockpit of that Harvard trainer spinning out of control three years before.

We buried Charlie Konvalinka in December 2004. His funeral was fourteen years almost to the day I had met him and Lorraine at their west-end Toronto home. The family asked me to speak at his memorial. To me, the man embodied all the qualities of Canadian veterans so infrequently applauded—their loyalty, their dedication, and their humility. Each anecdote I offered during my eulogy illustrated how overlooked instructors and other veterans had been during the war. And how silent they had remained about their service. But then I quoted from one of my interviews with Charlie.

"Remember," he had told me, "we instructors got no gongs, no medals for gallantry or bravery. We did, however, earn a more precious reward—the chance to live out our lives in freedom and peacetime."

Sometimes a veteran's reluctance to talk had more to do with personal philosophy than it did the aftermath of a World War. I can't remember whether it was the day she criticized the tattered condition of the red maple leaf flag hanging from my front entrance, or the Canada Day we celebrated her husband Willis's seventieth birthday on their porch, or when I first spotted one of her wartime portraits hanging in her front foyer, but it was one of those moments that spurred me to ask my next-door neighbour about her time in the military. Rodine Doris Mary Buckley-Beevers Egan doesn't mince words. She will listen to just about any point of view. But once she's made up her mind, she sticks to her guns. She's set in her ways and she's proud of that fact.

Pride may be her most precious attribute. Ronnie, as I've come to know her, takes great pride in her garden, her family and friends, her volunteer activities, and in the array of flags—the Union Jack, the Stars and Stripes, and the Canadian Maple Leaf—she flies from her house and on flagpoles across her backyard. She's even proud of her asphalt driveway, which she regularly shovels clear of snow in winter or sweeps clear of leaves the rest of the year, even though she doesn't own or drive a car. It's quite likely that her attention to detail, such as tending her flags, arranging her volunteer time, and keeping that driveway tidy, came from her wartime service on the home front.

I have always respected those who served at home in Canada during wartime, particularly the 1939 to 1945 period. Of course, few this side of the pond could compare their hardships to those that Allied families endured in Europe. After all, unlike the British who endured the Blitz, the Poles who witnessed genocide, or Dutch civilians who struggled through *razzias*, those who lived in Canada were a long way from the sharp end, thousands of kilometres from the shooting and the dying. Still, Canadian citizens at home exhibited a quiet determination that deserves recognition and retelling. During the war, Canadian families were exhorted to be careful what they said, to sacrifice and scrimp, to dig deep to finance the war effort, to knit socks and send packages to servicemen overseas, to save tinfoil, to buy bonds, to do volunteer work, to use less sugar, gasoline, meat, butter, and rubber. Or to take a job in a war production plant.

Canadian women in particular exhibited home-front commitment in so many ways. During the Second World War nearly a million women left their homes in the care of sisters, parents, or grandparents, so that they could take positions in the assembly lines of war production plants. In the United States, the woman who symbolized the migration of women into war munitions work became known as "Rosie the Riveter." In Canada, Rosie's equivalent was Veronica Foster, who worked at the Inglis plant in Toronto manufacturing Bren guns for the Canadian Army. As a poster girl for the Canadian support of the war at home, she was promoted as "Ronnie the Bren Gun Girl." It was clear to some, however, that women in war munitions achieved a great deal more than just propaganda points for the war effort. Lotta Dempsey wrote features for the *Toronto Daily Star* and as early as 1943 in one of her columns she noted the societal impact these home-front women were making. She wrote:

> You can tell your great-granddaughter some day that this was the time and place it really started: the honest-to-goodness equality of Canadian women and men in all the work of this country that is to be done; and the pay, and the kudos and the rights and the problems.
>
> And you can say that it wasn't done by club women at luncheons, or orators on soap boxes, or legislators in parliaments.
>
> It began to happen that hour when Canadian girls left desks and kitchens, elevators and switchboards . . . and stepped into overalls and took their places in the lines of workers at lathes

and drills, cranes and power machines, tables and benches in the munitions plants of Canada.

But my neighbour Ronnie Egan wasn't the Bren Gun Girl. It took quite some time to convince her, but when she finally consented to an interview about her war, she told me that she served in uniform. More than 100,000 women did. Some worked as nursing sisters. Thousands joined the Canadian Women's Army Corps, the CWACs. Just as many became members of the Canadian Women's Auxiliary Air Force, later known as the RCAF WDs or Women's Division. And thousands more women responded to the recruitment poster that read: "You too can free a man to serve at sea. Join the Women's Royal Canadian Naval Service." At age nineteen, Ronnie signed up with the WRENS. No question.

"Army was never thought of in my day, because we were always navy," she said, as she simultaneously stiffened her upper body. "My father was navy. And I was navy. Dad was a Conway boy* and that was that."

Ronnie explained that she enlisted at the local Royal Canadian Navy barracks, HMCS *Discovery*, in her hometown of Vancouver in 1942. The next year, she was sent to Guelph, Ontario, for basic training in the engineering department. Then she and about two hundred other WRENS were posted for duty to HMCS *Stadacona* in Halifax. She said they were the first WRENS to arrive as permanent staff at the Mechanical Training Establishment (MTE) offices of Atlantic Command in the port of Halifax. By 1944, she rose to the rank of Chief Petty Officer and was one of only four WRENS chosen to run the MTE. In a photograph she showed me, WRENS are lined up for inspection at the launch of a corvette in Halifax harbour. The tallest,

---

* The original HMS *Conway* dates to 1859 when the British Admiralty lent the twenty-six-gun sailing frigate for the training of merchant navy cadets. The name was handed down to subsequent Royal Navy "school ships," and its graduates automatically became members of the Conway Old Boys Club. Seventy Conways lost their lives in the Great War, 166 in the Second World War.

most erect, and most polished—from her cap to her greatcoat buttons to her leather shoes—is CPO Buckley-Beevers.

Ronnie's responsibilities were numerous. She fought the clerical war at HMCS *Stadacona*—handling training charts, filing the results, and keeping track of the ratings, the other WRENS at the Halifax base. Among her more unpleasant duties was informing the wife or girlfriend when a male relative or friend in the navy was in hospital for treatment of venereal disease. But that was balanced by other aspects of her service in perhaps the busiest wartime harbour on the eastern seaboard. She said from the moment she heard the boatswain's whistle each morning, she took to her job eagerly and seriously. When she could, in quiet moments off-duty, she would walk to where she could see Bedford Basin and "the most beautiful sight of all"—the armada of ships gathering there for the next eastbound North Atlantic convoy. But she derived greatest pleasure, she said, conducting drills on the parade square.

"I drilled the WRENS quite a lot," she said, her voice rising in a bit of a crescendo. "And for experience I took them into one of the big halls and even drilled the men. Putting them through their paces—close order drill, marching—and all the rest of it. I really enjoyed that."

The more she spoke, the more I began to understand where her strict attention to detail had come from, why her flags were always so orderly and her driveway so spick and span clean. But our interview soon revealed that the King's Regulations approach to things was just the tip of the iceberg. It turned out CPO Buckley-Beevers took more than drill square procedure seriously. Among other things, she was a stickler for proper military attire, insisting that her ratings wear lisle (cotton-thread) stockings while on duty and that silk stockings were strictly forbidden until off-duty hours. It was also evident that Ronnie did not appreciate not being appreciated either; once when a male Royal Navy officer suggested it wasn't appropriate for women to be serving at *Stadacona*, Ronnie lodged a formal complaint with her superiors and presently the British CPO was reassigned away from the Canadian base.

Nor was CPO Buckley-Beevers to be trifled with in the streets of Halifax.

"There was one instance when I had to take over," she said. "A junk dealer had a horse pulling his cart. The poor horse's ribs were showing and it had collapsed right on the main street of Halifax. They just wanted to drag the horse off in this condition. So there I am in uniform and I put my foot gently on the horse's neck. 'This horse will be shot or it will be attended to properly,' I told them. I was bound and determined the horse was going to be treated humanely. Finally, a policeman did come and shoot it and only then was it taken away."

The horse episode wasn't her only act of defiance in public either. In the course of my periodic conversations with my neighbour, I had discovered that Ronnie had served at HMCS *Stadacona* throughout the war, up to and including the time of the infamous VE Day riots in Halifax in 1945. I knew she and I had to explore that event, which turned out to be a black mark for both the navy and the citizens of Halifax.

Relations between the 65,000 permanent residents of Halifax and the nearly 55,000 transient navy and merchant seamen had not been the best during the war. Many Haligonians detested what nearly six years of war had brought their city—thousands of servicemen pouring through on their way to Europe; beaches fouled by oil from a harbour filled beyond capacity; rationing of everything from food staples to basic clothing; curfews and just general overcrowding. On the other hand, some servicemen and servicewomen complained that the food in the city was substandard, that rents were sky-high and general facilities non-existent. Some navy people claimed they were dreadfully exploited, having to pay premium prices for ordinary items and services. They claimed some Halifax merchants had even posted signs that read "No Sailors or Dogs Allowed."

At any rate, on the morning of May 7, 1945, when word leaked out that German capitulation in Europe was at hand, people in Halifax began abandoning their workplaces, and everything in the city was locked up tight. Thousands of civilians and navy personnel streamed into the streets. But there was nothing to see, nothing to buy, and nothing to do. Years of pent-up frustration and anger boiled over. And two days of rioting ensued.

At four o'clock in the afternoon (on the second day), May 8, 1945, Ronnie completed her clerical shift at the MTE. By that time she was married to Willis Egan, a Canadian army driver posted permanently to Halifax, and was making her way through the city to their lodgings away from the *Stadacona* barracks. En route, Ronnie and several female navy friends decided to shop in Zellers, one of the few stores that remained open that VE Day. The WRENS didn't immediately recognize how threatening Halifax streets had become. She said they leisurely made their purchases and stepped into the doorway to leave the store. They were suddenly confronted by a half-dozen drunken sailors who told the women to move aside. The seamen had decided they were going to torch the store.

In the blink of an eye, and with the natural authority of a parade square drill instructor, Ronnie announced, "Oh no you aren't!" I could just picture three or four WRENS, hands on hips, forming a defensive wall in the doorway, and like Horatio at the bridge, the defiant voice of Ronnie, the Chief Petty Officer in charge, telling the stunned navy men where they could or could not go. She said there was a momentary standoff, neither side appearing to flinch. But when Ronnie apparently repeated the order, the sailors retreated.

I couldn't believe the coincidence of the moment. Here was my next-door neighbour, not only an eyewitness to the Halifax riots, but also something of a hero for saving a store and probably its patrons from a fiery end. Equally coincidental, I had something to give Ronnie in return. During my search through the documents of Supreme Court Justice R.L. Kellock, who led an inquiry into the VE Day riots in Halifax, I had actually found an exhibit photograph taken of an inebriated sailor sitting on a cobblestone street during the riots. In the background of the picture, a Zellers storefront can be seen clearly, the very same building Ronnie and her navy pals had protected on VE Day. I knew not to ask her if she felt heroic over the episode. She would never have entertained such a notion.

"Did you consider making the navy a career after the war?" I asked her finally.

"As far as my experience in the navy goes, we were treated royally. We had clean sheets . . . good blankets . . . excellent meals . . . good living quarters. But when it was over, I said, 'I never want to see another file in my life.' I stayed there after the war for a while to help with discharges. But it was a case of joining up, doing my share, and that was it."

Ronnie Egan's modesty about her wartime service in the WRENS extended long after the war. One day in 2005, which coincidentally the federal government had designated "Year of the Veteran," Ronnie was enjoying a visit from her daughter, Carolyn. I dropped by about the time Carolyn was helping her mother fill out some sort of application. The form would entitle Ronnie to some financial assistance with repairs and maintenance of her hundred-year-old home. She might even get some assistance tidying (and shovelling) her driveway. Carolyn wondered whether Ronnie was entitled to the services outlined in the form. I looked more closely at the application, which was clearly marked Veterans Affairs Canada. I asked if she had ever filled out any such document before.

"No. Why should I?" Ronnie said. "I've never asked for handouts in my life."

I suddenly realized that former Second World War CPO Rodine Doris Mary Buckley-Beevers Egan had never applied for or received a veteran's pension, veteran's assistance, grants, land, education, indeed any veteran's benefits, though she was fully entitled to them all. As far as she was concerned, she had fulfilled her duty during the war, taken her honourable discharge, returned to civilian life with her army veteran husband, Willis, raised four children and a bunch of grandchildren. End of story. Though every November 11 she would faithfully pin her WRENS badge to her coat lapel and stand at attention in front of the community cenotaph paying her respects to war dead and veterans, she felt no need to dwell on her own wartime record. And certainly there was no need to expect payment for it.

To Ronnie, it was simply a matter of pride.

If I thought only veterans' pride led them to silence about their wartime experience, I was to learn otherwise from another of my BCATP interviews. One unexpected revelation during that research in the early 1990s was that many well-known people had served as wartime aviation instructors. Among others, actor Bill Walker and broadcaster Joel Aldred had instructed during the Second World War. So had real estate executive J.J. Barnicke and musician Buff Estes, former saxophone player in the Benny Goodman band. And though they extended their reputations in the aviation industry after the war, Max Ward, Wop May, Punch Dickins, and Russ Bannock rarely dwelled on their instructor service from 1940 to 1945. Then I came knocking with a notepad, a tape recorder, and a head full of questions.

Typical was my visit with long-time Toronto newspaperman and radio commentator Bob Hesketh, whose regular "The Way I See It" column on CFRB was extremely popular. It turned out he and Lawson Packaging executive Bill Lennox had instructed together at No. 9 Service Flying Training School at Centralia, Ontario, in 1944. Because of their close work as instructors during the war, the two men had enjoyed a friendship of more than half a century. Neither man considered his instructing service particularly pivotal to the war effort, but they agreed to be interviewed together.

When I turned the tape recorder on, Hesketh and Lennox first retraced their steps enlisting in the air force, getting processed at Manning Depot, being streamed into pilot training at Initial Training School, soloing at Elementary Flying Training School, and graduating from Service Flying Training School (SFTS). Moving their stories along to their days as instructors, I pointed out that they probably became pilot trainers because they'd graduated with such high grades in their courses. Lennox said he highly doubted that academic excellence made him a good instructor, just his calm attitude in the air. Hesketh also dismissed my suggestion, saying they'd probably drawn his name from a hat.

"Official records showed that the top ten per cent of every BCATP graduating class was ploughed back into the plan as instructors," I insisted. "Instructors were the best pilot graduates."

"I do remember . . . we used to use a practice field for approaches and landings," Hesketh said. "I don't know what happened, but . . . the guy testing me cut the single engine and said, 'Okay, make an emergency landing at that airfield.' For some reason I did the right thing and landed the airplane perfectly. I was probably lucky that day."

To illustrate my top-of-the-class point, I asked the two men to talk about what principles and techniques they used to teach their SFTS students to solo and graduate on single-engine Harvards and Yales, or twin-engine Ansons, Oxfords, and Cranes. Surely, Hesketh and Lennox had given their trainees some basics for survival once they got overseas. Both men shook their heads. They quickly refuted the idea that pilots who'd never gone on ops nor fired a shot in anger could teach students about dogfighting in a fighter or dodging anti-aircraft fire in a bomber.

"What about that theory about the quick and the dead?" I said. "You must have sensed you were giving them something, right?"

"I had a student," Lennox suddenly remembered, "that another instructor gave me for a washout [pass or fail] check. What I discovered was the instructor never let a fault develop. Every time the boy went to make a mistake, the instructor took control back. So the boy didn't know what a single-engine takeoff was [on a twin-engine aircraft] or stall recovery. He didn't let him react. . . . You had to teach them all you knew and let them make some mistakes."

Not everybody understands that reality, I suggested. Again, Lennox shrugged off any credit other than he did the job the air force expected of him and that was that. Then I asked the sensitive question about BCATP instructors not getting overseas. Lennox said he felt disappointed he never saw action. Hesketh said he was embarrassed every time his sons asked him about his wartime service. Nor did he feel comfortable at RCAF veterans' gatherings. Compared to the sensational stories of air combat, his instructor tales paled. He said air force reunions always made him feel like a bit player in a John Wayne movie. But then he said he'd share a story with me he was telling Bill Lennox as I arrived for the interview that day.

Hesketh recalled a visit to Toronto's Sunnybrook Hospital. He'd decided to get a physical checkup there and the general practitioner turned out to be a fairly young man. Sometime during the exchange of medical information, Hesketh said he had been a pilot in the RCAF during the war.

"Oh," the doctor said. "Were you one of those guys who rained death and destruction on those innocent people of Germany?"

"No. I was an instructor," he said. Hesketh had never encountered anybody with a negative attitude about what RCAF bomber crews had done during the war. He felt offended by the doctor's attitude. Hesketh told me he wished he *had* been on ops because he would have used that experience to set the young doctor straight. He told me, however, that his Sunnybrook visit did achieve something he hadn't expected. He felt then, more than he ever had before, that a BCATP career *was* worth talking about.

"It was the first time in my life I can remember being proud that I had spoken out about it," he said.

5

SETTING THE RECORD STRAIGHT

Aside from the rhythm of attending November 11 ceremonies every year, there are several other significant dates I try to observe in some fashion. On June 6, I generally call veteran friends who participated in the D-Day invasion. On July 27, because it's become the equivalent of Remembrance Day for Korean War veterans, I join them at the Wall of Remembrance in Brampton, Ontario, for the ceremony marking the anniversary of the truce in their war. Then, each summer on the morning of August 19, I traditionally contact Stephen Bell and pay him a visit. I don't generally have to remind him it's the anniversary of the Dieppe raid. But one year, when I phoned to make sure he was up for a visit, he said, "That's right. By this time on that day I had about twenty-three chunks of shrapnel in me and was an unexpected guest of the Führer."

Bell arrived at Dieppe during low tide that morning after an all-night crossing of the English Channel aboard a tank landing-craft (LCT). A wireless radio operator with the Calgary Tanks Regiment, Trooper Bell's "B" Squadron was supposed to land, before daylight, in simultaneous support of the infantry directly in front of the seaport of Dieppe. Instead, the LCTs delivered them fifteen minutes later than the first wave of infantry. Add to that, a mid-Channel skirmish with enemy E-boats and the element of surprise was gone.

Consequently, upon the Canadians' arrival, the Germans occupying Dieppe unleashed murderous fire from the town site, beach installations, and gun emplacements atop the cliffs that nearly encircled the port. Bell's tank, F2, was second of three off the LCT. Tank F2's assault lasted only a few minutes. It advanced less than six metres up the beach, where fist-sized chert rock caused the tank tracks to bog down, leaving the tank immobile and an easy target.

"We were hit on the turret just coming down the [LCT] ramp," Steve told me in our first interview in 1993. "This shell hit the top of it. Just blew the tank lids right off. All you could see up there was daylight."

Bell wanted me to understand the nature of his surroundings that morning, so he drew me a cross-section diagram of the tank. His drawing showed drivers Earl Snider seated forward right, howitzer gunner Bill Willard seated forward left, machine gunner Charlie Provis in the turret, lieutenant in charge Dick Wallace on a periscope to the left of the turret, and radio operator Bell to the right. Steve then added the Churchill's armament to the sketch—its main six-pounder gun (with ninety shells aboard), the BESA machine gun and its thirty boxes of clips (each holding 750 rounds), and the three-inch howitzer. When he finished the sketch, he explained ultimately that all that firepower simply got marooned on the beach.

"We were hit about fifteen or twenty times by high explosives. One time we were lifted right off the ground—a sixty-ton tank three feet off the ground—and dropped back down," he went on. "Knocked three of us in the turret out cold."

Things deteriorated from there. With the tank stuck on the chert rock, Bell joined another gunner, Johnny Booker, outside the vehicle, establishing a machine-gun position between some piled-up stones and the tank track. Bell and Booker took turns loading and firing the machine gun until a German shell crashed into the tank above them and temporarily knocked them out again. This time Bell had shrapnel and stone fragments in his legs, back, and buttocks. Both his ears were bleeding from the concussion of the explosion. Booker got hit in the legs. Bill Willard took bullets in the ankle, knee, and shoul-

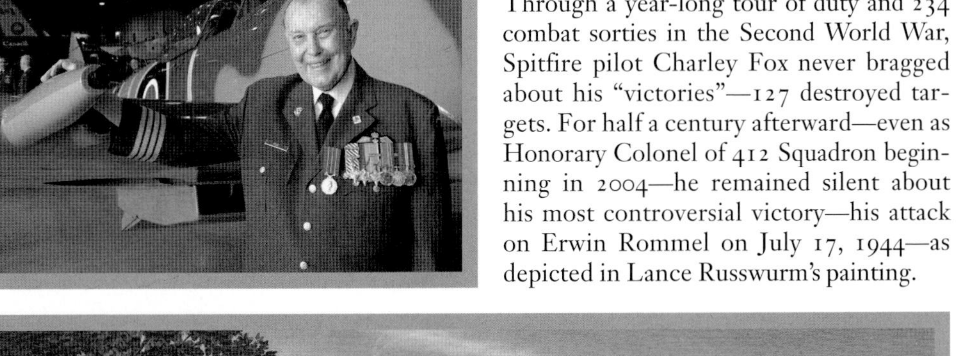

Through a year-long tour of duty and 234 combat sorties in the Second World War, Spitfire pilot Charley Fox never bragged about his "victories"—127 destroyed targets. For half a century afterward—even as Honorary Colonel of 412 Squadron beginning in 2004—he remained silent about his most controversial victory—his attack on Erwin Rommel on July 17, 1944—as depicted in Lance Russwurm's painting.

on given to Sgt. Alex Barris

s liaison Sgt ... ose normal
the chain ... Stations to
4 Barris exp ... ion to duty.
ation, he ha ... fect liaison
rides from ... articular
successful at ... he has
ere and adv ... So intense
ties that on ... 1945, he
Stations wer ... d. He took
en a direct ... became
om this comp ... al duty with
Sections du ... personnel,
ed these squ ... duties, sought
was instru ... discharge
y 1945, one ... eturn after
Regt in Cam ... 4 Barris
which were ... d booby
of this squa ... s of the
ining two we ... ged to ex-
d and further their evacuation through medical
pressed initiative and forsight in discharge of
has been greatly instrumental in the success and
ion in which he serves. His total disregard for
... r and above the

NOT A PASS · FOR INDENTIFICATION ONLY

WAR DEPARTMENT
THE ADJUTANT GENERAL'S OFFICE
WASHINGTON, D.C.

CERTIFICATE OF IDENTITY
TO BE ISSUED TO MILITARY AND
CIVILIAN PROTECTED PERSONNEL

BARRIS
ALEX P
32656882

Alex P. Barris
NAME
Tec 5
DESIGNATION
Alex P. Barris
SIGNATURE
J E Danah Capt.
COUNTERSIGNED
W.D. A.G.O. 65-10

PROPERTY OF U.S. GOVT.

DATE ISSUED JUL 1 1 1944

LOSS OF THIS CARD MUST BE REPORTED AT ONCE

(LEFT) The U.S. Army identification card revealed nothing of my father's wartime experience. Even his medic's gear let on little of his service as stretcher-bearer, first-aid medic, and unit leader. Only his military citation (buried in his personal papers some 60 years) revealed the true mettle of Tech. Sgt. Alex Barris.

(ABOVE) Every Byng Boy had left a battlefield wounded. Those entitled to that claim at this May 2007 annual dinner included (back row l to r) J.J. Donahue, Tim Ellis, Blake McCullogh, Roland Black, E.A. Bauer, Bob Likely, Alex Penman, Delbert Seely, C.F.A. Graham, Rex Fendick, Joe Slemin, David Dickson; (front row) George Pridham, Robert McLeod, James Turnbull, (the author), Robert Jones, Neil McKelvey, James Stewart, Ronald Cotterell, Phillip MacGillivray. (BELOW RIGHT) In 2007, at the 90th anniversary commemoration of the Canadian assault at Vimy Ridge, Canadian students (l to r) Robb Phillips, Cotter Allen, and Michael Riseley wear the names (white patch above chest pocket) of Canadian casualties sustained in the victory. (BELOW LEFT) When Saskatchewan homesteader Gavin McDonald wrote his life story, he omitted the years 1915 to 1918. Only when his two adult nieces requested he fill that gap did his First World War accounts come to light.

Since the Second World War, each year the Dutch government sends thousands of tulip bulbs to Canada for planting. In October 1994, students at Pickering College welcomed veteran Canadian tank commander Bruce Evans (ABOVE LEFT) and former Dutch citizen Anne (Keijzer) Pompili (ABOVE RIGHT) to explain that the bulbs symbolized Canadian soldiers' sacrifice during the liberation of Holland. (BELOW) Only when the students then planted the bulbs—as part of a TV news story—did they fully understand the meaning of remembrance.

(ABOVE) In August 1953, Canadians return from Communist POW camps in North Korea, where their wits were their only weapons. With Red Cross worker Ina McGregor (background) are (l to r) Paul Dufour, George St. Germain, Joseph Binette, Ernie Taylor, Len Badowich, Jim Gunn, Barry Gushue, Victor Percy. (LEFT) As an RCAF military pilot instructor, Charlie Konvalinka survived plenty of close calls in Canada from 1941 to 1944, but his subsequent introduction to operations at the Personnel Reception Centre (The Regent) in Bournemouth, England, proved to be an unexpected test of his moral fibre.

(ABOVE LEFT) Ronnie Egan deflected any credit for winning the home-front war, but when sailors and civilians rioted in Halifax on VE Day 1945 (ABOVE RIGHT), Chief Petty Officer Egan actually saved a downtown Zellers department store from destruction. (BELOW LEFT) RCAF vet Bob Hesketh always felt his home-front training stories paled next to his pals' overseas heroics, until a crucial day in a doctor's office. (BELOW RIGHT) Dressed in dispatch riding gear, during training in England in 1942, Don Kerr looked confident, with his emotions in check, for the D-Day landings. Visiting Juno Beach a second time—60 years later—proved tougher emotionally.

(ABOVE) Their German captors herded survivors of the doomed Dieppe raid across Europe to POW camps in the summer of 1942. (BELOW RIGHT) At a *stalag* in 1943, Calgary Tanks trooper Stephen Bell (right) traded ten cigarettes to a German guard for a picture of himself and signaller Lloyd Watt; in August 2007 (BELOW LEFT) he sat with the author.

(ABOVE) As dangerous as the D-Day invasion itself, was the filming of Canadian troops landing at Juno Beach by Bill Grant (BELOW RIGHT). Throughout the Second World War, the Canadian Army Film and Photo Unit sustained 26 casualties in Europe. (BELOW LEFT) CFPU personnel in France (1944) included (back row, l to r) Chuck Ross (others unidentified); (centre row) Ken Bell, Mickey Dean, Gordon Akeman; (front row) Lou Weekes, George Cooper, Gordon Petty.

der, then a mortar exploded close enough to tear Willard's torso open from the breastbone to the crotch; Earl Snider and Bell took safety pins from a first-aid kit and pinned the gash closed. Meanwhile, the gunner from Bell's tank, Charlie Provis, was dead from a bullet through the head.

It was now about 11 o'clock. The crewmen of F2 hadn't advanced at all, but had held their position for over four hours. Royal Navy LCTs began reappearing along the beach to pick them up, so Bell and Booker tried dragging wounded to the landing craft. As they did, Germans emerged from the town, pouring over the seawall. Wounded, exhausted, and out of ammunition, Canadian troops were surrendering all around them. Germans eventually confronted Bell and told him to drop the revolver on his belt. He obeyed, put his hands up, and began perhaps the three worst years of his life, as a prisoner of war.

"You could ask anybody who was on that beach and they'll tell you that water was just like red ink with blood," Bell said finally. "Bodies? You have no idea. Just like cordwood, just floating round and round. Arms, legs, it was unbelievable. If I hadn't seen it I wouldn't have believed it myself. The water coming up on the beach was foaming red with blood."

During our first visit, Stephen Bell had given me all I ever wanted to know about the role the Calgary Tanks had played during the Dieppe raid. Unlike other veterans, who sometimes needed the familiarity of a Legion hall or a few drinks to loosen their tongues, he didn't seem at all reluctant to offer every detail. It wasn't bravado. I think he knew I wanted to document the story as accurately as possible, so he looked me straight in the eye, calling up every image he could. And though he was a low-ranking trooper that day, he was quick to criticize what he considered the shortcomings of Operation Jubilee against Dieppe. He complained that the Royal Navy promise to knock out the menacing German guns above the beach had not been delivered on. He said the Royal Air Force didn't want to kill French civilians in the town, so it didn't saturate-bomb the port's defences. Ultimately, he blamed Louis Mountbatten, who he said anticipated the raid to flop since "he expected about seventy-five per cent casualties." In fact, the casualty figures for the whole force reached sixty per cent in men and one hundred per cent in tanks. Of eighty-five tanks, only twenty-four made it to shore. Bell said nearly thirty troopers in his regiment were killed and more than a hundred were taken prisoner. It took the Germans a full day to clear the beaches of bodies. Altogether 3,367 of the nearly 5,000 Canadians who embarked from England that day became casualties. More than 900 of those were killed in the bloodiest nine hours in Canadian military history.

My acquaintance with Stephen Bell began in 1993. All I had asked for was his personal account of the Dieppe raid. Maybe Steve recognized an eager listener in me, a way to set the record straight about Dieppe, about its aftermath, about its impact on his life. Maybe because he lived so far from any other Dieppe survivors (he said of more than 700 in his regiment, he was then one of only six still alive), he felt I was a touchstone for the experience. I offered him an occasional sympathetic outlet for those stories, where none otherwise existed. At any rate, the acquaintance continued through the next fifteen years with periodic meetings that became an education for me and grew into a strong friendship for both of us. We had plenty of reasons to visit each other over that time, not just interview sessions. Because we both read a lot of war non-fiction, we often swapped books we had liked.

Generally, when each August 19 arrived, I travelled the short distance to his country home and he reminisced about life before and after Dieppe. Other times he came to visit me in town. Since he loved cooking sauces—which his family insisted he not do in the house but at a stove in his private garage—he regularly dropped by my home in town with an armful of preserve jars containing his latest batch of homemade chili or spaghetti sauce. During those summertime or autumn visits, I would pull a couple of lawn chairs into the shade. He would roll a filterless cigarette or two. I would ask a few questions to get him started and another wartime tutorial would begin.

It turned out that Dieppe was barely the preface to Stephen Bell's war saga. For the next three years—from August 1942 until May 1945—he became a statistic in the Third Reich's elaborate system of war prisons. I have had the opportunity to interview scores of Canadians imprisoned during wartime. Their stories formed the basis of numerous articles I've subsequently freelanced to periodicals and newspapers since the late 1980s. Most men admitted to me that with time their incarceration memories became blurred or spotty. I quickly learned, however, that Bell lost track of very little during that time. The first night of his life as a POW, for example, he remembered sleeping on crushed bricks outside a cement factory in Envernieu. The second day, as the Germans marched them in a column, he remembered a French farm woman came out of her house and gave him fresh water to drink. Five days later, he told me, the Germans marched them to railway yards, loaded them into boxcars, and shipped them to the first prison outside Paris. The boxcar trip illustrated the way he would be treated for the duration.

"There were 125 men in each boxcar," he said. "Couldn't even sit down. Stood there, sweat just dripping off the ends of my fingers. No place to relieve yourself. When they stopped, they opened the doors, took out the dead guys, and put two buckets of water in. We had half a loaf of bread and one tin of meat. For six days and five nights. Going through Holland, we saw civilians standing, watching the POW train go by. They held up the V for victory sign with their hands. The Germans opened up with machine guns at these civilians. That really brought it home to me. This was for keeps."

By late September the Canadian POWs had reached Stalag VIII-B at Lamsdorf, Poland. Steve heard the camp held nearly 80,000 POWs, about 1,200 to each compound, about 150 in each barracks. Bell's deduction that the Germans meant business proved accurate. He remembered it was October 3 when they were marched out of their compound and told they would suffer reprisals for the attack on Dieppe. Their daily routine would include not only confinement but also binding. Each day, Bell said, he was tied to nineteen other men.

The Canadians were not allowed out of the barracks. Guards made sure nobody tried to loosen the ropes, and if a man had to use the latrine, he and all those tied together would have to go too.

"Within an hour of being tied up, our hands were black due to lack of circulation. We were tied from 7 a.m. to 6 p.m. every day," Bell explained. "After a month of this treatment, our hands and wrists were in terrible shape, bruised and [with] very little feeling. On December 6, 1942, instead of being tied up with ropes, we were handcuffed with about ten inches of chain between. This was less painful than the ropes, but did more damage to our hands and wrists during the two winters that followed, when the temperature dropped to minus 45.

"We got no Red Cross parcels. Our daily ration was a cup of mint tea, a couple of potatoes, a slice of black bread (mostly sawdust), and watery soup of carrots or sugar beets. I lost fifty pounds in the first twelve months. By the time the chains were removed in November 1943, I had dropped another twenty pounds. I went from 5-foot-10 and 180 pounds to 5-foot-9 1/4 and 110 pounds—skin and bones."

During one of our chats in the shade one summer day, Steve began to describe his escape attempts. He escaped five times in three years and was recaptured four times. First he swapped identity papers with a private on a work party; he escaped temporarily but was recaptured and spent twenty-eight days in a confinement cell. During his second escape, a guard shot him in the back, but Bell's web belt slowed the bullet down so it lodged between his ribs; following surgery, he spent another twenty-eight days in solitary on bread and water. Bell then joined a group digging a tunnel, but he was transferred to Stalag II-D before the escape attempt. At the new camp in Stargard, Poland, he escaped twice in the summer of 1944 but was recaptured both times. Finally, in February 1945, as the Russians advanced into Poland, the Germans abandoned the camps and began a forced march, using their prisoners as hostages.

"We heard that Hitler had given an order for all POWs to be shot," Bell said. That's when he and another Dieppe captive—Essex Scottish infantryman Murray Denneau—decided to pick a moment and run. Meantime, Bell had managed to salvage three-year-old army boots, army pants, and a civilian cotton shirt, and a wool jacket he'd traded for sixty contraband cigarettes in the camp. He had a scarf he'd knitted, leather mitts he'd made from cat skins, and an extra pair of wool socks. "We waited for the air force to come. When we were being shot at from the air, all POWs and guards got off the road as fast as possible . . . to get away from the bullets and rockets. We managed to get away. It was the middle of March."

The winter elements nearly made their escape a death sentence. The winter of 1945 across Europe was bitterly cold. Even late in the season, temperatures dipped to minus 40 degrees, and the damp weather left Bell and Denneau perpetually wet and shivering. They managed to survive for a week on frozen cabbage leaves, apples, and a few potatoes. On the verge of starvation and fully prepared to be handed over to authorities, they entered a German village and knocked on a door.

Stephen Bell is not a religious man but more a fatalist. As he prepared another roll-your-own in the shade of my backyard that day, he shook his head in disbelief over what he was about to tell me. Bell said he confessed to the woman occupant of the house, explaining that they were Canadian prisoners of war on the run. He told the woman she could turn them in, and that there was probably a reward, but they were nearly dead from hunger. Instead she let them in, fed them potato soup ("the best potato soup I ever tasted in my life"), and sheltered them in the basement. She had only one request in return: Could she bring a neighbour over to see them? They didn't care.

"This neighbour woman had letters from Gravenhurst, Ontario," Bell said. "Her son was a POW there in Canada. She said he wrote home to say how well he was treated, the bacon and eggs, the steaks. And through the Eaton's catalogue, you could order a radio or a chesterfield. She had two or three letters that she read to us in German. She had never seen a Canadian before. But she was so thankful that her son was in Canada and not a prisoner in Germany."

I figured the Gravenhurst letters story was the climax to Bell's escape saga and, since the war ended just weeks later, that the two

Canadians were quickly repatriated. I should have known their route home would not be that simple. He told me the woman in the village sheltered them in her basement for nearly a week, then stocked them with fresh food—bread, pork, hard-boiled eggs—and drew them a map to steer clear of the Gestapo. Two days later they ran into a squadron of Russian tanks, presented themselves to their Soviet Allies, and figured their troubles were over. But the Russians simply tossed them in with their thousands of German prisoners, being marched eastward "to Siberia." Bell and Denneau escaped yet again and finally made it to Lubec on the Baltic Sea coast, where they planned to steal an airplane and fly to England. Fortunately, they didn't have to complete that leg of their plan. They arrived in Lubec on May 11, 1945, only to discover the war was over—the Germans had capitulated on May 8—and instead of relying on their limited flying skills, they got a scheduled ride to England on an RAF transport plane.

It suddenly occurred to me that this ex-Saskatchewan farm boy, ex-Calgary Tanks wireless operator, ex-POW had likely developed quite an attitude about life. I sensed that his response to authority had changed drastically since the morning of August 19, 1942, at Dieppe. I surmised that Stephen Bell's transition back to the rigours of the military in England and eventually to civilian life in Canada was not a smooth one, that the culture shock, after three years of deprivation and confinement, would be pretty severe. I was right. After four days at a hospital in Oxford, he got twenty British pounds and a pass to London. By May 16 he was in jail and then paraded before a major, who asked him to volunteer for parade duty during a garden party at Buckingham Palace. When he refused, Bell got fourteen days confined-to-barracks. Then he remembered he was supposed to be married on July 5, but that got postponed. Finally, Bell related one of his last exchanges in a military uniform. He was again brought before a commanding officer.

"We want you to sign up for service in the Pacific," the man announced to him.

"To fight?" Bell asked in astonishment.

"Yes. To defeat the Japanese."

"Are you out of your fucking mind?" Bell blurted out.

After years of being told what to do by his Calgary Tanks superiors, by his German captors, and by the Russians, Bell said, he wasn't about to take any more orders. From anybody! He almost got charged with insubordination. But instead, he was shipped home, coincidentally arriving at the Quebec City docks on VJ Day (Victory over Japan Day) in August 1945. Stephen Bell doesn't have a high regard for military procedure or its bureaucracy, then or now. He was given his discharge on November 30, along with a five-minute debriefing and medical exam. Nobody asked him about his damaged eardrums, the remaining shrapnel in his back, the arthritis in his hands and wrists, the bullet wound in his ribs, or why he weighed only ninety-seven pounds. And although Canadian army doctors didn't bother to test him for battle fatigue (later known as post-traumatic stress disorder), they did apparently check to see if he had a hernia. A few weeks after his discharge, Bell collapsed on Bay Street in Toronto. X-rays revealed he had both pneumonia and pleurisy. He spent the next seventeen months in and out of the Christie Street Veterans Hospital.

"I was eventually placed on 100 per cent pension," Bell told me. "After six months, I was called to 55 York Street [an army office in Toronto] for a review of my health. I told them I felt fine most of the time, so my pension was reduced to 10 per cent. I was so happy about having a job, being able to work again, that it didn't bother me that my pension was cut off. I could make it on my own."

That last comment didn't surprise me in the least. Stephen Bell had made it pretty much on his own all his life. Though he didn't get married on July 5, 1945, as scheduled, Bell did get married at the end of the war. After a divorce, he married Marilyn Dobie from near his childhood home in Saskatchewan. He had four children. He worked at the post office, the railway, and as a pressman at the *Toronto Telegram*, and eventually established his own landscaping business. In retirement, the wounds of wartime came back to haunt him—bleeding in his ears and backaches from the concussion shell and shrapnel on the beach at Dieppe, swollen hands and wrists from being bound at Stalag VIII-B, and arthritis in every joint that was exposed to the cold and damp during three years of abusive imprisonment. In 2003 the Royal Regiment of Canada—not the Government of Canada, mind you—struck and awarded a medallion to honour Dieppe vets, among them Stephen Bell. The same year, doctors diagnosed him with cancer of the lungs, liver, and spleen and gave him months to live.

My friend defied the odds for more than five years. He stopped making and delivering chili sauce to my house in 2007. But we went on exchanging our favourite war books. Despite doctors' orders not to, he still rolled his own cigarettes and smoked them outside his house on the porch. And I still visited him on the anniversary of Dieppe to hear what really happened that August 19 day and in the three debilitating years that followed. I had to visit him earlier than usual in 2009, in early April, and in hospital, several days before he died of complications from the cancer.

Several things struck me about him at the end. While no doubt the disease had crippled him physically inside, I don't think it changed him outwardly. He still had a pretty full head of hair. His eyes still lit up when he saw me. He insisted on seeing a newspaper; he needed to know more than what was going on in that room. And even lying there in a hospital bed, his body language still spoke strength, calm, and self-determination—his wife, Marilyn, often said about her relationship with him: "You can't harness the wind." His demeanour suggested defiance, not defeat. And I wondered if he was that way because he'd been there before—in Europe, at the hands of his wartime guards. He'd learned to hide pain and discomfort pretty well, no matter how debilitating they were. He never let his captors win the psychological battle.

Nor was Stephen Bell angry those last days. Sure he complained about hospital treatment. Who doesn't? But I didn't see hate in his eyes. I remember his describing the way the German farm woman had treated him in March 1945, after his escape from the last prisoner-of-war camp. Although she could easily have turned him over to the Gestapo, she didn't. Instead, because her neighbour's POW son had been treated so well in Canada, she felt she should reciprocate. Somehow that woman's life-saving food and shelter had given back some of what three years of torture and deprivation in the camps had taken from him. There was a great deal more forgiveness in Stephen Bell than I ever expected.

"If it wasn't for that kind old German woman, I wouldn't be alive today," he told me once. "I have a lot to be thankful for."

Although I can no longer share August 19 with Stephen Bell in person to remember what he lost at Dieppe, I think I will always practise the life lessons that a veteran of his experience has afforded me.

I have my friend Charley Fox to thank for helping me set the record straight on Canada's largest expenditure during the Second World War—the British Commonwealth Air Training Plan—the subject of my book *Behind the Glory*. But there was more to the story, I discovered, than just Canada's $1.617-billion investment in the training of more than 200,000 men for the Allied air war. Among the myths Charley dispelled, for example, was the notion that BCATP instructors were second-rate flyers, that they didn't have what it took to fly operational missions overseas and so were relegated to teaching the basics to green, young cadets. In fact, the records proved just the opposite. The creators of the massive training scheme realized the unique talent required to translate manuals, maps, and syllabus (the training regimen air cadets had to learn) into skilled airmen. That's why the top 10 per cent of each graduating class did not go overseas into combat, but was instead trained further to become instructors for the next generation of BCATP trainees. The quality of the plan's instruction guaranteed its perpetual success. As proof, all I had to do was read Charley Fox's pilot logs.

Several pristine, blue-coloured, hardback volumes covered his flying career from his first flight as a BCATP trainee on January 5, 1941, until his last combat patrol on May 5, 1945, three days before VE Day. Each entry looked as though a calligrapher had penned it onto the page, the printing was so tidy and perfect. I asked Charley to share as much of his experience as a Service Flying Training School (SFTS) instructor as he could. I wanted to know what it was like to be one of instructor Fox's students at No. 6 SFTS Dunnville, between October 1941 and May 1943. I had had a glimpse of that instructor–trainee relationship during my "second seat" flight in a CHAA Harvard at Tillsonburg back in 1990. But I wanted Charley to explain how he taught young men, who had only soloed in Fleet Finch biplanes at Elementary Flying Training School, how to deal with the faster, more powerful, and much less forgiving mono-wing Harvard. I wanted to understand the psychology of instructing. Charley scanned his flight logs for a moment and remembered an Australian student who was on the verge of failing his course. The young student pilot had completed more than eight hours in the dual-control Harvards but had not soloed yet.

"I was flight commander at Dunnville then," Charley recalled. "I was going to have to wash him out of the course because his instructors couldn't get him to land." Charley explained that he took the young man up and tested him in all airborne procedures: instrument flight, stall and spin recovery, navigation technique, formation flying, as well as basic aerobatic manoeuvres such as turns, rolls, and loops. Charley said the student did everything perfectly. "But when it came time to land the Harvard, he'd let the aircraft get away from him. He'd start jiggling the rudder. The aircraft would turn too quickly. He'd touch a wingtip and spin right into a ground loop."

Repeating the process in hopes the trainee would settle down on the second attempt, he reacted the same way, over-controlling the rudder and ground looping yet again. Then Pilot Officer Fox had an idea. "Is this aircraft, Harvard No. 2784, the same one your instructor uses?" he asked.

"Yes," the Australian student said. "My instructor uses this aircraft practically all the time."

Charley said that he then approached a corporal serving with the ground crew at Dunnville station and asked him to go out to the Harvard on the flight line and (in front of the Australian trainee) take a look at the tail wheel of the aircraft. By agreement, the corporal would pronounce the tail wheel unserviceable. That would require the student to repeat the test, this time in a different Harvard.

"I don't have to check you out anymore. Take another aircraft," Charley told the Australian student and he sent him up solo in the second Harvard. The seasoned instructor was gambling that his impromptu psychology might give the student enough confidence to land the Harvard safely without an instructor lording over him from the second cockpit. Even so, Charley admitted the next few minutes, standing and watching from the ground, proved as nerve-racking for him as it must have been for the young Australian.

"He did the whole flight," Charley said, "and brought the Harvard down and greased it on the runway perfectly. So, how do you make young men into pilots? I don't know what happened to him. All I know is that he graduated. He got his wings."

It turned out that F/L Charley Fox's flight logs provided another important lead in my pursuit of the complete BCATP story. Often during my research, I had wondered how instructors in Canada coped with the unpleasant truth about flight instruction during the Second World War—that it did not offer its best practitioners any opportunities to perform glorious feats of arms or heroic deeds, but instead might confine a great aviation teacher to much dreary, monotonous, and boring work. Among flying instructor Fox's students, whose names were also entered in his pilot's log, was that of a cadet named Jack Kelshall. In the summer of 1942, instructor Fox had tested student Kelshall on instruments, takeoffs, and landings. Kelshall, Charley remembered, was not a Canadian and upon graduation from No. 6 SFTS Dunnville, Kelshall was posted to Training Command with No. 1 Central Navigation School at Rivers, Manitoba. I was curious to know more about this particular student.

Unfortunately, Charley couldn't pick me up in his car and drive me to Kelshall's home this time. It was in the West Indies. It took me some weeks, but I finally tracked the former navigational instructor down by telephone in San Fernando, Trinidad, where he had established a successful law practice after the war and was about to retire. I learned that among other things, private citizen Kelshall had one of the largest private libraries in Trinidad. That suggested to me that he was a meticulous collector. I hoped he might therefore also have saved some of his flight logs and diary material from his teaching days on the Prairies. When I explained my interest over the phone, the man was quite stunned that I would go to so much trouble in search of his stories about being a navigational instructor in the BCATP.

Nevertheless, at his suggestion, I composed a number of questions in a letter, sent it to him, and he promised that he would respond also by letter. Weeks passed and nothing came back. Four months after my original letter, I phoned again, only to learn that Kelshall had died within a week of his retirement. His wife, Anneliese Kelshall, said she had been haunted by the fact that there on his office desk was my unanswered letter. She promised to try to find something in Jack's extensive office and library of some 15,000 books. In May 1991, when I received the package from Anneliese Kelshall, I had no idea what I was in for. She had enclosed a number of newspaper stories and obituaries about her husband. They helped me understand the man's post-war dedication to serving the courts and the public in Trinidad. The letter attached said she had gone through his office files, however, and found only his pilot's log book, some personal diaries, and a series of political speeches. She lamented there was little to help me, but "I took a photostat of a graduation lecture given by Jack" when he was at Rivers, Manitoba. I read the two-page speech, simply titled "Graduation Lecture, Station Intelligence, Pilot Officer Kelshall—No. 1 CNS."

The speech began with his thoughts about "why we are fighting this war," about Hitler, about the Nazis, about atrocities, and about the battle for liberty—some of the politics to which Anneliese had alluded. Then Kelshall became very direct in his delivery. He posed a series of questions, essentially asking the graduating airmen, "What are we going to do about it?" It was evident that many of the men sitting or standing before him at Rivers were not destined for overseas postings but would remain in Canada to become the next generation of pilot and navigational instructors. Kelshall realized, as it had been for him, a posting to a BCATP station in Canada was not what any of them wanted. But, he surmised, it was up to him to motivate their sense of professionalism, inspire their commitment to the cause, and then to help them accept the thankless nature of their task.

In part the speech said:

> On those of you who are going to become instructors, a tremendous responsibility rests. The success of the war rests directly on the fighting efficiency and mental attitude of the men in our services. . . .
>
> If you make the effort to arouse, in each of the boys you will have in your charge, the determination to do his level best, the conviction that no sacrifice is too great—if you see that each one of them gets the very best training that it is in your power to give—then you are fighting against the Reich in the most powerful and the most effective way there is. . . .
>
> In your work as instructors, you will have none of the excitement of combat. You will have no hope or expectation of pretty little ribbons to pin under your wings. You will have no bright prospect of quick promotion or triumphal tours through Hollywood and New York. Nobody is ever going to throw ticker tape on you. The unswerving, driving energy needed to do a good job as an instructor must come from within yourselves. . . .
>
> It is not easy. It is not attractive. But, gentlemen, if you do a good job of instructing, the reward, though not material in nature, is very great. It lies in the knowledge that in this, the greatest and most critical conflict in the history of the world between the forces of right and wrong, you have been entrusted with a difficult and important job . . . that you have been worthy of the trust . . . and that you have done your part to the limit of your ability. It is worth it, gentlemen. Good luck to you all.

It was a brilliant speech. I read it over and over again. I could see him pounding it out on a typewriter in his office at the BCATP station in Rivers. I could hear him deliver it to those courses of graduating airmen proudly receiving their wings that day. It moved me, I'm sure the same way it must have moved them. More than that, Jack Kelshall's graduation lecture helped me to understand, more than I ever had before, why that generation of young men and women had felt compelled to enlist, serve in the Canadian forces, and go to war. Kelshall's keynote speech spelled out more clearly than ever the sentiment of the time: "No sacrifice is too great." In addition to that, Kelshall's clear understanding of the pivotal role of the instructor in the war effort was a beacon in my search to know everything about the BCATP story and get it right when it came time for me to sit at my keyboard and put it to paper. I knew I would have to quote his oratory at just the right moment in my forthcoming book. For days afterward, Kelshall's words kept ringing in my head. I felt the inspiration, motivation, and uplifting message of encouragement to his graduating class of instructors. I think it was the closest I ever came to understanding the makeup of those remarkable wartime aviators. It helped push me to the completion of my work.

Buoyed by positive reviews and strong book sales of *Behind the Glory*, early in 1993, I began accepting offers to speak about the theme at the root of the book—that BCATP instructors had largely been overlooked by historians, neglected even by their air force masters, and worst of all, forgotten by those they'd trained. Invitations came from TV and radio,* historical societies, veterans groups, high schools,

* When *Behind the Glory* was published, I did a national promotional tour—visiting ten or a dozen cities and giving perhaps 125 interviews. At a Winnipeg radio station, I sat in the lobby with several people waiting for the talk-show host to lead the next guest into the studio. Moments before my scheduled on-air interview, the host emerged and scanned the faces in the lobby with my book jacket in his hands. He looked perplexed. "Is Ted Barris here?" "Yes," I said. He laughed. He had the picture of me in the old flying jacket leaning against the cockpit of the Harvard at Tillsonburg in 1990. He thought it was a period photo of me in 1940 and that I was indeed a veteran promoting my reminiscences of wartime training.

and universities to elaborate on those accusations. Aviation stories seemed in vogue at the time and in particular tales of derring-do. While I had plenty of derring-do stories from instructors' flight logs, none of them included night bombing runs to Berlin, dogfights from the Battle of Britain, or sub-chasing sorties across the North Atlantic. More to the point, I sensed there was an appetite for events that had led to military aviation excellence overseas. The flyers who had given a fledgling air force its wings—those thousands of unsung BCATP instructors—seemed worthy of a hearing. It dawned on me that I had become their after-the-fact advocate.

Suddenly that winter I was contacted by the two co-chairmen of the Allied Air Forces Reunion. Both were RCAF bomber pilot veterans from Second World War Bomber Command, Pete Porter with No. 437 Squadron, and John Turnbull with No. 419 and No. 424 Squadrons. Since 1970, the Allied Air Forces Reunion (AAFR) committee had staged annual gatherings of veterans, exhibitors, active-service air crew, and aviation buffs alike to attend its weekend festivities in Toronto. Each autumn, the AAFR literally took over the Royal York Hotel on Front Street, booking rooms for many of its 12,000 members, erecting screening rooms to show both Hollywood films and documentary footage of Second World War sorties, and transforming the hotel's massive ballrooms into exhibit halls and banquet space. As was the reunion custom, each year the AAFR recognized different squadrons and those airmen associated with famous Allied airborne operations, such as Pathfinders, the Dambusters, Canadian No. 6 Group in Bomber Command, the Escape and Evasion Society, Home War Establishment, and so on.

"We were thinking of honouring those air crew in your book," Pete Porter told me on the phone. "Would you be interested in addressing the reunion about the instructors in the British Commonwealth Air Training Program?"

For perhaps twenty years or more, on countless early morning shifts, I had read the hourly national news on CBC Radio into every time zone and region in the country. I had done my fair share of TV hosting to national audiences as well. The fact that hundreds of thousands of listeners or viewers paid attention to my every word every time I turned on a microphone had never bothered me. Writing for newspapers or magazines with my byline prominently displayed had inspired the utmost respect for readers, but it had never unnerved me. Suddenly, having to speak to a ballroom full of Second World War air force veterans about their having neglected, forgotten, and sometimes even scorned Training Command brethren felt more daunting than any live broadcast or published byline. This would be very much like going into the lion's den and taunting the lion in broad daylight.

"Of course I would," I told the AAFR chairman. "But, if possible, could we meet with a former BCATP instructor or two to ensure the event meets with their approval?"

Porter and Turnbull agreed. The co-chairs met with several of my ex-BCATP instructor friends and me. The group laid out the plans for the twenty-third annual AAFR to pay special attention for the first time in its history to the service of veterans in Training Command. We insisted that the presence of the Training Command story be amplified with special posters, artifacts, photos, and literature in the exhibit halls. We negotiated an ideal time and place for my talk, which we suggested might be critical of the way other air force veterans had treated wartime training personnel during and after the war. We requested and got the AAFR to spend money on advertising the reunion in major air force publications and newsletters. And we made certain that the reunion committee employed every air force veterans' list it could find to ensure as many former members of Training Command as possible be notified of the event.

I rarely have a problem enjoying a banquet meal prior to giving a speech. I've always enjoyed the capacity to harness the nervous energy associated with live presentations and channel it into the talk. That tension, I've found, always works in my favour. At the October 2 AAFR banquet, however, I found it a bit tougher to digest the meal and even tougher to redirect the nerves I was feeling into the coming speech I'd composed. I felt a little like Jack Kelshall having to deliver the bad news of instructor postings to Canada to his graduating class. Nevertheless, as the Royal York hospitality staff finished serving the dessert and coffee, I was introduced and rose to address about 600 AAFR delegates and guests. They no doubt expected a fairly tame talk about the lesser known feats accomplished by their home-front comrades—the instructor staff of the BCATP.

After thanking the reunion committee for its kind invitation to address the membership and acknowledging the head table guests, I told the banquet audience that it was not going to get the speech it might expect. I told those present—mostly air force veterans—that I was going to challenge their sense of their own history. I then told three brief stories about encounters with veterans that had changed my sense of Canada's wartime aviation past and how they had also changed my life. I briefly described meeting Charley Fox in Tillsonburg where he challenged me to consider writing an official history of the British Commonwealth Air Training Plan. I then referred to a letter sent to me via the CBC from another BCATP veteran named Charlie Konvalinka, who pointed out "the role of the BCATP instructor had never been given the recognition it merited." And my third encounter described meeting a former BCATP instructor from the U.K., John Campsie, who said his reading of my account of the plan's extraordinary success made him "feel prouder of what we actually did."

I took a moment to point out what was behind *Behind the Glory*. Not so much to brag about completing and publishing the book, I merely wanted to illustrate to my audience of veterans the extent of my research and the breadth of my knowledge on the subject. I sensed that in order to criticize, I first had to lay out my credentials. I told them I had travelled 10,000 kilometres; communicated with sources in fifteen countries; recorded exclusive interviews with perhaps 250 veterans; sifted through photos, newspaper clippings, scrapbooks, unpublished records, diaries, flight logs, official and unofficial records; and then spent another twelve months writing the original manuscript for publication in the fall of 1992. I told them that critics had written positively about the book, but more germane, I told them several printings later, more than 15,000 copies were now in the hands of readers learning for the first time about the extraordinary achievements of BCATP instructors.

Then I told them the bad news. I accused my audience of ultimately insulting those men of Training Command.

"We as Canadians have all but omitted them from our history," I said. "In less than six years, the instructors and support staff of the BCATP trained nearly a quarter of a million aircrew. . . . BCATP instructors risked their lives every day of the war, not facing night fighters or anti-aircraft, but inexperienced green pilots. . . . Despite horrible losses in the air war overseas, nearly a thousand instructors and students lost their lives in training accidents and even military records don't acknowledge that."

I then turned to some of Jack Kelshall's words to punctuate my speech. I pointed out for those air force veterans who didn't know that BCATP instructors got no service medals nor ribbons for putting fully trained pilots, navigators, wireless radio operators, air gunners, bomb-aimers, and flight engineers into combat over Europe, North Africa, and the Far East. I added that there was no such thing as a tour of duty for instructors. They were on duty training until the air force told them otherwise, because in Kelshall's words, "no self or public interest, no personal inclination, no private benefit or gain" could dissuade the air force from its primary job of training aircrew for the victory overseas. Not only was serving as an instructor thankless, I told my audience, it also proved a detriment to one's overall flying career.

"If instructors didn't leave Canadian shores (and most of the 5,000 BCATP instructors did not), they were not considered 'veterans' and were therefore not entitled to health, land grants, housing, or educational benefits," I said. "And further, if instructors applied for positions in commercial aviation after the war, they were told 'No. You're not eligible. Those jobs are being held for operations airmen coming home from overseas,' the same aircrew the instructors had trained."

I let that sink in a moment, before I concluded the litany of mistreatment. I scanned the audience one last time.

"You and I are responsible for this neglect. Canadians have very little sense of their history. They have even less respect for those who made that history possible." I repeated that line, pointing at the vets in my audience. "You and I have even less respect for those who made that history possible.

"You see, I view these instructors as the skilled minds and hands that coaxed, tempered, and churned out nearly 250,000 air and ground crew for Bomber Command, Fighter Command, Coastal Command, and Transport Command. They were the invisible air force that gave Commonwealth flyers—*you*—the means to bring home victory. They were the people 'behind the glory!'"

Fortunately, I guess, there were enough Training Command veterans in the audience to deflect any of the anger some of the vets might have felt about my accusations, because many of them jumped up and applauded loudly. That seemed to spark most of the rest to follow. I thanked them for the praise but took a moment to acknowledge the three men in the audience whose challenge and encouragement had inspired me to write the book in the first place.

"They are three important reasons why my book happened and, in part, why the Allied Air Forces Reunion is finally honouring Training Command this weekend," I said to conclude. "I ask Charley Fox, Charlie Konvalinka, and John Campsie, all former BCATP instructors, to stand and be recognized."

Of course, the three former instructors enjoyed the unexpected attention. But they soon slipped back into their characteristic shell of modesty. I respected Charley Fox's modesty at virtually every turn. Implicitly I knew not to go into those parts of Charley's war that made him uncomfortable—death, loss, and bravery. But when we began appearing in public together more and more to share veterans' stories, I found his constant refusal to recount his own career achievements a bit hollow. After all, he had flown Spitfire fighter aircraft armed to the teeth with cannon and machine-gun shells into enemy territory for the better part of a year and a half. He had flown on some of his earliest combat operations with Canadian fighter ace George "Buzz" Beurling. He'd scrambled from Tangmere station, one of the storied Battle of Britain aerodromes in south England. He had provided air cover for Canadian troops, tanks, artillery, and the naval armada landing on Juno Beach on D-Day. He had led attacks into France and Belgium against German V-1 and V-2 rocket launching sites. His No. 126 Wing and No. 412 Fighter Squadron had spearheaded the advance north and east toward Germany. And he had flown his last official sortie on May 5, 1945, Liberation Day in Holland. With all that operational experience, I thought, it was time for Charley Fox, DFC and Bar, to take some credit for his remarkable record.

I don't know who was more surprised that I kept pushing him into the limelight, Charley Fox or Ted Barris. But the trust between us had grown so remarkably over those years of our friendship that I just sensed there were events he'd experienced that needed greater airing. In particular, something I'd seen in his pilot's logs—a note that had gone unexplained—had bothered me for a long time. In one of my first interview sessions with Charley, I had noticed an entry he'd made about a month after D-Day in 1944.

"What about this red mark recorded on July 17, 1944?" I asked.

"Don't know that I really want to go into that too deeply," he said.

"It says here 'armed recce' for one hour and fifteen minutes," I continued, "then one staff car damaged."

I had heard that there was a great deal of controversy surrounding an attack on this particular day. There were at least three, maybe four other fighter pilots—an American, a South African, and several other Canadians—all claiming they had shot up a Horch convertible (top down) containing a driver, three German officers, and none other than the Desert Fox himself, Field Marshal Erwin Rommel. But I wanted Charley Fox's version. It took a while for him to shed his characteristic modesty, but I finally coaxed the story out of him.

"It was late afternoon," he began, speaking slowly and precisely, "because we came out of the sun from the west. I saw the staff car going along an avenue of trees heading north at a good rate of speed. I called out that I was going down. Another fellow followed me down . . ."

"Who was with you?"

"Steve Randall. I was leading a flight of four aircraft. Two of us went down. I timed the shots so that I was able to fire and get him as the car came through a small opening in the trees."

"How close to the ground were you flying?"

"Down about ground level to shoot," Charley said, then added, "but what you do as soon as you're finished shooting, you're up over the trees and then you stay as low as possible until you get away from the area, in case there's support [returning ground fire] around."

"How many passes did you make?"

"Just one. Oh, I got him on that pass. We were moving pretty fast, but I knew I got him."

"What was all the controversy about?" I asked.

"We got back to base and we heard over the radio that Rommel had been hurt in a shoot-up of his staff car. The location was right. But what with double daylight saving time there in France, there was a dispute about the timing. . . . The Americans claimed that a Thunderbolt had done it. . . . Anther guy, the squadron leader from No. 411 Squadron, a Canadian from Down East, he said he got Rommel. I never made any noise about it . . . but it's always been sitting in my log book. It's not something you show off."

Over the years I'd known Charley Fox, whenever we'd spoken in public, I'd often invited him to speak about the events of July 17, 1944, but not until more recently had he chosen to take credit for the Rommel attack. He more often preferred to speak of his squadron mates, Steve Randall in particular, and the ones who didn't make it through the war. And in spite of the number of air force veterans all continuing to recount the way they successfully put Rommel out of the war, Charley never took the bait to challenge them either behind the scenes or in public. Finally, in April 2004, nearing the sixtieth anniversary of the famous strafing of the car, a Quebec historian offered proof that Fox had in fact been the one to strike the car with his Spitfire strafing, force it off the road near Livarot, France, and injure the Field Marshal, thus ending his career. (As he recovered from severe head injuries following the attack, Rommel was implicated in the plot to assassinate Adolf Hitler later in the year and was forced to commit suicide in October 1944.)

Author Michel Lavigne compared Charley Fox's log with the official RCAF and German military records to confirm the time, location, and military aircraft involved in the demise of the famous Field Marshal.

I guess my attempts to get him to speak openly about the Rommel incident were like those of a son coaxing a father to boast in front of the family. Initially, he didn't feel right about it. Anything that seemed like bragging in public was certainly out of the question, as far as Charley was concerned. Perhaps, the same way my father had turned to the emotionally safe humorous stories about boot camp in Kansas or going AWOL into Prague, it felt more comfortable for Charley Fox to speak publicly about the deeds of his comrades in 412 Squadron than to dwell on his own combat feats. It took the verification of the event on July 17, 1944, by another journalist to help Charley Fox go public more often about his wartime actions.

It is the film that epitomizes June 6. It is that indelible sequence showing darkened but clearly visible figures of Canadian troops silently exchanging last-moment instructions, moving ladders and rifles into final ready position, and patting the forward-most troops on their backs for encouragement. The doors finally swing open and the brighter outside light streams in. The first troops leap out of the landing craft. Ahead of them are the famous beach-resort houses of Normandy and 8,000 concealed German army troops intent on repulsing this attack on Hitler's Atlantic Wall. It is that iconic, point-of-view film of the greatest amphibious invasion in history—the D-Day landings.

"The footage is one of the most graphic depictions of combat ever recorded," wrote British historian John Keegan.

As celebrated as this remarkable movie material is, official history had somehow overlooked the story of its creation and its creator. For a while, my initial research on the subject revealed that this celluloid account of the Canadians' landing at the beach—code-named Juno—at about 8 o'clock on D-Day morning came from a static camera somehow bolted to the gunwale or the stern of the landing craft seen in the footage. Even museum sources I consulted noted that a motion-picture camera, facing forward to capture the activity en route to the beach, was activated by a seaman aboard the landing craft infantry (LCI). All official sources I consulted seemed to suggest that an anonymous sailor had merely pressed a button on the camera. The rest was history.

In 2003, as I worked feverishly to complete my manuscript about the Canadians' equivalent of Cornelius Ryan's *The Longest Day*, initially I felt content to accept most historians' versions of the filming. In fact, I had written up the section about the No. 2. Canadian Film and Photo Unit's locked-off cameras rolling blithely away capturing these historic images like passive witnesses to history. But something began to eat at my assumption. I began to worry that maybe there was another version of this story I had missed. Maybe the cameras had *not* been bolted to the LCI going ashore. Maybe somebody had *been* there manually framing the shot and more deliberately pressing the movie camera's start button.

From research, I knew that Ken Bell, the celebrated Second World War still photographer, had come ashore on D-Day with the 9th Infantry Brigade of the 3rd Canadian Infantry Division. I had seen some of his legendary F2.8 Rolleiflex photographs in other books. Bell's portfolio of stills, taken alongside the Canadian troops as they liberated northwestern Europe in 1944–45, makes up the heart of Ottawa's wartime collection at the National Archives. I discovered, however, that Ken Bell had died in June of 2000 and so searched out his widow, Mary Lea Bell, in Gibsons, British Columbia. She explained that her husband's memoirs about No. 2 Canadian Film and Photo Unit (CFPU) might have clarified how that famous D-Day motion picture film was shot. But Ken Bell had died before he had a chance to write about the CFPU's experience on June 6.

"You might try contacting one of Ken's fellow army photographers," Mary Lea suggested, "Chuck Ross in Edmonton."

It didn't take me long to find the former wartime cinematographer, living with his wife in a downtown high-rise overlooking the Alberta Legislature and the picturesque valley of the North Saskatchewan River. Born in Scotland and with just the slightest burr in his voice, Chuck Ross spoke with such clarity of his wartime experience, it was as if he had a photographic memory. In our earliest conversations in 2003, I delighted in his nearly instant recall of names, places, events, and the details of his time with No. 2 CFPU in northwestern Europe. That would be important if I wanted to clear up the mystery of the D-Day movie footage. But that's not where I began my first interview with the former Sgt. Ross.

When I asked for his account of events, he explained that he'd gone ashore in Normandy as a driver for Lt. George Cooper, a cine cameraman with the No. 2 CFPU. Cooper had filmed the Canadians during their liberation of Italy in 1943 and 1944. When Cooper landed on Juno Beach a couple of days after D-Day, he had two cameras assigned to him, so Ross learned to become Cooper's right-hand assistant—loading the cameras, reading the exposures, and preparing the lenses.

I then asked Chuck to walk me through the operation of the CFPU cine cameras used during the landings. They were Bell and Howell Model-Q Eyemo cameras. They shot 35-mm movie film; that's why the picture quality was so exquisite, he told me. Each camera was powered by a clockwork motor, which was wound up with a key, the same as a child's toy. The key was L-shaped with a handle; the operator inserted the key into the right side of the Eyemo and rotated it until the inside spring was wound up tight. Then he'd slip the key into a small slit pocket just above his right pant pocket. Chuck said that each camera magazine held about 100 feet of film or the equivalent of ninety seconds of shooting. I paused a moment before I asked this next crucial question.

"How much shooting time would one full winding with the key give the camera operator?"

"Oh, about thirty-five or thirty-six seconds," Chuck Ross answered.

"That's all. Only half a minute's worth of shooting," I said with surprise. And then I asked the next question equally carefully. "What do you think of the general belief that this famous film of the Canadians landing on Juno Beach was taken by a camera simply mounted at the back of the landing craft?"

"Not true," Ross came back. "It was shot by Sgt. Bill Grant."

"Not a sailor merely pressing the start button?" I wanted to be sure.

"No way." He laughed out loud. "With all that chaos, a sailor on the landing craft would hardly have the time or the ability to operate the camera too."

"Why then is the shot so steady?"

"Because the commanding officer Richard Malone [later publisher and editor-in-chief of the *Globe and Mail*] was most particular about his cameramen using tripods; if not, he blew his top."

Ross then described how his CFPU colleague, Bill Grant, had set up the camera and tripod several times inside the LCI during the run-in to Juno Beach. He had shot a complete magazine (about ninety seconds of film) as the Canadian troops prepared, waited, and (as the doors swung open) dashed from the landing craft. Ross said that Grant had then scooped up his camera equipment and two more rolls of unexposed film and scrambled ashore with the Canadian troops. There on the beach and shortly afterward inland, Grant had shot the rest of his movie film documenting the seaside village's complete liberation. Then, Ross told me, Grant packed his exposed film into cans that were marked "Press—Rush by whatever means possible—To Ministry of Information, London."

"Any way to verify that?" I asked.

"Sure. You can call the man who received and edited the film," Chuck said, "Staff Sgt. Ken Ewart."

I was in touch with the former Canadian army editor the same day. Fort Saskatchewan is situated just up the road from Chuck Ross's home in Edmonton. Again, I got some of Ken Ewart's background first. When the war began, he had joined the Loyal Edmonton Regiment. However, when the army learned that he had a unique knowledge of weapon sounds, it quickly realized Ewart would be invaluable matching the correct sound effects with the silent wartime film the cine cameramen were shooting in Europe. So the CFPU trained him to edit film at Merton Park Studios in South London, England. Early on the morning of June 7, 1944, just twenty-four hours after the film had been shot, Ewart received Bill Grant's movie footage.

"The first thing that had to be done was censor the film, keeping any [Allied] weapons in the dark," he said. "There was footage of troops crouched down inside the landing craft . . . jumping out the front of the landing craft, rushing up the sand dunes and into the first village."

"Any chance it was shot from a camera simply mounted on the back of the landing craft?" I asked just to be sure.

Just like Ross, Ewart laughed and said, "I received the cans of film with Bill Grant's name written on the outside. . . . Of course, for the newsreels, we took the best part of every scene. We didn't use everything he shot. We flashed the news. That's what we did."

Following the edit, Ewart told me, the scripting, dubbing, and sound recording were added and transferred to 16-mm film to complete the presentation that the public would see on movie screens around the world. Each newsreel consisted of about ten minutes of viewing. Within forty-eight hours of D-Day, people in Britain saw

Sgt. Bill Grant's film sequences, including the first images of Allied troops—the Canadians—landing in Normandy. Even before that, the exclusive film footage was flown across the Atlantic and shown to North American audiences.

"Theatres in New York were all showing the first newsreels of the landing. We had scored a complete scoop," Richard Malone wrote in *A World in Flames*. Then Malone went on to say, "Unhappily, the American theatres did not identify the troops shown landing on the beaches as Canadians."

About the time my book about Canadians on D-Day was published, I wrote a short essay for the *Globe and Mail's* Facts and Arguments section, entitled "The Shot Seen Around the World," reiterating my search for the true cinematographer of those famous movie frames. Both the book and the essay prompted responses from a long-established group of historians and photo buffs, the Photographic Historical Society of Canada (PHSC). In a newsletter published that same spring of 2004, PHSC contributor Robert Lansdale assembled his own documentation on the history of that famous footage in a piece entitled "20 Seconds of History—The D-Day Photos." He rightly took me to task over my reference to Ken Bell's "35-mm snapshots," pointing out they were stills from his trusty F2.8 Rolleiflex. He then paraphrased an interview he had done with Bell (published in 1994) in which Bell credits Capt. Colin McDougall, who was in charge of photographers for the Canadian Film and Photo Unit. McDougall, Bell explained to Lansdale, decided the idea of placing cine photographers among the highly trained troops in each LCI wouldn't work. Instead, the decision was made to statically position 35-mm Eyemo movie cameras toward the stern of several landing craft with navy crewmen triggering the shutters. So, Bell said, six cameras were installed.

"When Capt. McDougall hit the beaches," Bell told Lansdale, "he made a very dangerous search to retrieve the cameras. Two landing craft and their cameras were completely destroyed, but out of the rest came the historic footage. Films were rushed to HQ for processing and censoring then printed as 16-mm newsreels for worldwide distribution. But no one identified the troops as Canadian nor the cameraman as Canadian."

The PHSC mistakenly dismissed my conversation with Chuck Ross, "who I really think should be identified as Charles (Bud) Roos," Lansdale wrote. The man Lansdale referred to, Sgt. Bud Roos, came ashore on D-Day with the Regina Rifles, but his landing craft struck a mine, throwing him and his movie camera into the seawater and ruining his film. Elsewhere in Lansdale's story, he quoted a military history buff from Vancouver; John Eckersley's research concluded that the famous sequence seen following D-Day actually resulted from motion picture film captured from three different landing craft. Eckersley supported the "clamped Eyemo explanation," suggesting that "a static camera on a tripod would give the same imagery if the photographer reached up from a safe crouching position to trigger the camera."

Finally, in his newsletter article, PHSC writer Robert Lansdale introduced the potential for yet another Canadian cinematographer as the man of the hour that June 6 morning. Bill Poulis spoke to the PHSC in 1995 and reminded those present that the Royal Canadian Navy had assigned ten photographers of its own to capture images of the invasion from aboard the landing craft. Poulis refuted the notion of unmanned cameras rolling on the landings, suggesting (as Chuck Ross and Ken Ewart had) that busy sailors would have little time to wind up, mount on a tripod, focus, and start the Eyemos. Nor was it likely with the scarcity of cameras that the Canadian army would gamble with six units bolted to the gunwales of inbound landing craft. But Poulis recounted that he had had no trouble finding a spot aboard a landing craft to shoot one trip in with the first wave of troops and then a second run-in with more Canadians later in the morning. As for crediting Bill Grant with the landing footage, Poulis commented: "[It] is to my mind erroneous and simply not true. We all sent film back to SHAEF [Supreme Headquarters Allied Expeditionary Force] in special priority dispatch bags via the first ships we knew were returning to the U.K. For all I know, one of the two shots of soldiers leaving assault craft were mine."

Nevertheless, my research had yielded two sources who verified that Bill Grant had set up the camera and pressed the shutter button on the famous D-Day footage, not a random sailor aboard a navy landing craft. More than that, film editor Ken Ewart had recalled receipt of the "Press—Rush" containers with Grant's name attached. Then, by sheer coincidence, I found a third source. About the time I was stitching Grant's incredible story together, I received a phone call from an acquaintance, Carol Phillips, a bar steward at the Royal Canadian Legion branch in Lucknow, Ontario. She had mailed me an envelope containing her correspondence with Second World War dispatch riders. Among the responses to her inquiries about the men who rode motorcycles carrying messages during the war, she'd received a letter from Ottawa veteran Brian O'Regan. He recounted his days dispatching cans of film for the Canadian Film and Photo Unit: "On D-Day in Normandy," he wrote Carol Phillips, "I picked up on the beach a white-taped aluminum can containing cine reel #1 by Sgt. Bill Grant [and] the historic first film of Canadian soldiers in a landing craft approaching the beach, the ramp falling away as it hit the beach, and the first scenes of French buildings as the soldiers left the landing craft. The scenes were the first of the actual invasion to appear in newsreels around the world."

With three independent veteran sources—Ross, Ewart, and O'Regan—I felt comfortable dispelling the previously accepted version of history. A random sailor aboard a navy landing craft had not captured those famous frames seen in every D-Day retrospective on PBS in the United States, BBC in Britain, and the CBC in Canada every June 6 anniversary. It had been Bill Grant's courage under fire and ingenuity on the beaches of Normandy that had secured the footage. But my sources were fast disappearing. Grant himself was gone. Ken Bell was gone. Before my book *Juno* was published, Ken Ewart died. Only Chuck Ross remained.

"There isn't a day goes by that doesn't twig my memory of what happened back then," Ross said to a newspaper reporter in November 2003. "We recorded history."

Once embroiled in historical clarification, however, always embroiled in it. Three years after the publication of my book *Juno* and my Facts and Arguments essay in the *Globe and Mail* about Bill Grant's famous cinematography, more new data came my way in 2007. Unexpectedly, I received further communication from John Eckersley, the military historian who had concluded (in Robert Lansdale's newsletter article) that the famous D-Day landing sequence was a compilation of footage from several cinematography units on June 6, 1944. It appeared that the community of D-Day film expertise had grown. In his book, *D-Day to Carpiquet*, author Marc Milner also covered the filming of the Juno Beach landings. Contrary to previous wisdom that the film depicted members of the first wave of Queen's Own Rifles of Canada, however, Milner cited documents that, he said, proved the North Shore Regiment of New Brunswick was depicted. Apparently, close examination of the shoreline revealed the buildings to be those in St-Aubin-sur-Mer (at the west end of Nan Red sector) not Bernières-sur-Mer (in Nan White sector) as previously believed.

In the months that followed our original conversations about D-Day and the controversial filming aboard the Juno Beach landing craft, I learned that Chuck Ross had much more wartime viewfinder history to share with me. We kept in touch, and whenever I landed in Edmonton we would meet at his apartment overlooking the North Saskatchewan River valley or for lunch at the Petroleum Club, the prestigious meeting facility just north of downtown. It was during those follow-up conversations that I came to know more about the man who had learned to aim and shoot a movie camera at Canadian troops, while Germans aimed and shot guns at them . . . and sometimes him.

Chuck Ross was nothing if not meticulous and patient. In all our conversations about his experiences with the Canadian Army Film and Photo Unit in wartime Europe, he recognized my naïveté about the preparation that went into each exposed frame of 35-mm film in the 1940s. My insta-camera mentality had little understanding of what was required to shoot motion picture before the advent of load, shoot, and fire moviemaking.

He reminded me, for example, that after continuous use of 80 ASA Tri-X film in the Eyemo, the internal workings of the camera would get gummed up with film emulsion, thus slightly slowing down the twenty-four frames per second speed of the film through the shutter. To clear the internal mechanism of the camera of the excess emulsion, Ross learned to take a change bag (a double-lined, light-excluding bag with two arm-hole entry sleeves), zipper the camera inside the bag, and by touch alone, remove the camera cover, lift the film out of the Eyemo gate, wipe away the excess emulsion in one swiping motion, reset the film in place, replace the camera cover, and remove the camera from the bag ready to shoot again. He could do all that in forty-five seconds, he told me. He worked at break-neck speed partly to test himself sometimes, but most often to fulfill his commitment to the service of his unit. He admitted to a dose of self-preservation too.

"I never shot footage of anybody being killed," Ross said.

"Was that policy?" I asked.

"No. By and large they didn't show a lot of that footage," Ross continued, "because, if I may use this phrase, 'There but for the grace of God go I.' But there were times [cameramen] had to shoot that stuff, because we were told we had to get it."

The CFPU sustained its share of casualties; four cameramen and two drivers were killed and twenty others wounded during the liberation campaign. Ross recalled the unit losing Lloyd Millan, killed when the landing craft in which he filmed received a direct hit from a German 88-mm artillery shell during the liberation of Walcheren Island in Holland. Cine cameraman Terry Rowe died covering the landing of the Devil's Brigade at Anzio, Italy. Jimmy Campbell died in a mortar attack near the River Orne in France. And Chuck Barnett died when the Auster spotter plane from which he filmed the Rhine crossing was shot down by a German fighter aircraft.

Chuck Ross survived a few close calls, but when I asked for an explanation, he prefaced his remarks by saying, "What I experienced versus what the infantry, artillery, and tank boys went through was nothing." Then he recalled an incident in early July 1944, during the Canadians' push to capture the airport at Carpiquet in Normandy.

Ross and his superior, Lt. George Cooper, had stopped next to a Canadian self-propelled artillery vehicle, called a Priest.* Cooper had caught up with his brother-in-law, and the three men stood behind the Priest just talking. All Ross recalled next was the zing sound of a single bullet passing a few feet over his head—perhaps a German sniper's shot or an errant shell from a Schmizzer, a German machine gun—followed by the scream of its ricochet off the stone wall behind him. "It didn't nearly hit me," he hastened to add. "It hit the wall three feet away from me. That's a long way. But it just sticks with you."

At that moment, early in the liberation campaign, Ross didn't think about what the ricochet might have done. There wasn't time. The pressure was on everybody in the CFPU to be abreast or even ahead of the Canadians' advance beyond Carpiquet. July 11, 1944, didn't have the same resonance as June 6, 1944. But for the French civilians who survived the bombardment and fierce fighting in Normandy's largest city, Caen, it really did mean the beginning of the end of German occupation. And cinematographer Ross found himself right in the midst of the exhilaration of this pivotal day, with an Eyemo camera in his hands. The film and photo unit suddenly learned that General Bernard Montgomery was en route to the frontline fighting in Caen. Even as thousands of the city's residents huddled in the great church of St. Etienne in the middle of the city, Monty decided to rush to the site. He had decided to seize the moment and announce the liberation of the city in front of as many civilians (and cameras) as possible.

"[Montgomery] knew the value of publicity from the photographic angle," Ross said. "When he flew anywhere, the first two people off the plane were a British stills man [photographer] and a motion picture cameraman. . . . George [Cooper] was shooting with one camera and I was on a second camera. We were surrounded by

---

* During the Second World War, American military strategists designed a motor carriage for a 105-mm artillery piece. The British incorporated the self-propelled artillery vehicle (SP) into their arsenal, but because a machine gun was mounted in a pulpit at the front and to one side of the howitzer, they nicknamed the vehicle "the Priest."

French citizens. [The British and Canadian troops] were still trying to clear the Germans on the far side of Caen . . . but Monty was sitting up there on the back of a convertible with cameras running, telling the French they were now liberated."

That wasn't the only time Chuck Ross got a scoop by hanging onto the coattails of Bernard Montgomery. The Caen story had been one for the main course of our lunch at the Petroleum Club. He saved a Dutch liberation story for dessert. Shortly after VE Day (May 8, 1945), Chuck told me, Queen Wilhelmina made a triumphant and highly publicized return to Holland. Among her earliest semi-formal meetings involved receiving Field Marshal Montgomery at the family's summer residence, Huis den Bosch. When members of No. 2 Canadian Film and Photo Unit got wind of the meeting, Chuck Ross managed to commandeer a jeep, a driver, and a position in the motorcade right behind the Field Marshal himself.

"[Montgomery's] car was in the lead," Ross recalled. "I was in the next jeep and I said to the driver, 'Stay right behind him.' He did and we got through the gates while all the Dutch press were behind us [left outside] as they closed the gates to the residence."

With the rest of the press corps looking on in envy, the Queen and Prince Bernhard emerged from the summer residence to greet their liberator. With just enough time to set up his tripod to please his boss and a full magazine in his Eyemo to capture the smiles and handshakes, Ross had another Canadian exclusive. There remained one small detail. In order to condense the final version of the meeting, Sgt. Ross needed cutaway material, completely separate images an editor could use to capsulize Montgomery's meeting the Royals on film to a more manageable length.

"So I'm looking to get a cutaway [shot]. And here's two little girls looking out the window. It was the two princesses [Beatrix and Irene]. One later became Queen."

Chuck Ross revelled in unique moments such as that, but he wasn't one to brag. Too many of his friends in the CFPU had not come home to boast about cinematic coups during the war. But he made it seem as if the entire unit deserved credit for filming the D-Day landings or the Dutch royal family restored to its summer home. Not long after our original interview and its resulting correspondence, Chuck Ross confided that he'd been asked to speak about the history of the CFPU at a sixtieth anniversary of D-Day event. He worried that he didn't have the writing skills to deliver a satisfactory talk. He asked me to read his notes and to critique them. Of course, they were fascinating, but rather technical.

"Start with a personal anecdote," I suggested. "Show your audience what it was like to be on Juno Beach that day and in the Normandy campaign."

Chuck later sent me a copy of his speech, which deflected any of the credit for the film unit's valour away from himself. Much as I had attempted to do in my telling of the D-Day story, Chuck held up Bill Grant's extraordinary film footage "that scooped the world." But he also offered an image of the Normandy campaign most observers probably missed. It was a perspective only a veteran who'd peered through a movie camera viewfinder in wartime could have known. It was something only a cameraman with an eye for detail would have spotted.

"I will always remember a sergeant of the Regina Rifles," Ross said in the conclusion of that D-Day speech. "Leading his squad through a grain field, his face was young, but his eyes were that of a veteran who has seen all. Those men were his responsibility.

"Although today it is sixty years ago [that D-Day happened], for those of us who were there in Normandy, it will always be yesterday."

6

"PUT A HUMAN FACE ON WAR"

AMONG the guiding principles of my documentary work on Canada in wartime, I have tried to place animate objects above inanimate ones. It has always seemed to me the danger this kind of research and writing presents is an attraction to the hardware of war, rather than the human lives changed by it or lost to it. Far too often during my travels to museums, archives, historic sites, conventions, and reunions, I have watched people gather and ogle at how close to mint condition are the tanks, trucks, and airplanes on display. I have endured countless conversations among collectors about the relative lethal capabilities of this weapon over that one. And I have nodded silently when amateur and professional historians debate the impact of this military manoeuvre's contribution to victory or that strategic blunder's leading to defeat. Most of the time, I don't care to be seduced by war technology or battle analysis. But I have to admit to one exception.

The morning in February 1993, when fire struck a section of the Canadian Warplane Heritage Museum (CWHM) at Mount Hope (near Hamilton), Ontario, I was reading hourly national newscasts on CBC Radio. I recall broadcasting the story and conducting a news interview on-air about the destruction of three of the museum's prized aircraft—a rare Hurricane, an Avenger, and a Spitfire. Like the large volunteer membership of the CWHM, I suddenly sensed a feeling of loss of these priceless fighter aircraft, but also some relief that one of only two airworthy Lancaster bombers in the world was spared because it was in an adjoining hangar and was pulled to safety during the fire. Coincidentally, my book about the training of aircrew in the BCATP was just out, so I called my museum contact and asked if I could come to speak to the membership as a fund-raiser. At that meeting, I bought a CWHM membership and left a box of my new book behind to help raise funds for the museum—a small gesture in the wake of the huge financial loss of the aircraft.

But it did occur to me later that I had instantly reacted to the loss of the warplanes almost by reflex. I guess I rationalize my purchase of a CWHM membership that day and the donation of books, however, because in the loss of those aircraft I instantly saw the faces of so many fighter pilot veterans I'd interviewed. I saw the burned-up Spitfire and began replaying the Spitfire stories I'd gathered as an author and broadcaster over the years. It was as if the torched aircraft at Mount Hope symbolized the severing of yet another link with those veterans' legacy. Time and general neglect had already taken so many of them and their beloved aircraft away. The morning I spoke to the CWHM volunteers, all the Spitfire stories that air force veterans had ever shared with me came flooding back.

I remembered Canadian aviatrix Marion Orr, who ferried Spitfires around the U.K. for the Air Transport Auxiliary during the Second World War, raving that the power of the Spitfire taking off pressed her so hard against the cockpit seat that she'd climbed to 5,000 feet before she even knew it. I recalled journalist Scott Young's 1942 interview with George "Buzz" Beurling in England after he'd shot down a record of twenty-eight enemy aircraft in just fourteen days of fighting in the skies over Malta. Beurling told Young that dogfighting in a Spitfire "was like playing pool shots all the time, [knowing] which of the guns in which wing was aimed at what you wanted to knock down." I thought of Brick Bradford's miraculous return from a June 1944 sortie to photograph a bridge over the Salween River, in Japanese-occupied China. En route home he had to navigate his Spitfire through rain, snow, icing, turbulence, and thunderheads up to 42,000 feet with virtually "no instruments," landing the Spitfire at Calcutta with fuel tanks registering empty. In contrast, I recalled my conversation with former BCATP instructor John Trull, whose final pilot's log entry aboard a Spit on February 20, 1944, read: "My damned kite up and quit on me." An airlock had blocked the aircraft's fuel line, and although Trull survived the resulting crash landing, he spent the next six months evading the Germans in occupied Belgium before getting back to the U.K. In particular, that morning at the CWHM, however, I got thinking about an RCAF fighter pilot whose name had become as closely associated with the Spitfire after the war as it was during the war: Jackie Rae.

"The Spitfire's probably the most important aircraft of World War II," Jackie Rae told me in an interview at his Toronto home in 1990. "The first thing that comes to my mind is really how beautiful it looks. . . . Anyone who flew one, as I did, is romantic about the Spitfire because it was marvellous. It had no bad habits. It out-flew any enemy aircraft."

Although he was born in Winnipeg and originally wanted to study medicine, his first gainful employment when the family moved to Toronto was in show business, performing on-stage with his brother and sister as the Three Raes of Sunshine and later producing radio shows for a Toronto ad agency. Just age eighteen in 1940, as the Battle of Britain reached its climax, he entered an RCAF enlistment office on Wellington Street in Toronto and told the recruiting officer, "Nazism really disturbs me." Reflecting on this in 1990, he said, "It was a juvenile patriotic reason to join the air force, [but] I said I'd read a lot about the Battle of Britain and I wanted to be a fighter pilot."

At his Toronto home, Rae brought out his wartime journals, pilot's log, and attestation papers and pointed out that he'd completed his initial training at Toronto's Eglinton Hunt Club, his elementary flying at Sky Harbour training facility in Goderich, Ontario, and received his service (graduation) wings at Borden, Ontario. I commented that I didn't think those enlisting in eastern Canada were allowed to train in eastern Canada. He openly admitted that he'd rigged his papers.

"I was sitting in the room at the recruiting centre," Rae said. "There was no one but a corporal and myself, and on his desk were two stacks of files. One stack said 'West' and the other said 'East.' I asked, 'What does that mean?' He said the fellows in the 'West' file live in the east and we want them away from their families, so we train them in the west. And the fellows in the 'East' file, we bring from the west to train them away from their families.

"When he wasn't looking, I quickly flipped through the files. My file was in the 'West' pile, so I pulled it out of there and stuck it in the 'East,' so I trained no farther than 150 miles from home."

Cadet Jackie Rae may have rigged his training destinations, but as a pilot officer, he served two full tours on Spitfires in Europe. When he pulled out his clasp of service medals from the war, it included the Air Crew Europe Star, the 1939–1945 Star, the Defence of Great Britain medal, the Victory Medal, a Mentioned in Dispatches award, and his Distinguished Flying Cross. His pilot's log showed that he had moved to operational or combat flying for the first time in March 1942, just as Operation Jubilee was taking shape.

"Dieppe was my first big sweep, with 416, a Spitfire squadron," Rae said. The list of squadron leaders and flight commanders at No. 416 City of Oshawa Squadron, located at Hawkinge airfield near Dover on the southeast coast of Britain, read like a who's who of Fighter Command. Lloyd Chadburn, Wally Murray, Bob Phillip, Mac Macdonald, Dave Goldberg, "all leaders who had been through it and were vehement about how you should fly this airplane, how you should move that control column around, and turn the airplane inside out."

By midsummer of 1942, the momentum of the air war had changed. Rae said that instead of defending south England as Winston Churchill's famous "few" had done during the Battle of Britain, members of the crack 11 Group of Fighter Squadrons along the south coast went on the attack across the English Channel to meet the Luftwaffe over occupied France. During our talk in 1990, I was curious to know more about the actual dogfighting he'd experienced during his first days flying Spitfires. He said there was surprisingly little. Rae's Mark II Spitfire held only eighty-seven gallons of fuel, which limited the Spitfire's range—leaving England, flying across the Channel, taking on enemy aircraft, and returning safely to the English bases. However, with the addition of a jettison fuel tank to extend his flying time, Rae said he could take his aircraft to 35,000 feet and operate over the English Channel for between an hour and forty minutes and two hours and ten minutes.

"That still wouldn't leave very much time to provide cover at Dieppe on August 19," I suggested.

"Actual fighting?" Rae said. "It would be maybe three to five minutes. Very short. . . . The squadron did numerous sweeps that day over the beach, came back, refuelled, and went back over again."

With a strength of thirty fighter pilots at the Hawkinge station, Rae said the squadron sent twelve aircraft up at a time, that is, two flights of six Spitfires flying in three lines of four aircraft. He illustrated by splaying the fingers of both hands in front of me—the four fingers of one hand indicating a forward line and the four fingers of the other representing the following line of Spitfires. On contact with enemy aircraft, he explained, this formation would allow individual pairs of fighters to break off in pursuit, each Spitfire pilot protecting another's tail. Each sweep across the Channel included a squadron of a dozen Spitfires flying at 3,000 feet and another twelve at 7,000 feet. During the planned hit-and-run raid at the seaport of Dieppe, it would be the fighters' job to keep German strafing and bomber aircraft from attacking the infantry and tank corps landing on the beaches. I asked Jackie what he thought of his squadron's effectiveness, given the disaster taking place on the beaches at Dieppe that day.

"I remember we caught one squadron of Junkers 88s who were making a bombing run," Rae said. "We got 'em in time to force them to jettison their bombs into the sea. It cut down their threat considerably."

That night back at Hawkinge, Spitfire pilot Rae noted in his pilot's log that his squadron had completed seven sweeps across the Dieppe beach head. It had suffered no casualties. It had been attacked by twelve to fifteen Focke-Wulf 190s. One had fired at him and missed. On one sortie, the squadron had engaged seven Junkers 88s, knocking one down, destroying three more, and chasing the rest from the cover zone. I asked him how that first ops flight felt, his baptism of fire.

"It was very exciting," he said, "but I was scared, of course."

I pressed him to comment on actually shooting down an enemy aircraft in combat or, as it was known, "scoring a kill." As a Spitfire pilot Jackie Rae registered eight official kills in aerial combat. They contributed to his being awarded the DFC. Still, I wondered if he ever had a picture of the enemy pilot in his head.

"I was always upset when I shot down an aircraft," he admitted. "I was never proud. I was aggressive, true. There's no doubt about it. But when it actually came to the fact and you sit down in the evening . . ." He paused and apologized for making it seem so dramatic, but he wanted me to understand that it affected him. "I would be sitting in a room and say, 'Jeez, I just killed a guy' or 'I just shot down four guys in a Junkers 88.' It always bothered me.

"I think there were people who (I was going to say) liked to kill. It's not what I mean. They enjoyed that they had a victory—the fact that someone had been killed was a secondary thing. I know certain people who it would not disturb. I think there were many like me who were disturbed by what they'd done. . . .

"See, it's hard for me. When I think about the war, I could ramble [on with] stories that are funny, that would drive you nuts. And they're the things I just think about. I don't think about [the killing] much any more."

At Jackie Rae's funeral in October 2006, his nephew Bob Rae (the former Ontario premier) quoted the inspiring poetry of another noted Spitfire pilot, John Gillespie Magee; for me, the "eager craft [flung] through footless halls of air" in "High Flight" had to be a

Spitfire. It seemed the most appropriate way to pay tribute to the man and his wartime service.

Indeed, the toughest wound for any veteran to endure is to be forgotten. My years of research into the lives of Canadian men and women who served their country at war have introduced me to many who say the war maimed them physically. It stole the best years of their lives. Worst of all, however, they fear that the history of their war overlooked, neglected, or forgot them completely. Typically Canadian, those vets never complain, especially since they survived while so many comrades did not. But in quieter, contemplative moments, when I pushed them, they've gone so far as to criticize government, military, historians, media, and the public for allowing their service to go undocumented or unheralded. Several of my navy veteran acquaintances—Tom Atherton and Dan Bordeleau—never complained to me about their lot as merchant seamen during the Second World War. However, I think the status of their wartime service was aptly described by former Canadian naval intelligence officer Joseph Schull as "a life unrelieved by uniforms, recognition, or the shoreside amenities for naval crews." A Canadian Merchant Navy Association report to the Standing Senate Committee on Veterans Affairs in 1991, entitled "It's Almost Too Late," recommended that the Government of Canada "extend full veterans' benefits to all Canadian merchant seamen who served in dangerous waters in Canada's armed conflicts." I've often wondered out loud why such a report should have been necessary.

George MacDonnell, a member of the Royal Rifles of Canada who fought in the defence of Hong Kong in December 1941, wrote in his book *This Soldier's Story* that for a long time the Canadian government overlooked the mental and physical trauma he and fellow survivors experienced at the hands of Japanese prison camp operators. "Unemployability, alcoholism, chronic illness, blindness and shortened lives," he wrote, "have been the consequences of prolonged savagery, malnutrition and forced labour" in Japanese POW camps during the war. By 1998, lobbying by MacDonnell and other members of the Hong Kong Veterans' Association yielded federal payments of $24,000 ($18 per day for three and a half years of imprisonment) to survivors or their widows. If not forgotten, certainly this overdue stipend represents a half-century of shameful national neglect.

Shirley Smith (later Mills) would be the last to claim history intentionally ignored her. After all, the recruiting motto for her wartime corps, the Women's Division (WD) of the RCAF, was "Women serve that men may fly." The British Commonwealth Air Training Plan, Canada's largest wartime contribution, stretched RCAF resources so thinly between 1939 and 1945 that putting women in uniform became a necessity. So, following an Order-in-Council in July 1941, the government began recruiting women into home-front air force service. The next year, Aircraftwoman Shirley Smith Second Class joined the more than 17,000 WDs who served in the BCATP—packing parachutes, recording air cadets' flying times, preparing meals, posting weather conditions, handling communications in ops rooms, and organizing flyers' equipment (gloves, helmets, goggles, and boots). The WDs' satisfaction was pride in the job, a sense of contributing, and for Shirley Smith "it was the first time I felt like an individual and was treated as one." The WDs' only reward was recognition that their wartime work had been seamless, virtually invisible.

The same might be said for members of the signal corps, nursing sisters and medical staff, supply and services troops, mechanical and electrical engineers, air force ground crew, dispatch riders, artillery and armoured corps troopers, reconnaissance and intelligence staff, home-front armament workers, or, for that matter, the musicians, singers, dancers, and comedians who entertained troops behind the lines, sometimes within hours after that front line had been secured. Often, veterans of campaigns during the Second World War claimed their theatre of war got short shrift from politicians and military brass. Survivors of the Battle of the Atlantic, the Burma campaign, the Dieppe raid, North Africa, and other battles told me frequently their war was an invisible one. Indeed, the entire 1st Canadian Division, which helped liberate Italy between 1943 and 1945, has fought the ridiculous moniker "D-Day Dodgers" blurted out by a misguided British parliamentarian. For survivors of the hard-fought battles at Agira, Monte Cassino, Liri Valley, and Ortona, the sting of being forgotten is only part of the frustration.

Imagine, however, the unique frustration for a generation of Canadian servicemen and servicewomen whose entire wartime experience was not just misunderstood but universally ignored and described as such. For nearly 30,000 Canadian veterans, service on the Korean peninsula between 1950 and 1953 is generally referred to as "the forgotten war." When hostilities between North and South Korea escalated into all-out warfare in June 1950, Canada joined a sanctioned United Nations special force to restore the political boundary between the two nations. The three-year war of attrition killed 516 Canadians but largely went unnoticed even by Canadians. I was one of them. It took a while for me to recognize the phenomenon, but by the mid-1990s—as I focused more and more on Canadian wartime history—my war reference bookshelves housed several book and DVD titles dealing with the Korean War in those exact terms: John Melady's book *Korea: Canada's Forgotten War*, Joseph C. Goulden's book *The Untold Story of the [Korean] War*, the CBC TV's *Forgotten Heroes: Canada and the Korean War*, and Time-Life's documentary *Korea: The Forgotten War*.

I don't think I set out initially to undo Canadians' apathy about the war, but my curiosity was certainly aroused when I realized far too many Korean War veterans in Canada felt dissatisfied and even angry that no one had told their story. My publisher at that time expressed interest in my thoughts about a book on the subject, so, in the fall of 1996 I set out to find some of these men, meet with them, and listen to their stories. A contract for my book *Deadlock in Korea* soon followed and my library of tape-recorded interviews with Korean War vets grew quickly. One among the first of my interview subjects left the deepest impression on me. Ted Zuber was an apparent loner—a painter living in the wilderness near Seeley's Bay,

Ontario. He had served a complete tour in Korea as a sniper with the Royal Canadian Regiment. He had been credited with five sniper kills. He had been wounded by a grenade. And back in Canada he had transposed a number of his diary sketches from Korea into large-format paintings. Thirteen of them became official war art in the Canadian War Museum collection.

I had to meet Ted Zuber. He seemed equally interested in talking to me. First in the spring of 1997 at a regimental reunion and again that fall at his secluded house and studio north of Kingston, Ontario, we talked for several hours during each visit. Looking a bit like a backwoodsman with his thick head of silver-coloured hair and full beard to match, Zuber was articulate, honest, and blessed with a wry sense of humour. He never hesitated to answer any of my questions and recalled his Korea experience with what seemed photographic detail. I soon discovered why. Zuber said he was born in Montreal in 1932, the eldest of five boys. After leaving high school at about age 15, he said, he pursued what most called a trade, but what he considered a potential livelihood that might support his growing interest in painting. He apprenticed in Kingston, Ontario, with a former navy cameraman to become a commercial photographer. Before pursuing fulltime careers in painting or photography, however, Zuber said there was something he had to do.

"Growing up as I did during the Second World War," he said, "as a male, I was waiting for my turn to get into uniform and do my bit. . . . When the war ended, my friends and I felt we were all denied the opportunity. Not that we wanted to kill people, but we somehow felt we hadn't had a chance to prove that we too could be a man."

I soon learned that Ted Zuber had plenty of opportunity to prove himself. By August 1950, two months after the war began, he'd enlisted. Sixteen weeks of basic training at Camp Borden, Ontario, with nearly a thousand other recruits, led to special parachute instruction in Rivers, Manitoba, and a first jump he called "a highlight of my life." He did Arctic survival training "to defend North America against the Russians, of course." He thrived on everything the military threw at him, except for one thing: military discipline and protocol. Saluting, polishing, starching, pressing, and never questioning seemed counterintuitive. He needed to find a way to avoid that part of army life. The scout and sniper section provided the escape. He was still in the regiment, but he operated for the most part on his own.

I had interviewed very few military snipers before. All kinds of questions raced through my head: What skills did the army look for in a sniper? What temperament? How did they train a sniper? What weapons and techniques did he use? What was the psychological makeup of a successful sniper? Was it kill or be killed? But I began by asking Zuber how they chose him.

By the time Zuber got overseas in 1952, the war had deadlocked around the 38th parallel (pretty much where it began in 1950) into a war of attrition. Each side tested the other with hit-and-run attacks across a mined and barbed-wired no man's land. While the U.S. Army in Korea had abandoned the use of snipers per se, Canadian military strategists found snipers valuable under the stalemate conditions of the war. Zuber seemed to fit the bill. He explained that his photographic and artistic skills suddenly provided him a golden opportunity late that year when his battalion was already on active duty at the front. Because of his photography apprenticeship, Zuber immediately understood the optics of sniper scopes and geometric angles. His art experience helped him recognize perspective, distinguish man-made versus natural positions, and make field sketches that a camera couldn't capture. Photographs, he said, brought back too much detail, while he could be selective and generate sketches of specific targets.

In October he was invited to a sniper course. His training emphasized marksmanship, naturally, but also map-reading skills, spotting locations of military importance, and special techniques of stalking. The Lee-Enfield, single-action rifle was his weapon, and he learned to choose and clean each individual piece of ammunition, because the slightest scratch could alter a bullet's path through the air. He learned whenever he went into a position to look for two ways out and never to fire twice from the same position—"expected to do your duty with one round." In addition, Zuber said, he also learned that "it was perfectly legal militarily to execute a sniper in the field," so it was best not to be taken prisoner.

Again, I pressed for details. How did a Canadian sniper make sure he wasn't the victim of an enemy sniper? He said he was trained by an instructor, a Sgt. MacPherson, who'd gained experience as a sniper against the Germans in Holland during the Second World War. Zuber said his tools were simple and that he quickly gained a reputation for camouflaging himself better than anybody in the battalion. All he needed was his Lee-Enfield, his scope, a small spade, a plastic bottle with a half gallon of water, and burlap sandbags ripped into sheets.

"I picked out the most strategic position, the best observational point during daylight, [but] took myself out there at night," Zuber said. "I dug what is called a belly hide, about six inches deep and I'd lie flat in it [with] the rifle placed under me. I'd make a puddle of mud, in the hole I'd dug, and soak these pieces of burlap in it. Then I crawled into this—very uncomfortable, of course—and covered myself with these wet rags soaked in mud. When the sun came up, it dried me. You could literally stand in front of me, six inches away, and not see me. I became part of the terrain."

Zuber made it very clear he was trained as a sniper *in* Korea, *in* Korean conditions and *for* Korean situations. His job would be to get rid of Communist Forces' snipers before they could do any harm to UN forces (in particular, the Canadian contingent of those forces). Through the fall of 1952, Zuber's instructor, MacPherson, put trainees through intense marksmanship testing, reducing the number of sniper candidates from twelve to six. The sergeant instructor forced the successful candidates to pair off. On one hand, MacPherson trained them to be "responsible for no one but yourself," but on the other hand "to find out how each man thinks, so you know what *not* to expect from each other."

"I looked at this guy next to me and he looked at me and I said, 'God, you're ugly.' He said, 'You're not so bad yourself.' I said, 'You wanna marry me?' He said, 'Okay, we're married.' And he and I became sniper partners. His name was Al Craig, from Fredericton, New Brunswick. We became bloody good friends."

"How critical was that partnership?" I asked.

Ted Zuber's face flashed immediately with a specific memory. Not long after he and Craig had finished their training, Zuber explained, the Royal Canadian Regiment battalion was rotated into a vulnerable position along the fifteen-kilometre-long Commonwealth Division front line—known as the Jamestown Line—between United Nations' troops to the south and Communist Chinese and North Korean forces to the north. The specific position was known as The Hook, so named because it jutted hook-like from the main front line out into no man's land in the Sami-ch'on valley. As the battalion moved onto The Hook, the sniper team carefully chose its positions out in front of the main trenches—Zuber in a bombed-out machine gun position and Craig at a position known as the Ronson Feature, a few hundred metres to Zuber's left and at a slightly lower elevation. The Canadian snipers rigged a communication line between field telephones linking the two sniper outposts. There they waited for opportunities to knock out sniper positions on the Communist side of no man's land.

"That's where Al saved me," Zuber said.

This particular day, Zuber got a call on his field phone from Craig, who wondered why his partner was allowing a Chinese sniper to move toward him. Zuber thought Craig meant the Chinese soldier they both could see 600 yards across no man's land jumping up and down in an enemy trench. No, Craig meant the Chinese sniper just over 100 yards in front of Zuber's position, in his blind spot. The Canadian team suddenly realized Zuber was being stalked. The enemy team wanted Zuber to shoot at the man in the distant trench so the man in the blind spot could knock off Zuber. The Chinese hadn't spotted Craig.

To counter the Chinese threat, Craig directed Zuber's line of fire to the parapet closest to the sniper in the blind spot "about 125 yards to your front, not quite 11 o'clock," Craig said. When Zuber had lined up that spot, Craig prepared to fire a shot at the Chinese soldier in the distant trench. He knew he wouldn't likely hit him, but that shot would likely distract the sniper in front of Zuber.

"Al fired a shot," Zuber said. "The Chinese sniper [in front of me] lifted his head to see why the shot came from down there. He lifted his head right into my sight, so I blew him away. Boom."

I suggested to Zuber that this kind of warfare seemed a bit like tit for tat. He admitted sometimes that was true. I asked for an example, and Zuber recalled another instance involving a young corporal, John Gill, serving directly under the commanding officer of the regiment, Lt.-Col. Peter Bingham. The C.O. treated Gill like a son. Zuber remembered that around the end of December, Gill had gone out on a night patrol into no man's land. Such patrols often ventured out beyond UN lines to spy on the Chinese, sabotage their land mines, or bring back information by capturing a prisoner. This night, Zuber said, Gill was the last in a line of a dozen men coming back through the friendly wire and minefield. A Chinese sniper sighted him and shot him through the head. The next night, when a Canadian patrol went out for his body, it discovered Gill's dog tags had been taken—the sure sign of a sniper.

Not long after Gill's death, in one of his first sniping assignments, Zuber recalled spotting a Chinese soldier working his way through trenches 300 yards across no man's land in front of his position. Zuber realized the man was a sniper because of the equipment he carried, including an American carbine and infrared snooper scope he'd apparently salvaged from a battle with U.S. troops. Zuber homed in on the man, took aim, but missed with his first shot. Remembering his training, Zuber should have accepted his defeat and moved on. But because Zuber's shot hadn't hit the ground near its target, the Chinese soldier had concluded the shot was an errant bullet. The man suddenly reappeared, resuming his walk through the Chinese front trench as if nothing had happened.

"I'm certainly not conscious of any difference in my emotional structure that moment from the moment before, but, of course, I'm an old hand at it now," Zuber said. "I did not miss the second shot. I got him. He just spun. He actually lifted off the ground . . . and fell out of my view on the forward side of the hill into what we called 'dead ground,' part of no man's land.

"Our patrols were advised to do a sweep over the Chinese sniper's body and bring back any intelligence they could. Well, they brought back the [U.S.] snooper scope and Cpl. Gill's dog tags. This was the guy that had killed Cpl. Gill."

Two days later a package arrived in a clean, unsoiled sandbag for Zuber. He opened it to find a note from Lt.-Col. Bingham himself. "Congratulations, Zuber," the note said. "Take two days off. Find a cave." Attached to the note was a bottle of Haig & Haig Scotch, from the commanding officer's private stock, a thank-you gift for killing the sniper who'd killed Gill.

Zuber's luck ran out early in 1953. One night, while his RCR battalion was still stationed at The Hook, Zuber took the opportunity of a break in the action to catch up on some sleep in a tunnel beneath the position. Beside him underground were a combat engineer, two South Korean labourers, a signaller friend of Zuber's, and about twenty new recruits. The reinforcements had just begun preparing their weapons for the night's deployment. One of the men was told to prime a box of a dozen grenades in the tunnel. It was about midnight when one of the grenades he had primed slipped from his hands. The grenade had a four-second fuse. Instead of shouting an alarm or tossing the grenade away from those in the tunnel, the recruit panicked, dropped the grenade, and ran out of the tunnel. The explosion decapitated one of the Korean workers, broke the engineer's leg in two places, blew the signaller's foot off, and peppered shrapnel into the back of Zuber's legs and buttocks.

"It's something you never see in the movies, Ted," Zuber suddenly wanted to make clear to me. "No matter how realistic the movies get, they don't show the concussion. There's no pressure in the movie theatre. All these stupid explosions you see in the movies, with all these flames. It's all crap. It's not like that at all. It's the blast!"

I asked Ted Zuber what else Hollywood movies don't show. He went on to explain that he, with shrapnel wounds all over his back, and the surviving South Korean labourer, with severe chest wounds, were taken to the jeep head, a spot as close to the front lines as vehicles were allowed to travel. A jeep with two stretchers transported the two wounded men to a regimental aid station, where medics and medical officers (doctors) could administer first aid. When Zuber directed a medic to the South Korean first, an officer noticed the medic attending the labourer and shouted, "Hey! Our own first!"

"Something struck me," Zuber said to me. "I would appreciate that decision if I was really hurt. But I also remember being emotionally torn. So how should I feel after what [the doctor] had just done to this corporal medic? And to the South Korean?"

I reacted with equal horror as Zuber described the South Korean's last moments, the creaking sound of the man's unconscious struggle to breathe and his eventual stillness in death. And then I wondered about Zuber's point about emotion. I wanted to know how there was ever any room for emotion in such situations. I remembered a passage from John Keegan's *Face of Battle*, suggesting that First and Second World War soldiers exhibited inhumanity and lack of emotion because of "their sense of littleness, almost of nothingness, of their abandonment in a physical wilderness, dominated by vast impersonal forces, from which even such normalities as the passage of time had been eliminated." With death and destruction at every turn, I asked Ted Zuber how he had managed to sense and express such normal human feelings. How had he been emotionally torn?

"Emotion was a luxury we had learned in the first few days, few weeks at least, to give up," he readily admitted. "You never thought of dying because you learned how to live without that thought. For example, I never heard a dirty joke the whole time I was in Korea. . . . It just went completely out of your world. . . . Emotion was something you just didn't tolerate."

In some ways, Ted Zuber wasn't fully able to reach that conclusion until after he'd returned home to Canada. I was curious about how he had taken to capturing his Korean War experience in paintings. He told me over the course of his year in Korea that he had completed between seventy-five and a hundred drawings. Most he said consisted of field drawings—enemy positions in perspective with compass bearings and distances—sketched onto a drawing pad. In addition, on his own time, he sketched buddies resting, showering, hanging their laundry, writing letters home, and a few portraits behind the front lines, in what they referred to as "the reverse slope." He said that many of those sketches had been stolen when he was wounded. However, he managed to send a few, perhaps a dozen, home. Years later, when Zuber committed himself to putting his Korean War impressions on canvas, he suddenly realized those original sketches lacked something.

"I looked at them and they were emotionless," he said of the revelation. "In an exaggerated way, they were about as interesting as a topographical map. . . . The drawings were totally useless to me. I never used any of them in my paintings. I wasn't allowing myself to say anything while I was there. So the one thing I injected later was the emotions."

That's when I realized one of my own shortcomings as a chronicler of war history. In half a dozen books, several hundred thousand words of manuscript copy, recounting battles from at least three different wars, I had innocently attempted to introduce an anachronism to the veterans' wartime experience I was presenting. Rightly or wrongly, in my accounts of battle and warfare, I had tried to include whatever emotion I sensed my interview subjects might have felt at the time. It's a common interview question: "How did you feel at the time?" Clearly, at the time, many of them could feel nothing. They were numbed—for better or worse—by the training, the demands of duty, the reflexive reactions to combat—and felt nothing. That might have accounted for their survival. The mask of battle suppressed all their feelings too. Since so much of my book source material has consisted of interviews long after the actual events have taken place, the vets have had time to reflect on their battle experiences. Fifty years later, they had a chance to account for their fears or elation, recapture the adrenaline of their combat, or approximate their abhorrence to the violent scenes they witnessed. And when I came along and asked "How did you feel?" they may well have superimposed emotion into the history long after the fact. The revelation was both unsettling and clarifying. I worried about the potential for misrepresenting history, at the same time I recognized my work was helping both veterans and readers grasp the picture of the moment—as it happened and via reflection.

Whether by design or circumstance, Ted Zuber had to rely on hindsight to introduce emotion into the subjects of his Korean War art. Not that his rear view compromised his art in the least. Each depiction of the war, based on his experience at Hill 187, Hill 355, The Hook, and the 25th Canadian Field Hospital, offered detail and context to every Korean War veteran's recollection of a tour of duty. It also connected with Zuber's art audience. An Ottawa industrialist purchased thirteen of the paintings and donated them to the Canadian War Museum. During my second visit with Ted Zuber, he told me a subsequent Korean War painting would soon be published nationwide. Veterans Affairs had chosen his painting *Holding at Kap'yong*, depicting Princess Patricia's Canadian Light Infantry's heroic defence of the road to Seoul, in April 1951, as the centrepiece for a commemorative poster in time for Remembrance Day 1997.*

My encounters with Ted Zuber inspired my creative juices no end. With a book contract in hand, I travelled the country seeking other Canadian veterans of the Korean War. En route, I met hundreds of men and women—infantry, artillery, tanks, naval crew, air crew, doctors and medics, nurses and Red Cross workers, intelligence troops, POWs, service corps, war correspondents, and entertainers—who'd never talked about their tours of duty in Korea. Suddenly, I sensed, they were more eager to talk, prepared to reveal

---

* When the Canadian government finally awarded Korean War veterans their service medals on November 11, 1991, Ted Zuber received his. A month later, he also received the Kuwait and Gulf service medal for his work as war artist during the Persian Gulf War the previous winter. He is the only Canadian with service medals from those two theatres of war.

their feelings (of the time or in hindsight), and give their war more exposure. Every step of my journey into their war I also began feeling pressure, a sense of obligation. Little by little, my research was taking on crusade-like proportions. Korean War vets began expecting my phone call. Many searched me out. I was grateful. But there seemed to be strings attached. My research no longer simply provided the foundation for a book. In the minds of my interviewees, I was finally going to pay tribute to Canadians who resented their war being considered merely "a police action" to protect the UN Peace Charter. I was going to erase the chauvinism among their First and Second World War brothers, who considered Korea merely a "conflict" and therefore not nearly as difficult or as dirty a war as theirs. I was going to undo fifty years of the Korean War being tagged as "the forgotten war," raise public awareness, and put a human face on their war.

That phrase—"put a human face on war"—took on even greater significance the deeper I waded into the Korea veterans' stories. As I journeyed across the country that year, I discovered another book about the Canadians in Korea was in the works. A committee of the Korea Veterans Association of Canada (KVA), based in London, Ontario, for some years, had attempted to assemble photos, diaries, and questionnaire material into a manuscript—called "The Korea Experience"—for publication. They were still searching for a publisher. After some discussion, the committee agreed to entrust me with its library. That virtually doubled my veteran base to nearly 500 individual entries. The project began taking on overwhelming proportions. And several deadlines loomed. In order for the book to be in bookstores by the fiftieth anniversary year of the war—2000—the research, writing, editing, assembly of photographs sections, etc., had to be completed by early 1999. I had less than a year to pull the rabbit out of the hat.

In addition to the coming half-century anniversary of the war, the KVA had an equally important milestone to prepare for even sooner than that. After many years attempting to interest the federal government and the Canadian military in a national monument to Korean

War dead in Ottawa, and without success, the veterans had decided to do it themselves. The KVA had already struck a comfortable relationship with a large cemetery facility near Brampton, Ontario, northwest of Toronto, where Korean War veterans might be buried together if that was their wish. Then, once again failing to interest federal or provincial authorities in assisting in the funding of such a memorial, the KVA accepted an offer to secure a section of the Meadowvale Cemetery for its planned national war memorial—a Wall of Remembrance.

The two-hundred-foot-long, two-foot-high curving wall of grey granite would follow a natural hillside bowl on the cemetery grounds. Adorning the wall from west to east, 516 bronze plaques would replicate the grave markers erected at the Commonwealth War Cemetery in Pusan, South Korea, displaying the name, rank, service, and date of death of each Canadian killed during the war. It took three years to raise the budgeted $300,000 for the KVA wall. Donations came from Legion branches, other military associations, trusts, corporations, individual businesses, service clubs, community organizations, individual cities and towns, individual politicians (though not a penny from either the federal or provincial governments), but by far the largest portion of the Wall Fund was raised by the Canadian veterans of the Korean War themselves.

I met the man who took on the responsibility for co-ordinating the inauguration of the Wall of Remembrance, about a month before the unveiling actually happened. The fact that he had volunteered for such a mammoth task, I soon learned, was second nature to him. Herb Pitts grew up during the Second World War in Nelson, B.C. His father, Herb Sr., enlisted when Herb Jr. was ten and returned when he was sixteen. Pitts the elder served as a medic with the 16th General Hospital, but he also organized the medical unit's band, fire department, and policing unit. Pitts the younger signed up for everything too—high school sports, Boy Scouts, church choir—but with two siblings and a modest income from his father's post-war drugstore business, Herb considered the option of military college to help pay for his post-secondary education. First at Royal Roads, in

Victoria, then Royal Military College in Kingston, Herb was about to begin his third year of study as the Korean War entered its middle year, 1952.

"A telegram [from the army] came," he said. "It said: 'You did well during the tactics phase of your training. We're prepared to commission you immediately as a 2nd lieutenant if you join the army now and volunteer for service in Korea.'"

It was an offer he couldn't refuse. Just twenty-two, Lt. Pitts sensed the commission represented a significant step into a noble profession—in the armed forces of one's country. He acknowledged there were also elements of patriotism in his decision, as well as meeting a challenge and embarking on an adventure. A commitment to Korea would move him from theory in the classroom to "real soldiering" in the battlefield, he told me. And, as Ted Zuber had said, a tour of duty in the army represented "a test to prove oneself."

The Royal Military College had streamed Pitts toward the armoured corps; he left Canada aboard a Canadian Pacific Airlines flight fully expecting to serve as an artillery officer with Lord Strathcona's Horse in Korea. The moment he arrived there, that summer of 1952, however, he learned the army was short of platoon commanders and he was immediately reassigned to the 1st Battalion of Princess Patricia's Canadian Light Infantry. He spent his first few hours in Korea exchanging artillery uniform and insignia for infantry, "trying to look like a Patricia" for the 11th Platoon of "D" Company now under his command. The "real soldiering" he'd volunteered for began during his first patrols to protect the most contentious location along the Commonwealth Division front, a prominent hill at 355 metres above sea level. Hill 355 was known among Commonwealth troops as "Little Gibraltar."

Prominent, protected by line after line of barbed wire and land mines, and manned by hundreds of Commonwealth troops dug into a network of trenches, Hill 355 appeared impenetrable. To think so, Canadian troops knew, was folly. A quick study at the front line, Herb Pitts learned that PPCLI strategists sent a variety of fighting patrols—observation patrols, ambush patrols, reconnaissance patrols, or escort patrols—out into no man's land below Hill 355 almost every night. Soon after he arrived at the front, Pitts explained, he volunteered to fill in for a fellow platoon commander, leading an escort patrol that would provide protection for engineers laying mines in front of Gibraltar. His platoon's job involved establishing a "firm base" or well-armed, secure position from which the working patrols and mine-layers could venture and to which they could return in an emergency.

I knew that any fighting patrol situation in no man's land was extremely dangerous. I sensed that Pitts was facing his first real test this night in front of 355. I wondered how he had dealt with the responsibility and tension during his first action in Korea.

"We were placed on a spur well out in the valley at the foot of the [enemy] Chinese positions," Pitts said. "Neil Rhodes did his final [reconnaissance] from our position, took his fighting patrol through us and did his thing. It didn't turn out to be successful.... We started to hear a tremendous amount of shuffling and yelling out around us. We couldn't tell who it was. We learned that Rhodes had casualties. So our job was to get them back through us safely and then stay as long as we could. The voices around us were not friendly. Our next job was to get ourselves safely back because there was some light mortaring beginning."

Pitts began a kind of leapfrogging manoeuvre in reverse or as he described it "thinning ourselves back." He sent part of his platoon to shadow Rhodes's evacuation of casualties. Then he directed the rest of his men to pull out section by section—half a dozen men at a time—until the last four members of Pitts's mobile firm base in no man's land consisted of two riflemen, a corporal, and himself.

"We heard this murmuring much closer to us now," he said. "So we each took our two grenades we're carrying and threw them on opposite sides of the hill. The grenades went off and we started to run. We got to the next position, dropped, listened, and there was more palaver going on. Then flares started going up. We caught up with Rhodes's platoon, were assured his platoon was clear, and moved back completely. Our job was to get him clear and we did without casualties."

What became obvious as Pitts described this and other actions to me was that the young lieutenant was not prepared to commit his men to any action he wouldn't first take on himself. That strong sense of personal involvement appeared to become Herb Pitts's calling card in Korea. He had come to the war relatively late. Peace talks had been underway at Panmunjom for over a year. It was only a matter of time before a truce and maybe even a peace treaty might be announced. Many United Nations troops, particularly those coming to the end of a full tour in Korea, felt end-of-war apprehensions. They didn't want to become the last needless statistics so close to the completion of service in Korea. In that additionally tense environment, Pitts the new reinforcement had been given the responsibility of planning, organizing, and leading patrols much like the one in front of Hill 355. And rather than telling his men "I order you," the platoon commander took his fair share of turns as the nightly patrols rotated through the battalion. By setting an example, Pitts hoped to earn the trust and respect of his men. It nearly cost him his life.

Coincidentally, the weekend of the wall unveiling at Meadowvale Cemetery in Brampton—July 26 and 27, 1997—the producers of the Ontario-wide weekend morning program *Fresh Air* on CBC Radio invited me to their Toronto studios to host the show both Saturday and Sunday mornings. I agreed on condition that immediately after the Sunday morning broadcast, I be allowed to dash to Meadowvale Cemetery in time to take in the official opening of the Wall of Remembrance. In spite of his being the MC for the ceremony Sunday, Herb Pitts agreed to an on-air interview with me on the morning of the unveiling. I sensed he had a greater understanding (than other Korea vets) of the need for the commemorative wall and a greater capability to explain why it was equally important for Canadians to recognize its importance too. During the course of our interview, Herb described the perseverance of the KVA to conceive, design, and underwrite the wall. He outlined the elements of the ceremony and the pride and anticipation of MCing the event. I sensed I had time for one more question in the broadcast before both he and I dashed from the studio to witness the unveiling at Meadowvale.

"Herb, many of our listeners were born after the Korean War," I said as a conclusion to our on-air interview. "They can't picture either the war or the men and women who served there. It's been called 'the forgotten war.' Do me a favour. Put a human face to your war."

Herb Pitts paused and then chose to tell another of his Korean War stories. The few minutes he took to explain the events of November 30, 1952, in my mind, were among the most riveting of my career as a broadcaster or listener, for that matter. Pitts prefaced the story by paraphrasing an order he'd received from Lt.-Col. Herbert Wood at a command post at The Hook. Wood had asked Pitts to invite volunteers to train them for the dangerous job of laying new barbed-wire barriers in front of the position. Volunteers assembled from members of the battalion, from every company of the Princess Patricia's, including two men from his own platoon. In typical Pitts fashion, he decided the volunteers should spend as much time together as possible—tenting together, eating together, and talking together—as well as train to lay as much barbed concertina wire as possible across hundreds of metres of exposed hillside in front of The Hook on a given night. The position might be under fire. The ground—already frozen—might be snow-covered and treacherous. The operation would have to be completed in two nights over ground that had previously been mined. For the task, Pitts divided his team into three groups of ten men, each under a corporal. The standard for laying triple-roll concertina wire fence was one hundred yards in ten minutes *in daylight*. After two days of training behind The Hook, a team led by one of the volunteers from Pitts's platoon, Cpl. Frank Mullin, was able to lay the one hundred yards of wire in nine minutes *in the dark*.

"Throughout the training," Pitts said, "we were kidding that whoever maintains the best times will get to lay the wire closest to the enemy lines. It was a carrot. You've done the best [so] your team deserves the [more dangerous] honour."

Pitts went on to describe the actual operation on November 30. A convoy of trucks had arrived, unloaded the concertina wire and iron pickets. With the equipment were scores of Korean labourers who would haul the gear forward for the wiring parties. Pitts said he made one last recce trip forward through the lightly snow-covered path to the point where the wiring parties would begin working. He then returned to the staging area to lead his men. In full darkness, just after 10 o'clock, Cpl. Frank Mullin's party, the one winning the right to be first, headed down the pathway into no man's land to begin laying and securing the wire. As usual, Lt. Pitts was in the lead, Cpl. Mullin next, followed by a radio operator volunteer, Pte. Jacob Batsch. In the darkness, Pitts heard someone slip and fall behind him. Concerned about any noise, Pitts whispered to Mullin that he take the lead, then retraced his steps to discover that Batsch had fallen on slippery ground. He helped the radio operator to his feet just as there was an explosion at the front of the column of men.

"I turned around and Mullin was horizontal in the air," Pitts explained in the interview. "What had happened was that Mullin, in following steps in the snow, put his foot slightly off the path and set off a [bounding Betsy] mine.* The mine took off his head. There wasn't another mark on him. The fellow behind him, Batsch, had one mark on him. It was a hole in the centre of his breastbone, close to his heart. I reached over and grabbed Batsch and said, 'What's the matter?' All he could do was cough. I pulled back his parka and I saw the wound in his chest. I thought, 'My God!' He died within ten seconds in my arms."

---

* Bounding Betsy (or Bouncing Betty) is an anti-personnel land mine developed prior to the Second World War. Each consisted of a cylinder or can (about ten centimetres in diameter) atop a post (about twenty-five centimetres in length). When triggered, one explosive launched the cylinder into the air about waist-high, where the second explosion scattered a lethal spray of steel balls and/or nails in all directions. Front-line troops referred to the jumping mines as "de-bollockers" for obvious reasons.

As traumatized as Pitts must have been, suddenly his platoon commander instincts kicked in. He got on the radio and called for stretchers. Then he turned his attention to his PPCLI wiring parties and Korean labourers. Most of them hadn't even witnessed a shot fired at close range before. Suddenly, just minutes into their first operation, they were facing the corpses of two men killed in front of them. The entire crew of PPCLI volunteers had stopped. The labourers sensed trouble and began retreating up the hill. Pitts said he had to keep emotions under control, keep the wire parties moving, and get the job done. Pitts ordered the Korean officer supervising the labourers to draw his pistol and demand they resume the operation. Eventually, with the two casualties moved back, the line of labourers calmed down and the group advanced into the valley. Within a few hours, the rest of the wiring party had laid 1,800 yards of concertina wire. Two nights later they repeated the process, only deeper into the valley and closer to a Chinese outpost.

"The job was completed," Herb summed up in the CBC studio. "We had re-wired the critical area, at the expense of two soldiers, with a bunch of men who were strangers to each other and to the war. . . . The men took the risk the [commanding officer] and I expected us to take. I don't know what makes men put their trust in one another. But after five or six days together, training and conducting two operations, [the wiring party] all dispersed to various parts of the battalion. It's a tribute to our young soldiers . . . to Cpl. Mullin and Pte. Batsch."

As in all my encounters with Herb Pitts, he had not given himself much credit. In thanking him for helping me and my radio listeners see the kind of war Canadians had experienced half a century before, I pointed out that Herb Pitts had later received the Military Cross for his service in Korea. The citation attached to the award commended Pitts for "his coolness and leadership," while Pitts modestly insisted "it was recognition bestowed on me on behalf of the contribution of others around me." I wished him and the thousands of veterans gathering for the opening of the Wall of Remembrance a smooth, meaningful event. I said I hoped that the ceremony and the reunion of Korea veterans helped keep the memory of men such as Mullin and Batsch alive.

Several hours later, that Sunday, the forty-fourth anniversary of the Korean War armistice, I found Herb Pitts in the throng at the Wall of Remembrance ceremony. He was dressed in his veteran's blazer and flannels with his medals—including the Military Cross—on his chest. As he prepared for his duties in front of the memorial, I thanked him again for his story and his candor. A convoy of buses had shuttled people from a staging area in Brampton to the Meadowvale Cemetery all morning long. Nearly 600 Korea veterans from across Canada had made their way to this event. Nearly a thousand others—families, friends, media, politicians, and interested spectators—gathered in silence near the circular walkway in front of the wall or on the grassy hillside that enveloped the wall from one end to the other.

Then came a most extraordinary moment. Following the dignitaries' speeches, the reading of a special poem in honour of the occasion, and much wreath laying, the veterans, who had been quietly waiting in parade formation in front of the monument, were invited to approach the wall. Just the veterans, alone with their thoughts at the many bronze plaques, began removing poppies from their lapels and pinning them on the wall. Some bowed their heads and closed their eyes. Others saluted smartly. Many wept openly. Then, in spontaneous response to the veterans' individual and collective grieving, many family members left their places adjacent to the memorial to join the vets in front of the wall.

I noticed two women emerge from the grassy hillside and make their way through the sea of veterans in front of the wall. One of the women caressed an eight-by-ten framed photograph of a young man in uniform. The picture was facing out. The two middle-aged women then held each other for emotional support as they knelt before the bronze plate commemorating someone they knew, perhaps the man in the photograph. Presently, a Korean War veteran worked his way from the clusters of men at the wall and appeared to introduce himself to the women. The three were suddenly suspended in a frozen pose of recognition. They quietly embraced each other and tears flowed freely. I stared at the three of them hugging for several minutes, feeling as perhaps they did, that they were the only ones at the wall. They were so totally focused on each other's faces and conversation. I sensed there was a story there. I had to know it.

The two women, Barbara Differ and Hazel Regan, were sisters. The framed photograph was a portrait of their brother, Bill Regan. Early in July 1953, Regan's 3rd Battalion of the Royal Canadian Regiment had moved onto Hill 187 along the Commonwealth Division front. Sometime on the night of July 17, the sisters had learned by telegram that their brother, Bill Regan, had been wounded and taken to a M.A.S.H. unit where he died on July 24, just three days before the armistice at Panmunjom. That's all the information the official records ever afforded them. In all the years since the war, none of Bill Regan's six sisters could discover anything more about their brother's wartime death.

"In 1991 we went to Korea," Hazel Regan told me in an interview at the Wall of Remembrance reception later that day. "All of us except one [sister] went to Korea. We sort of expected while we were in Korea that we would meet someone who knew my brother and how he died. We found nothing. . . . In my heart, though, I always knew someday we would meet someone."

That someone, it turned out, was the veteran who had approached them at the wall that anniversary Sunday morning in 1997. His name was Clyde Pryor. I later learned (as the six sisters had) that Pryor had served in Bill Regan's section of the RCR. Pryor said the Chinese artillery fire was particularly intense this particular night in July 1953. The shelling had broken a number of ground-laid communication lines. A volunteer pioneer patrol was assembled to work its way out into no man's land and repair the severed lines. Though both men were resigned to doing the repair, they sensed it didn't require two specialists, just one. Pryor said he and Regan flipped a coin to see who would go. Regan lost the toss. Then, Pryor told the sisters, during the repair operation the Chinese shelling resumed and Pte. Regan was mortally wounded.

"But for the toss of the coin, that would be me," Pryor had told Hazel Regan as he pointed to the framed picture she held in her arms that day. In fact, Pryor admitted one of the reasons he'd come to the unveiling was the hope of finding a Regan family member at the wall that day. "If not for the coin toss," he repeated, "I wouldn't be here. Your brother would be."

What an incredible coincidence, I thought. On a night so close to the end of the war, a young man from Toronto, Bill Regan, is felled by enemy shell fire. His family receives only the minimum notification, that he has died while on active service with the Royal Canadian Regiment. The soldier's comrade is equally devastated, knowing he might well have been killed that night, not Regan. Despite every attempt to learn more about his death, the Regan family finds nothing, not even by going to Korea. When Bill Regan's parents died some years after the war, the surviving sisters had a stone laid at their gravesite. The inscription included their brother's epitaph: "Bill Regan, 1933–1953. Killed in Korea. July 24, 1953. Pax." Then, at a ceremony and tribute created by Bill Regan's surviving comrades, attempting to give Canadian-bound mourners a place to grieve half a century later, purely by accident Bill Regan's sisters meet the man who last saw their brother alive on the battlefield. He helps them carry the burden of grief. He fills in the empty spaces in the picture of a man's last hours. Recognizing the final coincidence, that Hazel carried Bill's picture to the wall and Clyde had seen it, I had just one last question for Hazel.

"What ever possessed you to bring the framed photo of your brother Bill here to the wall unveiling today?" I asked.

"Because of what you said," Hazel answered. "You said it on the radio this morning. You wanted to put a human face on war. So I brought Bill's picture."

7

FRONT ROW SEAT TO HISTORY

MY JOURNEY with veterans has taken me from coast to coast in search of their stories, from home front to the front lines, from their enlistment to their demobilization, and from the theory of training to the reality of the sharp end. Throughout that experience, I have listened, learned, and been enlightened about Canada and Canadians in wartime. Occasionally I've been enlisted too. As I've suggested here, since I began meeting with veterans, I have periodically been invited to support, endorse, and even advocate for them—to raise awareness, to raise funds, and even to raise the flag, so to speak.

I have to admit Garth Webb's *cause célèbre* took a little longer to win me over. I first met the tall, ex-artillery officer one Saturday morning in the late 1990s. As I frequently did, I was sitting in as substitute host of the radio program *Fresh Air*. Late in the program, during the playing of a disc of music, in lumbered Webb with his briefcase of promotional literature and a handshake as big as a bear's. I invited him to sit in the guest's chair, and moments later we began our conversation about his incredible plan—to build a museum in France to commemorate the service of all Canadians during the Second World War. He called it the "Canada Normandy Project." His premise was not new. His optimism was.

"Tens of thousands of tourists visit Normandy and the invasion coast each year," he explained in the interview, reading almost verbatim from the brochure he had in his hands. "But Canada's contribution to the D-Day landings and the liberation of Europe is largely ignored."

In truth, the "tens of thousands of tourists" had little to do with the genesis of Webb's idea. That had actually come from children. As many Canadian military outfits had done in the decades after the war, members of Webb's 14th Field Regiment of the Royal Canadian Artillery kept returning to Europe on revisits. They paid their respects to the war dead at many of the Commonwealth War Graves Commission cemeteries in France, Belgium, Holland, and Germany. They reminisced about the way they were a generation ago. And they enjoyed the hospitality of European citizens who had not forgotten what a Canadian citizen army had sacrificed to liberate their cities and countryside. Most enthusiastic in their sense of gratitude were the children of those liberated communities. In one Dutch town Garth described to me, the young people showered the vets with flowers, embraced them like long-lost relatives, and sang songs of freedom in their honour. When the children had finished their demonstration of affection, Webb asked them if, in return, they'd like to come to Canada. Somehow the regiment raised the money and the children enjoyed a three-week tour of the country. The next step, it seemed, was a return visit, sending Canadian children to some of the places those Canadian troops had liberated.

But aside from the towns themselves, some empty beaches, a few tired-looking commemorative markers, and perhaps streets named in honour of the liberation or Canadian troops and their regiments, the vets wondered, "What would the children actually see?" Garth's Canada Normandy Project was born in that moment. He proposed that his fledgling organization would purchase a building in Bernières-sur-Mer adjacent to the famous "house on the beach" depicted in all those D-Day stills and movies. Garth told my radio audience the site would include a café, a terrace, and an interpretive centre. Inside that facility visitors would encounter artifacts borrowed from the Canadian War Museum, as well as newsreel footage, photographs, audio recordings, and touch-screen computer terminals telling Canadian veterans' stories from D-Day to the Battle of the Atlantic to the Italian campaign. I told him I could picture the site perfectly. What I couldn't picture, I suggested, were the millions it might require to actually finance the project.

"Oh, it's going to happen," Webb said, nodding his head with certainty.

"How much have you raised so far?" I asked.

"We expect the Canadian and provincial governments, corporations, and the Canadian public will be very interested in donating to this cause."

"If you say so," I said and I thought, "What a pipe dream."

And he smiled, as if to say, "Just watch me."

The next time I encountered Garth Webb, a couple of years later, he had invited me to a luncheon at the Queen's Own Rifles of Canada Officers Mess inside the Moss Park Armouries in downtown Toronto. Since I was teaching at Centennial College then, at the end of a mid-day class I had to dash to the luncheon from the east end of the city, but paused long enough to grab a notepad and a tape recorder. I was merely planning to observe the latest meeting of Garth Webb's project committee to see how his plans were coming along. I learned at the luncheon that Webb's "pipe dream" had evolved to something quite tangible. Instead of borrowing artifacts, renting the famous Queen's Own Rifles house on the beach, and installing interactive computers inside, the entire enterprise had a board of directors, a critical path, a budget, a design, and a new name. The "Juno Beach Centre" had moved too. Instead of relying on favours from the town of Bernières for a potential site there, Garth Webb had found civic allies in the neighbouring community of Courseulles-sur-Mer. Its mayor and council had identified with the wishes of the Canadian veterans to erect a substantial commemorative facility and in 2001 presented a former campground—located between the beaches and the town—as the site for the Juno Beach Centre. Target opening date was June 6, 2002.

Not surprisingly, I got caught up in Garth Webb's vision and optimism. The 15,000-square-foot centre, built of concrete and steel wrapped in a titanium and glass exterior, would consist of a series of pods that (from the air) approximated a pentagon or maple-leaf design. Inside, exhibit specialists would create five multimedia displays to illustrate Canada's worldwide contributions during the Second World War. The idea was to pay tribute to Canadians who had participated in every theatre of the war and dispel what board member Lise Cooper called "a Steven Spielberg perception among French young people . . . that the Americans won the war." The Juno Beach Centre had already commissioned Colin Gibson to sculpt a bronze memorial—Remembrance and Renewal—to welcome visitors to the site.

I quickly discovered that the luncheon I was attending was not a media event, but a meeting of the centre's fund-raising and awareness-raising committee and would I consider joining the cause? As I witnessed the centre's renderings, blueprints, and budgets being reviewed, I put away my journalist's tape recorder and realized I was munching on a sandwich amid a who's who of Canadian veterans. Among them were retired generals Lewis Mackenzie and John de Chastelain, retired judge A.G. Lynch-Staunton, historian Terry Copp, and long-time veterans' advocate Cliff Chadderton, not to mention numerous D-Day veterans, including paratrooper and Legion of Honour recipient Jan de Vries, Croix de Guerre winner Donald Jamieson, signallers Don Kerr and Bill Warshick, gunner Ken Darling, and, of course, artilleryman Garth Webb. All the troops seemed present and accounted for. The plans looked great on paper. All that remained were the dollars to make the Juno Beach Centre happen. How could I not offer assistance?

I offered whatever reporting and broadcasting skills I thought might help. Not long after I joined the committee, Wal-Mart Canada agreed to raise more than $3 million for the centre. It invited Canadian veterans into its 213 retail stores across the country to promote and sell commemorative bricks—each inscribed with a donor's name—to be incorporated into a series of outdoor kiosks at the centre. The company also created a series of TV ads shot on location in Normandy and hired a production company to interview D-Day veterans on camera for the displays inside the interpretive pods at the Juno Beach Centre in Courseulles. I volunteered to research and conduct the interviews. We recorded a number of sessions, and among the most interesting, it turned out, was my videotaped interview with Garth Webb.

One of the first myths he dispelled, in our recorded conversation, was that the Depression in the 1930s had left everyone in the Canadian west poor and hungry. Garth's childhood years in Calgary were relatively carefree, supported by a father who was a schoolteacher and a mother who ran a small business. When the war came along, he said, all his chums wanted to enlist in the air force. He chose to go to Queen's University initially, then transferred to the Canadian Officers' Training Corps, and joined the army in 1942. By the following year, Webb was overseas as a gun position officer reinforcing the 14th Field Regiment as it prepared for a major operation everyone knew was coming. Webb and his crew trained on the self-propelled (SP) vehicle nicknamed the Priest. They got acclimatized to each other, waterproofed the chassis, and practised firing the SP gun while aboard landing craft offshore.

"Everybody knew the invasion was coming," Garth Webb told me, "but nobody knew where the hell it was we were going. It was originally scheduled for June 5 [1944,] so on the night of the fourth we had a peek at all the [top secret] stuff. We didn't know where the hell Normandy was."

When Operation Overlord finally got the green light for June 6, Garth Webb learned everything he needed to know about Normandy as he and his artillery crew crossed the English Channel aboard a tank landing craft. He discovered that his objective was the Nan White sector of Juno Beach supporting assault troops of the Queen's Own Rifles and Le Régiment de la Chaudière. Interviews I'd done with other D-Day participants had educated me about the fear and anticipation troops felt during the crossing, not to mention the seasickness. Every channel swell and trough, every hour and minute of waiting, and every imagined enemy ship or plane played on their fears. Not Garth Webb. When he wasn't studying the firing plan for the morning landing, he said he was checking and rechecking the condition of the Priest and handing out anti-nausea scopolamine pills to his seasick artillery crew.

"Guys that waited all night wondering, 'Am I going to live through tomorrow?' They had more concern and fear than I did. I was too busy. The same when we landed. Everybody talks about all these casualties on the beach and the confusion. I looked where I was going and walked right through it. I was too busy to stand around counting. . . ."

Webb's D-Day story seemed almost pedestrian. In fact, he said his story made him "a lousy interview." At about H-Hour-plus-90 minutes (H-Hour being the launch), Lt. Webb and the rest of his "C" Troop of self-propelled artillery landed at Bernières-sur-Mer. On the beach, his 14th Field Regiment moved quickly into the town to establish a secure base. Any German return fire was limited to mortars and sporadic machine-gun fire on the beach, he said, and was relatively ineffective and harmless. Garth described meeting a reconnaissance officer who led several of the regiment's Priest gun crews through the village. The officer told them not to worry about farm fields just beyond; he even pointed out there couldn't be land mines because a cow was wandering in the pasture ahead. This was all sounding rather ominous when I asked, "What happened?"

"There were no land mines," Webb said, "but there was an 88 way out in the field."

Later, when I read the war diary of 14th Field gunner Wes Alkenbrack, I learned that 700 yards directly ahead of Webb's Priest and three other Canadian SP guns was a German 88-mm gun. It was dug in and strategically sited to cover all exits from the village, with its barrel at ground level and skillfully camouflaged with earth and brush. The enemy gun had been positioned there for some time, but in all the excitement among townspeople celebrating their new-found freedom, no one had bothered to inform the Canadians about its presence. At 11:30 a.m., as four SPs from the 14th Field Regiment emerged from the southwestern part of the village and out into the open pasture where the cow was grazing, the German gun crew fired and scored a direct hit on the first one. Webb saw some of its crew immediately jump from the Priest for cover as the Germans scored a hit on the second SP. Then they hit the third self-propelled gun and it erupted in a huge explosion.

"The 88 blew up three of our guns, and on two of the guns, the crew were all killed," Webb explained. "This was the first day of the invasion. Just two and a half hours ashore . . . and we saw a lot of people killed right in front of us."

He ended his account of the battle with a list of the crewmen who died: Bob Sciberas, K.J. Hooton, R. Goff, C.A. Massey, A.F. Clavelle, and W.J. Dupuis. But, he added, the urgent need to keep moving and gain ground left him and the other SP crews no time to dwell on the shock of their losses. He paused. I wondered why he would say that he didn't think his story made a very good interview. I thanked him for going through such a difficult memory. To give him a couple of seconds to collect his thoughts on camera, I offered some reactions to what he'd said. I suggested that maybe his recollection of staying busy during the nighttime crossing of the channel, then ignoring the carnage on the D-Day beach as they landed, might have been a defence mechanism. Staying focused on the task at hand had perhaps suppressed any emotion he might have felt given what he saw. Perhaps, all these years later, assessing his actions as unspectacular—making him "a lousy interview"—he was illustrating a similar defence mechanism blocking out the tragic loss of his fellow gunners late that D-Day morning.

"I don't know what I blocked out," he admitted. "It's hard to describe the role I had. I told you I came out of university. I had this cushy deal of being an officer right away. . . . Everybody knew some of us would get killed. But we didn't ever worry about it. . . ."

Garth Webb taught me a lot about the way the memory of war works. I guess he also showed me how strong his training had been leading up to the invasion. If he and his battery mates felt invincible, it was partly due to their youth, but I learned it was also the result of their belief in what they'd learned as volunteers. Garth told me about meeting some American vets after the war. He said they revered their generals, in particular George "Blood 'n' Guts" Patton, for his sense of abandon in order to achieve victory. But those same vets also deduced that such commanders weren't very concerned about their men either. By comparison, Garth Webb felt that Canadian troops had commanders who cared about the rank and file men and that their army didn't use abandon, but preparation and organization to achieve victory. Webb may not have known exactly where Normandy was, nor what tough slogging lay ahead, but he did have confidence in himself and the training of his comrades. "We were good," he said. "We were going to save the world."

Maybe it was that same sharp focus, that ability to shut out impediments to reaching an objective that was at work sixty years later as Garth Webb went about building a commemorative museum on Juno Beach. What I had once dismissed as a pipe dream became a reality because he never lost sight of it. He always expressed faith in getting there. He had had a front row seat to history and wanted fellow veterans to share their view and for the Canadian public to benefit from that experience. The volunteers who listened to the former artillery lieutenant's plans to build a Canadian museum in Normandy picked up on that drive and couldn't help but join in the cause. One thing was certain for me. No matter what my journalistic instincts might tell me, I never doubted Garth Webb's conviction again.

The subsequent Juno Beach Centre committee meetings I attended at the Moss Park Armouries in Toronto reflected the momentum of Webb's enthusiasm and the power of his positive thinking. Working groups had fanned out across the country to spread the word, show off the plans, and raise more funds through those commemorative bricks. More than 11,000 were sold. Ultimately, the Juno Beach Centre opened a year later than planned, in 2003. But that gave other committee members more time to complete their work. Jan de Vries, a 1st Canadian Parachute Battalion private who had jumped into Normandy in the pre-dawn darkness on D-Day, spoke at city halls, town councils, and school assemblies. Bruce Melanson, from the Royal Canadian Legion, led scores of fellow veterans into corporate centres, malls, and plazas to take cash donations. And Don Kerr, a lieutenant with the Royal Canadian Corps of Signals who landed on D-Day with the British at Gold Beach, wrote to provincial politicians, some of whom he knew personally, reminding them of the regiments that had come from their regions during the war and appealing for government grants. The millions of dollars I expected Garth Webb's original dream would never attract began to flow because enough Canadians—as individuals and as organizations—recognized that supporting the Juno Beach Centre was the right thing to do.

The grand opening at Courseulles-sur-Mer—on June 6, 2003—offered the thousands of Canadians and French visitors all the pageantry and patriotism they could have hoped for. The titanium and glass of the Juno Beach Centre glistened in the morning sunlight. The Canadian maple leaf and French tricolour flags fluttered symmetrically in the offshore breeze. The Remembrance and Renewal sculpture and kiosks of commemorative bricks beckoned everybody closer. Aircraft, parachute teams, dignitaries, speeches, band and choral music, wreaths, and ceremony all contributed to the launch of the centre in fine style.

It was the veterans who made the christening of the building so indelible, however. I spent the day watching their faces, listening to their flashbacks, doing more interviews for the centre's archives. Each man—like the bricks in the kiosks—offered another personal snapshot of Canada's wartime story in Europe. Among the D-Day images I saw that day was a photograph of a self-propelled gun crew camped in Normandy. It showed bombardier Doug Allen, signaller Ken Darling, gunner Cowie, and gun position officer Garth Webb. During Garth's speech to the dignitaries, veterans, and well-wishers that day, he described the equal thrill of being on the beach both in 1944 and in 2003. He reminded us about his first visit on D-Day:

"It was like the Grey Cup and the Stanley Cup and the World Series all played on the same day, and I'm not only there, but I'm playing!"

By the end of that same summer, I had finished my book *Juno: Canadians at D-Day, June 6, 1944*. I had chosen to try to take the reader chronologically—blow by blow—from final invasion preparations in south England in early June to the end of fighting on the sixth. The publishing house worked quickly to ensure that the book—incorporating all the stories, photographs, and maps I'd gathered over more than thirty years of researching and interviewing—would hit bookstores in early spring 2004, just in time for the sixtieth anniversary.

Meantime, *50Plus* magazine and its parent organization CARP (the Canadian Association of Retired Persons) in tandem with Merit Travel asked if I would host a tour to attend the sixtieth anniversary ceremonies in Normandy. My head full of so many powerful memories from the Juno Beach Centre's opening the year before, I immediately agreed. Because I had discovered so many compelling stories associated with the invasion, I felt sure that others would be drawn to the locations where it actually took place. I hoped the tour might attract some D-Day veterans as well. Prior to the anniversary, I completed a national book tour and spoke to numerous veterans groups, historical societies, and school assemblies eager to acknowledge and celebrate the anniversary. I also accepted an invitation to co-host television coverage of the June 6, 2004, ceremonies with Lloyd Robertson on CTV. The whole country was suddenly caught up in D-Day fever.

Perhaps not surprisingly, a lot of that fever consisted of images that looked more like a Hollywood movie than what veterans had described to me in years of interviewing and research on the subject. Too many of us born after the war had a Darryl F. Zanuck view of D-Day. His movie adaptation of Cornelius Ryan's best-selling book *The Longest Day* seemed larger than life, but generated powerful mythology. It was difficult to portray the nighttime airborne jumps and landings on D-Day with anybody other than Richard Todd as

Maj. John Howard seizing the Orne River bridge or Red Buttons as Pte. John Steele, the American paratrooper stuck on the roof of the Sainte-Mère-Eglise church. And in the mind's eye, how could the charge up the beaches of Normandy not be led by the likes of a cigar-champing, bullet-resistant, nerves-of-steel commander like John Wayne? What was most difficult to dispel, perhaps, was that the invasion on June 6, 1944, had included anybody other than the Americans and the British. As in the movie, the Canadian contribution to the D-Day victory, in too many people's minds, was a minor subplot. Only those Canadians who had bothered to search beyond the international stars and thousands of extras of Zanuck's movie or the Canadian veterans of that operation themselves knew otherwise. Fortunately, when our Normandy tour group of forty-three travellers left Canada, it included nine veterans, five of whom had experienced D-Day first-hand.

What astounded me during our ten-day trip, however, was that even our D-Day veterans didn't realize how much they had contributed to the success on June 6. On the flight to Paris, for example, I learned from a conversation with John Clark that he'd been a stoker aboard the Royal Canadian Navy destroyer *Iroquois*. During operations just prior to D-Day and on June 6, he and his shipmates had plied waters at the western entrance to the English Channel. Though his responsibilities lay principally below decks, he recalled seeing the destruction of several enemy gunboats, and in particular, German sailors abandoning those vessels. What stoker Clark hadn't seen were the 7,000 other ships, tucked into every harbour, inlet, bay, and cove on England's south coast, waiting for the signal to launch. Thanks to the efficiency of crews, such as those aboard *Iroquois*,* the D-Day nautical operation—code-named Neptune—could launch without fear of German gunboat attack.

---

* According to a Canadian Press story in October 1944, during twenty-eight days of operations during the Battle of Normandy, HMCS *Iroquois* steamed 10,000 miles, fired more than 3,500 rounds of heavy ammunition, and sank 23 enemy ships in the Channel area.

No doubt Wilf Pound had a clearer view of the Neptune operation than stoker Clark. He served as a Royal Canadian Navy helmsman aboard an infantry landing craft on D-Day morning. LCI crews had but one responsibility—to get assault troops safely ashore. Some of the crews manning these flat-bottomed transport vessels had already helped put Allied troops ashore in North Africa, Sicily, and Italy, so they bragged to their military passengers that they'd put troops ashore in Normandy without getting so much as their trousers wet. A slight exaggeration perhaps, but it was clear when our tour visited the shoreline adjacent to Bernières and Courseulles that even Wilf was impressed with the open water they had covered to get the invasion troops to shore.

Incidentally, as tough as Wilf remembered it was to make it to Normandy in 1944, his wife, Melba, explained that they almost didn't get there in 2004. At the time, Wilf's deteriorating respiratory health required keeping an oxygen tank handy. Consequently, half a dozen D-Day tours to Normandy for the sixtieth anniversary had refused to accommodate the Pounds that spring. We agreed to try to get Wilf and Melba to Juno Beach. The trip obviously invigorated them. Wilf shared his experiences with others on the tour and he rarely needed the extra oxygen.

Another veteran accompanying us was Viola Boyd, who'd served with the Canadian Women's Army Corps. During the war, she worked in a transport pool, driving a two-and-a-half-ton truck (she called it "a deuce and a half") wherever it was needed around Aldershot, England, where the Canadian army was headquartered. At the time of our trip, Vi's visual impairment required that she have a companion nearly all the time. Her stepson David gave her that assistance, but he also provided insights to the Canadian soldier's experience in Normandy that few of us expected. His father, David Boyd Sr., served as a corporal instructor on Bren-gun carriers with the Canadian Scottish. David Jr. reminded the tour travellers that among the Canadian objectives for D-Day had been the Carpiquet airport, some ten kilometres inland from Juno Beach. History shows that German counterattacks and resistance proved stronger than expected immediately after D-Day, especially around the strategic Carpiquet airport, so bitter fighting postponed the Canadian liberation of the airstrip, tarmac, hangars, and other buildings until early July.

Among the rituals I introduced into our daily bus touring around Normandy's historic sites in 2004 was that anyone aboard the bus wishing to make a comment or share a veteran's story should feel free to use the tour guide microphone at the front of the bus. Initially shy to accept the invitation, our veterans and others on the tour eventually began to offer D-Day anecdotes from their own experiences or those of a family member more freely. Several days into the tour, David Boyd suddenly asked for a moment at the bus mike and offered his father's Normandy war story as related to him by his uncle:

"Dad and his Bren-gun carrier crew were requisitioned by the Royal Winnipeg Rifles to support their riflemen in the battle for Carpiquet airport," Boyd said. "The airport was built for German bombers . . . the runways heavily reinforced with metal, like re-bar, to hold up under the great weight and speed of the fully loaded bombers."

David explained that Col. Kurt Meyer and panzer (tank) troops of the 12th Hitler Youth SS, guilty of massacring twenty-three Canadian prisoners at Abbaye d'Ardenne on June 7, had been assigned to defend Carpiquet. Equally lethal was their weapon, the 88-mm gun, which fired armour-piercing shells spaced periodically with tracers (phosphorous loaded shells) to help the gunner sight a target.

"Dad's carrier was running at top speed in a zigzag pattern toward the Germans," David Boyd continued, "when a tracer shell cracked hard against the runway surface, and as it spun like a flying flare along the surface it went directly under the carrier, between [its caterpillar] tracks. Dad roared out a single order: 'Bail out!' As he pulled on the brakes . . . Dad and his three-man crew leaped out, rolling as they landed. Dad got to his feet, hunched down, and ran in the same zigzag pattern he had used when steering the carrier toward the enemy, running away from the 88s."

David explained that his father's next recollection was waking up, strapped to a stretcher outside a medical tent. Medics had finally caught up to the shell-shocked corporal striding zigzag, wild-eyed, and speechless with his hands fluttering across his face. When the medics directed him to psychiatric treatment, he protested that he wasn't crazy and demanded he be returned to his regiment. He got his wish but, as David pointed out, also the worst possible posting.

"He was assigned to a grave-digging team. He followed his friends all the way to Germany, burying friend and enemy as they fought toward victory."

David Boyd's depiction of his father's trauma left the tour group stunned and quiet on the bus for some time afterward. His intention hadn't been to shock us, but I think it helped all of us understand what had drawn him and his stepmother Viola to Juno Beach that first week of June. Clearly, David's father had endured incredible shock and loss in Normandy, and in the veteran's absence, his son felt compelled and, I think, privileged to pay family respects to him and his fallen comrades. It was a feeling common among several of the veterans and those family members present.

Veterans in Normandy during that first week of June were as plentiful as the poppies dotting the countryside. Because this was the sixtieth anniversary observance of D-Day, the media were everywhere. Early in the tour we included a visit to Le Mémorial de Caen, the modern museum exploring war and peace in the twentieth century, located in the Norman city of Caen. As we assembled inside, beneath a full-scale replica of a Typhoon fighter aircraft suspended over the main foyer of the museum, one of the U.S. network TV news crews noticed our veterans, in particular, the tallest of them—six-foot-five-inch Fred Sampson.

"Lofty" (as we began to call him) stood head and shoulders above most tourists in the entranceway. Add to his prominent stature an English accent and devilish laugh and the media gravitated to him. And the moment the cameras rolled, the young people in the museum—hundreds of school-age children also taking in the anniversary—homed in on him too. Suddenly, it was a Lofty love-in. The kids wanted his autograph and the media wanted his story. And he was pleased to oblige. He teased the children, saying he'd flown to Normandy on D-Day with no engines. Then he proceeded to describe the Horsa glider he piloted behind a four-engine Stirling tow plane. Since the museum had plenty of D-Day photographs and movies playing, Fred was able to point to images of the aircraft he flew to Normandy in the early evening of June 6. He told them he had orders to "crash-land" the glider. That usually got a laugh too, but that was the way his cargo was delivered.

Lofty's red beret and blue blazer with his parachutist's wings and service medals pinned across his chest attracted crowds wherever he went that trip. When we visited Sainte-Mère-Eglise, where the U.S. Airborne had landed in the darkness on D-Day morning, the American tourists just wanted to hear Sampson's accent. At the Pegasus Bridge museum, where British infantry had crash-landed in gliders after midnight on D-Day morning to capture the Caen bridge in fifteen minutes, Fred was mobbed by tourists and history buffs all wanting to be photographed next to him. With a bit of false modesty, he obliged. As he did, he regaled them with a recounting of his VIP trip the night before to a special commemorative cocktail party and dinner hosted by Prince Charles, colonel-in-chief of the British Parachute Regiment. It had been a tough social schedule, he told them, and he had limited himself to just a few salutary cocktails. Although he never took more credit than he deserved, Lofty never failed to rise to the occasion.

Another veteran on our tour proved to be just the opposite sort of personality. Lorne Empey had never considered his work on the night of June 5 and into the early hours of June 6 to be particularly remarkable. Below decks, in the engine room of Royal Canadian Navy minesweeper HMCS *Minus*, sixty years before, stoker Empey's war had consisted of minding engine boilers, pressure gauges, and lubricating oil. Above him, crewmates on *Minus* (and a dozen other RCN sweepers) were clearing mines from the 150 kilometres of water between England and France. Working in the dark all night, those sweeper flotillas had ensured unmolested passage of the invasion armada. Only at the end of his watch, when he had climbed into the dawn light above decks and saw the number of ships flowing through the safe lanes *Minus* had cleared, did Lorne Empey realize the magnitude of D-Day.

"Within seconds, the entire area lit up with a thunderous roar [of naval guns firing at the German defences on shore]," Empey said. "There was now nothing for us to do, but become witnesses to a tremendous spectacle, one which has not been matched by anything since."

That view from the deck of *Minus* left an impression. Lorne was prepared to admit that. But it was only as our D-Day tour group travelled across Normandy and visited the five Allied landing areas, that veteran Empey understood what youngster Empey had accomplished. At one point our tour bus pulled into the visitors' location at what had been the American landing beach, code-named Utah. All our travellers, including Lorne, hiked past the tourist museum and the food stands to the water's edge. The beach at Utah was barely above sea level. Anyone on the beach—including the German occupying armies in 1944—had a panoramic view of everything—the sea, the land, and the sky—in all directions. Virtually nothing could escape one's view in that flat, open stretch of sand. As they walked on what had been Utah Beach, Lorne and several of our vets met a British veteran. I overheard their conversation.

"I didn't know the Canadians landed on D-Day," the man said.

"Sure they did. On Juno Beach," Empey said. Then he pointed to the horizon to the northeast. "And our Canadian navy was out there."

The flotilla of Royal Canadian Navy minesweepers, in which his ship HMCS *Minus* served, had in fact cleared German mines ahead of the American troopships and landing craft en route to Utah that night of June 5 and morning of June 6. And because the Englishman didn't know that, Lorne was quick, even proud, to point it out. Suddenly his role on D-Day took on some significance. I could hear it in Lorne's voice. For my benefit later, he indicated exactly where he'd watched the D-Day landings occur.

"We moved out behind the battleship *Texas*, dropped our hook, and watched the battle," Empey explained. "The invasion was on!"

A couple of nights before the D-Day anniversary ceremony at Juno Beach, I sat for several hours and interviewed the one air force veteran on our tour. As a Halifax bomber pilot, F/L Bill Novick's closest comrades-in-arms would have been a navigator, a bomb-aimer, a flight engineer, a wireless radio operator, and gunners with him thousands of feet above Europe en route to nighttime targets deep inside Germany. But a few weeks before D-Day, Novick explained to me, his No. 433 Squadron began preparing for a target in occupied France. He and his crew were told the bomb bays of his aircraft would be loaded with high-explosive ordinance. They would be flying at a much lower altitude than ever before. And their route to the target would be extremely circuitous. Only when the master bombers pulled back the curtains in the pre-operation briefing to reveal the Normandy coast did Novick and the rest of 433 Squadron discover their precise objective.

"We were sent out west around Wales, then to France by way of Cherbourg and then to the city of Caen," Novick told me. He later learned the reason for the western route to end up at the eastern edge of the invasion beaches was to avoid the massive stream of transport aircraft, gliders, and fighters flying by the thousands straight from England to the Normandy invasion area. "We were flying for the first time ever at 3,000 feet. . . . Our time on target was 5:30 on the morning of the sixth . . . and it was impressed upon us how important this target was. Our squadron of sixteen planes was assigned to bomb the bridge at Caen over the River Orne."

When I quizzed Novick about the strategic importance of the bridge, even he admitted initially he didn't know. Later he learned that destruction of the bridge would prevent a division of German panzers from crossing the River Orne through Caen to mount a counterattack against the Allied troops landing on the invasion beaches of the Normandy coast. He explained that on the final run in to the target, his bomb-aimer had hesitated to drop the high-explosive payload because he thought the smoke markers had not framed the target properly. The sixteen Halifaxes circled and sighted on the target a second time, eventually smashing the River Orne bridge and making it impassable. At that moment in our interview, Novick paused and smiled at the thought.

"What were you just thinking?" I asked him.

"In this week's *Time* magazine, there was a sixtieth anniversary supplement for the D-Day commemorations," he said. "They had individual people talking about their experiences. Lo and behold, there's a former German tank commander who said he was on the other side of Caen. He was told to race to the beaches, but he couldn't get his tanks across [the river] because the bridge had been bombed. I smiled reading that. I said, 'Hey. That was me up there.'"

On D-Day anniversary morning, as our tour bus made its way to the commemoration, we crossed a massive traffic bridge on our way through Caen. I happened to catch Bill Novick's attention as we passed over the bridge. He was smiling and nodding. This was the bridge he'd taken out sixty years ago that very morning.

Although most days aboard the bus there was plenty of buzz as members of our group shared map interpretation, pointed out historic sites, and offered wartime stories, June 6, 2004, was slightly different. I had expressed openly my concern for being delayed by security measures en route to Juno Beach for the ceremony. With so many dignitaries present—from France, Britain, the U.S., Canada, and Germany—the gendarmes had informed us that all buses and passengers had to be checked and cleared in Caen before advancing to the beach ceremonies. Consequently, not everybody in our tour group was happy with my call for a 5 a.m. departure from the hotel. The bus ride through the early morning mist was unusually quiet, although my wife, Jayne, and I did acknowledge three anniversaries among our travellers—three women with birthdays all on that day, one—Elaine Jackson—actually born June 6, 1944.

It occurred to me, as well, that our tour group was approaching the unknown of the security checks at virtually the same moment Canadians on sea and in the air had approached the unknown Normandy coastline on D-Day. I hardly had to encourage navy vets John Clark and Lorne Empey, airmen Bill Novick and Fred Sampson, and landing craft helmsman Wilf Pound to think back to what they were doing exactly sixty years before. No doubt the reminiscing during the days leading up to the anniversary had rekindled enough good and bad memories. At any rate, to our surprise and delight, our tour bus was among the first to the Caen checkpoint. We were quickly cleared and told to move on to Courseulles-sur-Mer. We arrived so early at Juno Beach Centre that the Mounted Police were still setting up their checkpoint at the main gate. So we waited several minutes to be the first group admitted to the ceremony grounds. That our tour group would have the pick of the thousands of assigned chairs and bleacher seats seemed to make up for the 4 a.m. wake-up call. However, it wasn't until later that I learned how our veterans got an exclusive view of the entire ceremony. While I went off to join Lloyd Robertson for on-air colour commentary on the anniversary ceremony, I missed the second invasion at Juno staged by our tour vets. David Boyd later told me what had happened.

Being the first visitors on the site, he explained, our group of nine veterans, their spouses, and caregivers arrived at the front of a section of spectator chairs with a sign that read: "Reserved for veterans and escorts." All appropriately dressed with medals and ribbons showing, our vets immediately claimed and settled into the front-row seats. Before long, the other rows of reserved seats, not to mention the massive bleachers behind, quickly filled with veterans and ticket-holding guests. It also wasn't long before an RCMP sergeant approached our vets in the reserved area to explain those seats were intended for veterans and their families.

"What the hell do you think we are?" one of our vets said to him.

"I'm sorry," the Mountie said, "but these are for the vets the government sent over."

In an instant, Fred Sampson rose from his seat—all six-foot-five-inches of him at ramrod attention and towering over the young RCMP—and said, "Not to put too fine a point on it, son, the government paid our way over here sixty years ago and we don't plan to change seats."

"Okay, gentlemen. Don't shoot the messenger. I'll pass that along."

About ten minutes later, an official from the Juno Beach Centre arrived to try to move them again. David Boyd described her as "smartly turned out in a black suit and clearly intending to take charge. . . . All she lacked to look like an over-rated corporal was two stripes and a clipboard." With all the authority she could muster she announced, "I want you to know that I am acting on orders from the prime minister. You will have to move, right now."

Boyd, seated next to his veteran mother Viola, began to record the woman on video. He said he couldn't contain himself. "That's pretty bold of the P.M., kicking veterans around with an election in three weeks."

The spokeswoman immediately slapped her hand over the camera lens telling Boyd to "turn that off!" She wheeled away and walked directly to the RCMP officer who'd previously requested the vets to move on. David said the woman grew quite agitated, pointed back at the vets in the front row and, following a quick confab with the Mountie, disappeared into the crowd. Moments later, the Mountie approached our vets and announced, "You people can stay where you are, although some might say you're in the wrong seats!"

Wrong or not, Lofty's intimidating stature, David Boyd's video recording, and our veterans' iron will not to be moved meant they got the best seats in the house. They got to watch the dignitaries arrive; witnessed inspection of the troops; enjoyed the speeches, music, wreath laying, and Queen's and Governor General's walkabout all from the front row. They came away with all the video, camera snapshots, and hands-on memories a group of veterans could ever have hoped for. Like the original June 6, this one in 2004 turned out to be "the longest day" of our tour, but the most rewarding.

Two days later our tour made its way back to Paris for the plane trip home. Again the security measures appeared extensive. A group of three young security officers—they couldn't have been more than twenty years old—had automatic machine guns resting across their chests. We joined long lines waiting to be checked in for our Air Canada flight to Toronto. The lines moved horribly slowly. I sensed our vets, at the end of an emotionally and physically draining week, were flagging. I seized the moment and requested VIP assistance to the "Canadian D-Day veterans" in our group. Coincidentally, one of the women at the ticket counter had a French newspaper and recognized Fred Sampson in one of its published photographs from the D-Day ceremony at Juno. It turned out the young woman's grandfather had been in the French Resistance. She got emotional as she related how her grandfather had always expressed gratitude for the Allied liberation of France. At any rate, our vets were suddenly expedited from the ticket counter to the waiting lounge near the boarding gate to the aircraft.

It took about an hour for the rest of the tour to catch up with our VIP veterans at the gate. But once on the plane, we all settled into our economy seats for the flight home. I was just beginning to relax, feeling at long last the excitement of the trip was over, when I heard an announcement on the plane's PA system: "Would tour leader Ted Barris please identify himself to flight steward?" My reflex reaction was that someone was missing, someone was ill, or that we were on the wrong plane or something. The chief flight steward approached and spoke to me quietly. He said that there were a number of seats available in first class and did I have any travellers who might enjoy being upgraded. There were just enough first-class seats for all our vets and their escorts.

"A few minutes later," David Boyd remembered, "[we were out] of those narrow-arsed seats in economy . . . and comfortably seated in plump, wide seats [in first class], being served glasses of champagne and orange juice. As we raised our glasses in a collective toast to a memorable pilgrimage, one of the vets called out to me, 'Hey Davie, we're in the wrong goddamned seats again!'"

If the Sixtieth Anniversary of D-Day tour introduced me to veterans who latently realized their individual contributions to launching the invasion of Europe in 1944, the Sixtieth Anniversary of Dutch Liberation tour, the following year, introduced me to the families of veterans who had finished the job in 1945. The Canadians who had participated in the liberation of Antwerp, who had joined Operation

Market-Garden to break into the heart of Holland, who had driven the Germans from the Scheldt estuary, who had participated in the Operation Manna food drops, and who had restored the royal family to its home in Apeldoorn, became the focus in 2005. About a third of our tour group of 138 people consisted of veterans. The rest were the spouses, daughters, sons, nieces, nephews, and cousins of those Canadians the Dutch called their "angels of freedom."

With thousands of veterans, mostly British and Canadian, trekking around the countryside to museums and cemeteries that first week of May 2005, Dutch citizens were doing all they could to make their Second World War liberators feel welcome. As at Normandy the year before, during the "Thank You Canada and Allied Forces" festivities in Holland, organizing officials, dignitaries, and the media seemed to be around every corner. And when a group of local officials invited our tour group to join a liberation ceremony in the town of Baarn, east of Amsterdam, on the evening of May 4, we all felt quite honoured.

We had no idea what we were in for.

At about 7:30 in the evening, our three tour buses pulled up to a crossroads some distance from the downtown core of Baarn. As we climbed out of the coaches, I remember noticing how quiet it was. Even though there were crowds of people waiting for us, no one spoke above a whisper. Several event organizers quickly separated the veterans in our group—nearly forty men and women—from the rest of us and escorted them to the vanguard of a procession that was forming. The rest of us joined several hundred men, women, and children—Baarn townspeople—making up the remainder of the parade.

We were told we were joining what the Dutch called "The Silent March" and were asked not to talk. The only sounds any of us could hear were the calls of birds and the clatter of our feet steadily marching over the cobblestone streets. Strangely, the marching seemed to grow in intensity. From my vantage point in the procession, I could see suddenly that our numbers were growing. While the veterans continued to lead the way through serpentine streets toward something ahead of us, the ranks of the rest of the parade were swelling. People were emerging from offices, apartment buildings, and individual homes to join us, all without speaking a word. I could feel the anticipation growing just by looking into the townspeople's faces. Something was about to happen.

It was nearly 8 o'clock when we passed the old town hall on the last block before reaching Amalia Park in the centre of Baarn. We couldn't see into the park because the greenery for which it is famous blocked our view. Then our procession emerged from behind the wall of trees at the entrance to the park. As we did, like the penultimate downbeat of a symphony, our arrival was heralded by the sounds of bells ringing in every corner of the town. Church bells, schoolhouse bells, firehall bells all chimed out together. This was the moment when Netherlanders each year paid tribute to civilians and soldiers who had given their lives to the liberation of the country in 1945. And there before us, standing in tribute at the entrance and throughout Amalia Park were no fewer than 6,000 townspeople. They broke into spontaneous applause as the Canadian veterans in our group came into view. They continued to applaud until the last of the procession had made its way into the park for the climax of the Silent March ceremony.

As a man of fifty-six, a child of the post-war, never having experienced the trauma or loss of war directly, having grown up in a culture that did not readily accept the sight of grown men showing emotion openly, and now cast in the role as leader of a national tour of Canadian travellers and vets, I felt very self-conscious about the tears welling up in my eyes. I was completely caught off-guard by the appearance of an entire town turning out that evening to welcome 138 strangers to perhaps its most cherished of annual rituals. I remembered thinking that I had stood through scores of Remembrance Day services. I had delivered several eulogies to veterans I'd befriended and then see die in their eighties or nineties. I had managed to keep my composure through countless pipers' laments and the playing of "O Canada" during painful memorials so many times. But here, in front of people I did not know, in a place to which I had no real attachment, and for an event I'd never witnessed before, the tears flowed. I couldn't stop them. But I wasn't alone. As I glanced around our group, I saw plenty of red eyes and handkerchiefs.

The ceremony at the park contained many of the components we'd become used to this liberation week. Flags flying at half staff. Buglers performing "The Last Post" and bands playing Dutch and Canadian national anthems. Aircraft formations roaring overhead in the missing man formation. Adults standing solemnly with heads slightly bowed. Children attentive to every nuance of the ceremony. Dignitaries speaking to the veterans who'd liberated their communities and restored their freedom. And while most of the messages were delivered in Dutch, the mayor of Baarn managed a final salute to the vets in English.

"To you the pride of Canada, our liberators, we thank you for our home," she said.

As the formal ceremony ended, most of those present began to press forward toward the cenotaph. It was just a worn, wooden cross, about a metre tall, embedded in a wall of stones, but it appeared that everybody wanted to pass in front of it before leaving the park. I joined the line of people slowly but steadily passing by the cenotaph. Next to me in the crowd, I noticed a man and woman together carrying a bouquet of roses. Instinctively I reached for the poppy I was wearing on my coat, removed it, and gestured to the man's lapel.

"May I give you this?" I asked, hoping he understood.

"Certainly," he said. "Thank you."

As I pinned the poppy to his coat, he told me his name was Harry Roos, the Dutch word for "rose." He explained that he was born after the war—in 1949—the same year I was born. In fact, our birthdays were a month apart and his two daughters were the same ages as my two daughters. "Not all my family made it through the war," he said. "An older brother was killed, so May 4 is very important to my family." About then, we were nearing the head of the line.

"What's the significance of the cenotaph?" I asked.

He explained that the wooden cross dated back to the end of the war. When the town fathers got around to rebuilding the park, in

1947, they added the stone wall around the cross. Every year since then, the Silent March ceremony has culminated in a remembrance ceremony at the park. Whenever possible, veterans have been invited to be thanked. He was glad the Canadians had come this year. It was now his turn in front of the cross and stone wall. Harry Roos paused, bowing his head a moment, and then he carried out his annual ritual, laying a rose for each member of his family—four of them—at the foot of the cenotaph.

The Silent March helped illustrate to me something I'd heard and read about for years—that the Dutch have utmost admiration for what Canadians accomplished during the Second World War and that they reaffirm their gratitude every year. Every generation. I remembered Canadian friends of Dutch descent telling me that when they'd returned to the central Netherlands city of Eindhoven, their Dutch relatives insisted to city officials that their street be repaved, flowers freshly planted, storefronts painted anew, and Canadian flags hung for "the liberators." The same sense of sparing no effort or expense prevailed through the entire week we travelled around the country in May 2005. The Dutch seemed to roll out the red carpet wherever we went. At the Anne Frank House in Amsterdam, special arrangements were made for us to proceed through block-long lineups of tourists to explore her refuge on Prinsengracht Straat while others waited. In Groesbeek, home of the country's largest Canadian War Cemetery, local musician and composer Theo Diepenbrock knew we were coming and arranged a tribute luncheon and serenaded our veterans with their favourite wartime tunes. At the insistence of amateur museum curator Kees Traas, the town of Nieuwdorp (at the western end of the Scheldt) turned out to greet us with a civic ceremony, a meal, a tour of the museum, and a tribute at the local memorial park. And the icing on the cake: Despite a bone-chilling, pouring rain on the May 8 VE Day parade in Apeldoorn, none of its citizens left the curb of the two-kilometre-long parade route until the final veteran had passed and been applauded.

That's how Harry Roos's generation—the Dutch born during or just after the war—continued to pay their respects to their Canadian liberators. Coincidentally, as our ten-day tour unfolded, I discovered that many of those Canadians—about the same age—who'd chosen to join us for the 2005 tour had similar intentions. About the third day of the tour, several of our travellers requested a quick side trip across the Dutch border from Nijmegen into western Germany to the Reichswald Forest War Cemetery, where 700 Canadian airmen killed during the war were buried. One middle-aged couple in our tour, Gary and Eleanor MacLean, searched out and found the gravesite of his father, Gordon MacLean. As Gary described it, on August 17–18, 1943, eight Mosquito fighter-bombers flew a diversionary operation to Berlin while a main column of nearly 600 bombers attacked the V-2 rocket factories at Peenemunde, Germany. Even though forty-one Allied aircraft were shot down that night, including Gordon MacLean's Mosquito, Allied Bomber Command described the operation "a successful raid [that] set back the V-2 experimental program by at least two months." More important for Gary MacLean, however, was the personal realization of a lifelong wish—arriving at his father's military gravesite—sixty-two years later.

A few rows away, in the same Reichswald cemetery, another middle-aged traveller in our group also completed a pilgrimage that morning. As a boy during the war, Paul Van Nest remembered his cousin, just a teenager, going off to war. Glenn Brooks trained to become an air gunner and served with the Halifax bomber crews of No. 426 Squadron based in northern England. Because Paul Van Nest had later acquired such a passion for war history, he searched records to discover that his cousin's squadron flew on the night of October 6–7, 1944, to attack industrial and transportation targets in Dortmund, Germany. Two of the 523 bombers sent that night were lost, including the Halifax in which Glenn Brooks was tail gunner; he and the flight engineer were killed, three other crewmen were captured and imprisoned, and another was missing-in-action.

Attending his cousin's grave meant a great deal to Paul Van Nest six decades later. Here was a man, who himself had led dozens of tours to U.S. Civil War battlefields and graveyards, at long last taking the tour that led him to his cousin's burial ground. Here was a true student of war history, experiencing the toughest lessons of war—loss and closure. I watched as Paul quietly placed a small paper Canadian flag beside the tombstone. He wrote down all its engravings, including the epitaph: "I have fought a good fight. I have finished my course." Then he crouched beside the stone so that I could take a few photographs to document the concluding chapter of Glenn Brooks's life in Europe. As we stood there full of emotion, Paul described how his cousin's death had played out at home in Canada.

"I remember the women in the family breaking down and crying and then hugging each other," he said. "I'd never seen them hold each other so tightly, so desperately. I've never forgotten that."

A couple of days later, our tour travelled through southwestern Holland, through the regions of Zeeland and West Flanders. There, in the autumn of 1944, Canadian infantry and armoured corps troops fought along the banks of the East and West Scheldt estuaries to clear the eighty-kilometre approach to the port of Antwerp. The liberation had cost nearly 4,000 Canadian lives. That day, May 6, happened to be the eightieth birthday of Lorne Empey, the Canadian navy vet who had joined us the previous year on the D-Day tour. A little less intimidated by the bus microphone this tour, Lorne recalled leaving his farm home in Saskatchewan to join the navy when he was just seventeen. Someone piped up, "Why did so many underage men enlist?" Lorne simply shrugged and pointed out, when the war broke out, one brother joined the air force, another enlisted in the army, his sister became an army nurse, and his father moved to Esquimalt, B.C., to build corvettes in the shipyards. That left him to run the entire farm operation, at age seventeen. Like so many, he was itching to get a meaningful job in the war effort, get into uniform, get paid a working wage, and eat three square meals a day. So, when the navy accepted his underage enlistment, Lorne was shipped for stoker training out to Esquimalt, where coincidentally the rest of his family was living.

"I'd like to comment on that," came a voice from the back of the bus. Jim Ronan, like Lorne Empey, was back for his second battlefield tour with us in Holland. From the moment we'd met during the

D-Day tour, I felt a strong attraction to Ronan. He was always well informed on the details of this battle or that regiment, which kept me on my toes. He enjoyed poking fun (often at me) when it was appropriate. And unlike Lorne Empey, Jim Ronan was not the least bit bashful. His voice a little raspy, his manner a little brusque, Jim Ronan generally waited for just the right moment to speak, but never hesitated to offer his opinion about wartime service. Whenever he spoke he always expressed unwavering pride and admiration for any Canadian soldier. But no matter which of the services was being discussed, Jim was always quick to point out that none of the war effort on the ground could have succeeded without the contributions of his outfit—the Royal Canadian Electrical and Mechanical Engineers (RCEME).* Ronan, like Empey and so many others, had enlisted underage.

"I originally registered to join the army in 1942 at age fifteen," he said. "I got a draft notice in 1943 and was deferred as a farm worker. . . . After D-Day, I went to the local armouries in Barrie to join up. They finally sent me a letter and I reported to the [Canadian National Exhibition] Horse Palace in October. My starting pay was $1.10 a day [about $33 a month]."

Ronan was barely seventeen at the time. He trained as a driver/mechanic at Camp Borden in Ontario, with hopes of getting overseas as a reinforcement in the Canadian Armoured Corps in 1944. But his foster father pointed out to authorities Jim was still too young to serve. He was threatened with jail time and a reduction to "boy soldier" status at seventy cents a day. Cooler heads prevailed and he stayed in uniform as a runner at an armoured corps training centre until the war ended. In 1947, after he'd turned twenty, however,

* As proudly as Jim Ronan proclaimed the wartime contribution of his RCEME comrades, he was ultimately more modest about his personal contribution to military history. In 1971, he helped administer the retrieval and restoration of a Duplex Drive Sherman tank, which sank just offshore during the D-Day landings at Courseulles-sur-Mer in 1944. The plaque next to the mounted DD tank is "dedicated by the First Hussars to the memory of all who participated in this operation." If not a D-Day vet, Ronan was certainly a D-Day history vet.

Ronan got his chance. He joined the engineers and served three months in the Korean War, at the ripe old age of twenty-five. He later continued his uniformed service with a United Nations peacekeeping tour of duty in the Middle East in the 1960s. What made Ronan's comments about joining up underage all the more intriguing was that on this second trip to European battlefields (designed principally for older adults), Jim had chosen to bring three of the youngest members of his family: his son Patrick and two of his grandchildren—Ross and Emma, who was just nine years old.

"My aim on this trip is twofold," he explained, "to honour fallen comrades, some of whom I trained with in Canada, and to give some of my descendants insight as to how war affects those involved."

They learned that and more. But they also gave the tour something unique in return. Not surprisingly, the younger Ronans carried with them the trappings of their generation—cell phones, electronic games for the longer bus rides, and a laptop computer instead of handwritten diaries or journals. A few days into the trip, their grandfather announced to the tour that Patrick, Ross, and Emma had set up a website to which they would feed daily dispatches publishing their observations and reactions to what they were seeing. They also volunteered to post photographs and messages from members of the tour to their families and friends back in Canada. Far from being outsiders and out of touch with the history of sixty years ago, the younger Ronan family members soaked up every moment they witnessed and then shared them with a wider audience on the Web. Once again, I found myself overwhelmed by what our simple idea of returning to historic Second World War locations was creating for the post-war-generation travellers with us on this trip.

En route to the Scheldt estuary battle sites, we stopped at the Canadian war cemetery near Bergen op Zoom. Nearly a thousand graves were arranged there in an open meadow sheltered by mature pines and lined by floral gardens. Once again, families completed long-anticipated pilgrimages. John and Betty McGuire, from Lindsay, Ontario, placed Canadian flags and a bouquet of roses at the base of a tombstone commemorating Sherbrooke Fusilier John McGuire

Sr. At another plot, Patricia Williams completed her journey from Creston, California, by placing flags at the marker of her uncle, infantryman John Moffat, killed in November 1944, as he and his regiment began the final phase of the liberation of the Scheldt estuary. This was not Pat's first stop at a family military plot this week, however. Three days earlier, she told me, she had placed flags in Groesbeek cemetery at the grave of artilleryman Lloyd Muter, killed exactly two weeks after her uncle John. Lloyd Muter was Patricia's father.

"I was born March 16, 1944, and my father left for overseas on March 20, 1944," Patricia told me later. "He likely had time to hold me once."

She explained that her uncle had served as a lieutenant with the Calgary Highlanders and her father as a captain with the Royal Canadian Artillery. They both had participated in the assault on the causeway to Walcheren Island, the last German stronghold in the Battle of the Scheldt. John was killed on November 1, Lloyd on November 14. Patricia said that her mother had received the two telegrams notifying her of their deaths on the same day. Since she had now visited both graves, I asked Patricia if the trip had given her some peace of mind, some solace. Given the loss her family had experienced, I expected a heart-felt response.

"I never really felt an emotional connection with my father. I wanted to. I certainly tried," Patricia admitted. "I knew stories that people told me about him, my mother, my uncles, my aunts, but as hard as I tried, my father was just someone else's stories."

I found it extraordinary that a woman would travel all that distance, visit the grave of her father and of her uncle, killed during the same campaign, and feel an emotional vacuum. Patricia explained that she had come to Holland once before, trying to connect with her father's wartime story. Even then, in 1974, when she met and shared a meaningful time with the Dutch family that had "adopted" Lloyd Muter's grave, she still had not been able to form an emotional bond with him. She tried digging into his war history, requesting and researching his personal military records to understand what his artillery battery had experienced. But she said that merely amplified the problem. Her connection with her father was always an intellectual one. What added insult to the injury, she pointed out, was that the Canadian soldier who'd returned her father's effects to Calgary later married Patricia's mother and became her stepfather. The relationship ultimately was not a happy one, and Patricia had always wondered what life would have offered had her birth father, Lloyd Muter, come home safely at the end of the war. A few weeks after the 2005 Dutch Liberation tour was over, I received a remarkable note from her. Things had changed.

"It wasn't until being home for about three weeks, when I looked at his picture in our living room," she wrote, "that I suddenly felt a heart connection with my dad. By going on the [Liberation Tour] and talking with other Canadian warriors, walking the Scheldt area, his last battleground, and participating in the ceremonies and rituals, I forged a connection with him. I didn't have to rely on someone else's recollections of him. I had done something to make him real and alive to me. My taking this trip was essential for me to feel that he did live and fight and die.

"Something magical happened while I was on that pilgrimage," Patricia said finally. "It was a profound life change."

Our journey to Holland for the sixtieth anniversary of the country's liberation never stopped surprising us. At Nijmegen, where we stopped beside the bridge over the River Waal, the second of three bridges involved in the famous Operation Market-Garden (the "bridge too far" operation), veteran Les Robinson posed for a photograph with Earl and Judy, his son and daughter-in-law from Hamilton, Ontario. The moment sparked a vivid memory. Throughout the liberation campaign, Robinson explained, he had driven transport trucks loaded with explosives forward to the front lines. Dangerous enough. But in the last days of the war, he said, he had illegally assisted Dutch civilians to get through Nijmegen. It involved dressing a young woman in a military uniform and transporting her past military checkpoints, so that she could be reunited with her family.

Several of our travellers who'd left Holland after the war to emigrate to Canada reminisced on the bus microphone about life in the last days of the German occupation. Ann Vos, a retired nursery school teacher from Owen Sound, Ontario, shook her head when she recalled "the hunger winter" of 1945. She described life in Rijnsburg for her parents, herself, and seven brothers and sisters starving without meat, vegetables, bread, or milk. They survived on a few potatoes, boiled tulip bulbs, and tea made from nettles, until the famous food drops of Operation Manna in late April 1945. I asked her what the lasting impact of that experience was.

"I have a soft heart," she said. "I'm a believer in being generous. Whenever I see street people asking for money, I always give them money. I appreciate the little things."

Survival for Mac Traas's family at the end of the war proved even more perilous. Over the bus mike, Mac chronicled the way his family moved from tolerance of the German occupation to active resistance. At seventeen, during a *razzia*, he was taken off the farm and sent to a forced labour camp in Germany. When he returned several years later, his brother had joined the Underground, and the family assisted the Dutch Resistance retrieving weapons dropped by Allied aircraft into occupied Holland. His mother was forced to feed German billets on the main floor of the farmhouse, while in the attic members of the Underground used radio equipment to communicate with England.

"On April 14, 1945, the Germans conducted a major raid on the farm," Traas explained. "We were hidden and it took the Germans nine hours to find us. They carted us off. I was twenty years old and my mother wanted to kiss me and told me to pray. I said, 'No. I'll die like a man.' I was more afraid of being captive then, than being dead.... The Germans had threatened for every German killed, they would kill ten civilians.... The German SS and paratroops were out of control. They took my mother and sister.

"'Have you seen any Canadians?' they demanded.

(ABOVE LEFT) RCAF pilot Jackie Rae and his Spitfire were trained and designed for airborne killing; confronting the combat reality, however, was neither in the syllabus nor the cockpit manual. As deadly as sniper (ABOVE RIGHT) Ted Zuber's aim was at the front during the Korean War, when it came to his later sketches and paintings, he admitted his sight had missed a vital detail. Ultimately, his paintings, including "Reverse Slope" (BELOW), gained official status as Canadian war art.

(LEFT) Herb Pitts went to Korea to put his classroom soldiering to the test; he returned with a Military Cross, but said "it was recognition . . . on behalf of others around me." (ABOVE) Sisters Barbara Differ and Hazel Regan mourn their brother Bill Regan (in framed picture) killed in the Korean War. They learned more about his death at the Wall of Remembrance christening, July 27, 1997, than they ever imagined. At the Juno Beach Centre opening (RIGHT) former artillery officer Garth Webb claimed he made "a lousy interview." In truth, his memories of June 6, 1944 (BELOW, middle) illustrate the human toll on D-Day.

(ABOVE) Navy helmsman Wilf Pound (left) and stoker Lorne Empey claimed they were just small cogs in the grand D-Day scheme, until they walked the Normandy beaches to see what Operation Neptune accomplished. (BELOW) Exactly 60 years after their veteran comrades secured the D-Day beachhead at Juno Beach, these Canadian vets (and family) claimed front-row seats at the anniversary tribute: (l to r) Sam and Bernice Reid, Fred Sampson, Jim Ronan, Dave and Violet Boyd, Bill and Vita Novick.

(ABOVE) Fred Barnard (left) had never told his D-Day story—storming ashore with the Queen's Own Rifles alongside his brother Don—until a chance meeting on the eve of the 60th anniversary of the invasion. (BELOW LEFT) In 2007, French ambassador Daniel Jouanneau presented the Legion of Honour medal to Fred Barnard in an emotional ceremony at Toronto's Moss Park Armouries. (BELOW RIGHT) No one was more keen to serve in uniform than Jim Ronan, who registered at age 15, tried to get to Europe as a reinforcement at 17, got to Korea with the engineers at 20 and completed several peacekeeping tours in the Middle East. Pictured in Italy in 1963, on his way home, he held the rank of Warrant Officer II.

Though Roland Pearce (ABOVE LEFT) and Hal Merrithew (receiving medal) served together on the front line in Korea only briefly, the legacy of one night's action earned them medals and finally (LEFT) a reunion half a century later. Both tug pilot Walter Schierer (BELOW RIGHT) and Fred Sampson (in doorway), the glider pilot he towed to Normandy, almost bought it on D-Day; it took 60 years before each could tell his death-defying tale to the other.

(ABOVE) Just 22 days before the Second World War ended, Petty Officer Terry Manuel faced his greatest test of the war—surviving the sinking of his torpedoed minesweeper *Esquimalt* in the North Atlantic. (BELOW LEFT) Operating Room Assistant Tony Burns was in such pain from his wounds in Normandy in 1944 that he said, "I took the rosary my father gave me, covered my head with a blanket, and died." (BELOW RIGHT) When he leapt from the transport aircraft—on D-Day morning—paratrooper Jan de Vries remembered waiting for "an eternity" to land; in fact, it took a few seconds. Sixty years later, the French awarded him the Legion of Honour.

The principal objective of patrols in Afghanistan (ABOVE LEFT) was to root out insurgents. (BELOW) Canadian troops did not expect an F-16 laser-guided bomb explosion (taped-off area) during a training exercise at Tarnak Farm. For his quick response to the incident, medic Bill Wilson (RIGHT) and his team received citations from the Deputy Chief of Defence. Brian Decaire (ABOVE RIGHT) survived the friendly-fire attack and later, as a Search and Rescue specialist, received the Medal of Bravery at Rideau Hall in Ottawa.

(RIGHT) Jeff Peck admitted that army service in the Afghanistan war zone in 2002 changed him; he didn't realize how much, until he accompanied the body of a comrade along the Highway of Heroes (ABOVE) in 2007. (BELOW) Hon. Colonel of RCAF 412 Squadron Charley Fox and the author share a moment at the annual 78th Fraser Highlanders "Bear Hackle" award ceremony in 2008; both were previous recipients.

"'No,' she said. And the German who was holding her shot her.

"We gained our freedom, but Mother Traas, a mother of the Underground, was gone." Mac and many onboard the bus were in tears as he finished the story.

On the final night of our Holland tour, during our traditional Farewell Dinner, there were even more tears—some of sadness, some of joy. With 138 people seated at tables in the hotel's largest dining room, we had taken over the building. Again, I began the festivities by reflecting on some of the highlights of the tour—the veterans we had celebrated, the events in which we had participated, the civilians we had met, and the coincidences we had encountered. We soon discovered that our tour had one last secret to reveal. Among the last to offer his thoughts and gratitude for the tour was an elderly veteran from Quebec. Ron Charland had served in Holland as a sergeant with Le Régiment de Maisonneuve. Moustached and always smiling, Ron said he'd been wounded twice. He told me his body still contained pieces of shrapnel from the Scheldt campaign. He even carried one piece in his pocket, he said, for good luck. On several occasions during the tour, when he and I had spoken together, he had explained his utter surprise and delight that an entire population, every generation, could be so completely involved in this tribute to the Canadians who had liberated the country sixty years before.

During one of the major events our group attended, the Remembrance ceremony at Groesbeek Canadian War Cemetery, Charland had wandered toward the front-row seating reserved for Dutch and Canadian dignitaries as well as those veterans speaking or being recognized during the ceremony. An RCMP officer posted there inquired if Charland had a reservation for the VIP seating area. Of course, he didn't. But one of our tour guides, an energetic and bright young guy named Corne Bibo, solved Ron's seating problem. Bibo commandeered a wheelchair and rolled Charland to the very front "like a king" to join the VIP section for a close-up view of Governor General Adrienne Clarkson, Queen Beatrix, Princess Margareit, and Victoria Cross winner Pte. Ernest "Smoky" Smith.

Enjoying the VIP vantage point, however, was not the real reason that Ron Charland had come to Groesbeek. He had lost a close friend, Edouard Paquette, killed in Holland in January of 1945, and once the huge formal ceremony was over and most of the crowds had left Groesbeek cemetery, he wanted to share some quiet time at his pal's grave. For some reason, however, the grave was hard to find, even with the aid of the Commonwealth War Graves Commission locator book. Eventually, however, Ron found the grave.

"That's not all I found," he told the Farewell Dinner. "I could not believe my eyes. . . . Someone had already placed a Canadian flag on his grave. I said to myself, 'That flag looks odd. It looks as if it may have been coloured by a child.' I reached down and turned it over and found a message on the back . . . signed by Patrick, a Grade 3 student in Oshawa, Ontario. I was touched that a Canadian child would send such a wonderful message to my fallen comrade."

What Ron Charland did not know was that Patrick's message had arrived at Edouard Paquette's grave thanks to a fellow veteran on our tour, quite by accident. Following his visit to Juno Beach in 2004, Lorne Empey (and his wife, Dorothy Deluzio) conceived a way to involve school-aged children in these battlefield pilgrimages. After some searching, they approached the Grade 3 class of André Doiron (Dorothy's son-in-law) at Father Joseph Venini School in Oshawa to create flags and write messages to Canadian soldiers killed during the Second World War. One such message read:

"Dear Canadian Soldier, I am writing to thank you for sacrificing your life so that others could be free. You gave your life for people you did not know in a land far from home. Canadians will always be proud of you. . . ."

Lorne and Dorothy then carried the twenty hand-coloured Canadian paper flags with messages on the backs, each laminated by teacher Doiron, to Holland in 2005. They randomly placed the children's flags at each of twenty graves in Groesbeek cemetery, offered a silent prayer, and snapped a photograph of the flag and grave marker to take back to Canada. No camera could possibly have captured the gratitude in Ron Charland's face that evening at our Farewell Dinner. He was so moved by the child's apparently personal gesture to Paquette that he could barely stay on his feet.

"I stood there and cried," Charland told the tour group. "Then I thought my buddy wouldn't mind if I exchange this wonderful flag with one I was carrying. So, I took it . . . a memento I will cherish for the rest of my life."

Like so many of the unique gestures displayed during our return to Holland, the torch of remembrance had been passed from one generation to another. And it had moved each one of us to the core.

8

REUNION OF TWO

We were both in the right place at the right time. I didn't expect to find anything noteworthy standing in line at my local bank branch, that summer of 2003. About the only discovery I was likely to make at the teller's wicket was how much more I owed on my credit card than I expected. The queue slowly shrank. Ahead of me, just an older man and at the front of the line, a friend of mine from in town. He noticed me and asked what I was doing.

"Writing a book about Canadians on D-Day," I said.

"Big anniversary next year, I guess," he said.

"You're right. It's the sixtieth."

Then it was my friend's turn for service at a teller's wicket. That left only the older fellow and me. As we moved up in the queue, he turned to me.

"I was there," he said quietly.

"A veteran, are you?"

"I was there," he repeated and then continued, "on D-Day."

Coincidental encounters with witnesses to history, for me, are not unusual. Researching and writing non-fiction features, broadcast documentaries, and books over the years of my professional career, I've enjoyed my share. For instance, a chance meeting with former hockey commentator Howie Meeker revealed that he was on the ice with Bill Barilko the night the Maple Leaf hero scored his Stanley Cup–winning overtime goal in 1951. In a chat with former CBC TV producer Bob Jarvis, he explained that Gordon Lightfoot's legendary song "Canadian Railroad Trilogy" was born in a conversation Jarvis had with then prime minister Lester Pearson. And while researching international contacts and the Internet to track down artifacts and accounts of the battle of Vimy Ridge in April 1917, I discovered a unique one—a gavel carved from oak wood salvaged from the Vimy battlefield itself—was housed at the Masonic Temple in my own hometown.

Still, converting chance encounters into usable script is not always guaranteed. In particular, as I've explained before, getting a veteran to recount wartime experiences can prove impossible. When asked, "What did you do in the war?" most veterans of the First and Second World Wars and the Korean War, I've found, rely on surefire rules of engagement in an interview. They never tell the stories of death and devastation. They just tell the offbeat tales that are sure to leave their audience laughing about the insanity of it all.

To my surprise, however, when I asked the veteran I met in line at the bank that day if I could come by his home for a talk, he agreed.

"But I've never told my D-Day story to anybody," Fred Barnard said. "Not even my daughter."

It may seem facile, but I've found the secret to interviewing veterans (and for a half-dozen military books, that's nearly 3,000 interviews) is honesty and preparedness. I've learned not to rely on clichés, such as buying the vet a beer or two at the local Legion to loosen his tongue. More often, a quiet, one-on-one conversation (preferably at his home) revealed more than chatting over drinks. My experience suggested it was more productive to know the source and know the language of war. Before I visited Barnard, I learned that on June 6, 1944, when British, American, and Canadian troops launched the greatest amphibious invasion in military history, Barnard was a corporal in the Toronto-based Queen's Own Rifles of Canada regiment. I discovered that his company of assault troops went ashore at Normandy, France, in the first wave. They faced crack German troops entrenched in concrete bunkers, armed to the teeth and intent on throwing Allied invaders back into the sea.

Despite all that, when I visited Barnard at his home my first question was "What was it like growing up in east-end Toronto during the Depression?" An obvious icebreaker, it relaxed the man right away. It told him I wanted more than tales of blood and guts. It demonstrated interest in both the storyteller and the story. It also gave each of us a road map into the minefield of his emotions and horrific reminiscences. As well, by the time Cpl. Barnard had brought me back to the Canadian invasion area, code-named Juno Beach, on June 6, 1944, I knew that his kid brother Donald Barnard was just a few feet away in the same landing craft with him.

Not by accident, but by design. Unlike the American forces, which had encouraged commanders not to allow members of the same family to fight side by side,* in the Canadian forces a man could complete documents to "acquire" or transfer another family member into his regiment, indeed into the very same company or platoon. The Canadian Army considered it a morale booster that engendered solidarity and esprit de corps. And so, while there were three years' difference in the brothers' ages, Fred saw the commanding officer of the Queen's Own Rifles (QOR) and signed paperwork to transfer his twenty-year-old brother, Donald, into the QOR. The regiments were so community based, in fact, that not only were Donald and Fred Barnard on the same landing craft that June morning, so was Gord Arthur, a neighbour who'd grown up with the Barnard boys on Sutherland Avenue in East York, a borough of Toronto.

---

* During the war in the Pacific—on November 13, 1942—a Japanese submarine torpedoed and sank the light cruiser USS *Juneau* as it attempted to resupply Marines on the island of Guadalcanal. Five Sullivan brothers died in the sinking; the brothers had insisted on serving together despite a U.S. Navy article issued in July 1942 forbidding "commanding officers to forward requests from brothers to serve in same ship/station." In the Steven Spielberg movie *Saving Private Ryan*, a character implies that the so-called Sullivan law requires U.S. military authorities, following the deaths of three of four Ryan brothers in combat, to retrieve the surviving Pte. Ryan from Normandy. In truth, no regulation or legislation was ever passed following the loss of the Sullivans.

"As we were going down the ramp," Fred Barnard said in our conversation, "I yelled to my brother, 'Give 'em hell.' And the next thing I know I'm in four feet of water. . . . There were all these obstacles sticking up. And mines. And landing craft being blown up. . . . Bodies everywhere. Then I saw my brother Don . . . lying on his back as if he was asleep. There was just a black hole in his uniform right in the middle of his chest. No blood. He must have died instantly."

I've witnessed many grown men cry. Most vets feel no need to apologize. Perhaps having revisited the horror with someone they don't know but have come to trust, they feel no embarrassment. Unlike for a family member, the vet doesn't have to protect a stranger's emotions. Very often, however, there are tears on both sides of the microphone. What's more, in recent years, upon reflection many veterans consider dealing with war demons therapeutic. They view it as a chance to get distant, past events off their chest. And since most have a greater awareness of their mortality as veterans than they did at the time of their service in wartime, they feel they're contributing to historical record. In that sense, they are using the historian as much as the historian is exploiting them. They see the exchange as a fair bargain.

The day I visited Fred Barnard, he shared several hours of reminiscences. He pulled out a shoebox full of yellowing documents and pictures, including snaps of himself and Donald in army uniforms. He showed me the Canadian Pacific telegram his mother, Janet, received from the minister of national defence regretting "to inform you that B137985 rifleman Donald McKay Barnard has been officially reported killed in action sixth June 1944. Stop. If any further information becomes available it will be forwarded as soon as received." The shoebox contained his father's soldier service book from the Great War, magazine articles about the Queen's Own and its service on D-Day, and for a while it had also contained Fred's medals. But he'd recently decided to mount and frame them with a wartime portrait for the den wall.

"Thanks for listening to my story," Fred Barnard said, as I left his home that day.

"No," I insisted. "Thanks for stopping me in the bank."

Finding eyewitnesses to history in Canada, I've discovered, can be that coincidental. Reacquainting some veterans with their past can be equally coincidental and often cathartic. I'm sure not a day had passed in Fred Barnard's eighty-plus years that he didn't think of his younger brother Donald, lost on Juno Beach on the first day of the invasion. But I sensed that our chance meeting in the bank had also given him a convenient excuse to talk about Donald, and to state the importance of their sacrifice on D-Day. Our Saturday interview at his house and our sojourn through that worn old shoebox had been Fred's first lengthy reunion with Donald in a long time. I had perhaps just been the catalyst for this reunion of two.

There were *two* coincidental meetings between airmen Bill Davies and Frank Boyd. The first happened in 1943, on the Niagara escarpment just outside Hamilton, Ontario. It was midway through the Second World War when the demands of wartime aviation had transformed the tiny farm community of Mount Hope from a sleepy southwestern Ontario village into a virtual beehive of wartime activity. Each day the skies over No. 10 Elementary Flying Training School (EFTS) and No. 33 Air Navigation School (ANS)—both housed at Mount Hope—filled with scores of yellow-painted training aircraft. The drone of Fleet Finches, Harvards, and Ansons taking off and landing seemed relentless as hundreds of air force recruits in training—sprogs, as they were known—hustled from H-hut barracks to flightline and back learning the technologies and techniques of military aviation. And every few months (eight weeks for pilots, 900 hours for navigators) scores of leading aircraftmen—schooled in the ways of war in the sky—moved on to the next phase of the British Commonwealth Air Training Plan. The BCATP was Canada's largest Second World War expenditure.

Absent from the Second World War canon of Canadian military history, I sensed, were the extraordinary tales of young airmen who came to train from across the Commonwealth—Britain, Australia, New Zealand, Rhodesia, South Africa, India, and Canada—and their unheralded teachers, the BCATP instructors. In the late 1980s, I attempted to find some of these remarkable aviators, who not only knew how to fly or navigate military aircraft expertly, but who also knew how to pass that expertise on to others. The pressure on instructors to perform and cadets to achieve was palpable. If an instructor couldn't quickly get his sprog pilot to solo or his observer cadet to navigate in daylight, at night, in fair weather or foul, the system washed the student out, failed him. It was too expensive and too risky to do otherwise. Victory in the air over Europe, North Africa, and the Pacific demanded it.

In the spring of 1991, my search yielded two letters from Bill Davies in Toronto. He had attended an Aircrew Association of Canada meeting, at which I had requested members contact me with BCATP stories. Davies wrote that he was born in Liverpool, England, blessed with an aptitude for mathematics, and graduated with a degree from Leicester University. In 1941, he explained, he had enlisted in the Royal Air Force, crossed the Atlantic in the troopship *Queen Elizabeth*, and was first sent to No. 5 British Flying Training School in Clewiston, Florida, for pilot training. All went smoothly until word spread that Davies had shared a conversation with a black waiter in the dining hall, offered him tips, and even shook his hand when the man announced to Davies he'd been accepted into the U.S. Army and would be leaving the base. Davies got hauled up on the carpet before a bigoted British commanding officer at the Florida school.

"I received the biggest dressing down I had ever had in my life—I can vividly recall his spittle splashing onto my service shirt as his face was red and contorted with anger," Davies wrote. "I had stood for a few minutes shaking the hand of the black youth. . . . I was never formally charged. I was marched out and . . . within forty-eight hours given an unscheduled flight test and although I thought I did very well, was failed and washed out from further flying!"

Not dissuaded, Davies explained in his letter, he'd found his way to Mount Hope, where he began training to become a navigator. His aviation observer's career might well have ended equally unsatisfactorily, were it not for his encounter with a remarkably capable and understanding instructor. Frank Boyd had himself graduated from the BCATP in 1942, after training on Airspeed Oxford aircraft at the Service Flying Training School (SFTS) in Medicine Hat, Alberta. Instead of the hoped-for posting overseas to operational flying in the air war over Europe, like so many skilled graduates of the plan, Boyd went where the air force assigned him.

As a staff pilot for sixteen months at No. 33 Air Navigation School, Flight Sergeant Boyd flew several flights training navigators every day and clocked more than 1,200 hours in the air. Most combat pilots in Bomber Command or Fighter Command in Britain wouldn't accumulate half that much flight time. And while observer cadet Davies didn't previously know the experience level of his instructor F/Sgt. Boyd, he came to recognize it quickly on November 12, 1943. As a test of his navigational skills—using instruments and visual bearings—Davies was assigned to navigate a cross-country flight—from Mount Hope (100 kilometres west) to St. Marys (back 100 kilometres east) to Caledonia and (north 10 kilometres) home to the base—aboard a twin-engine Anson training aircraft with experienced staff pilot Boyd at the controls. His job was to simply fly the route given by student navigator Davies.

"We took off from base at Mount Hope at 0900 hours," Davies wrote. "After leaving St. Marys, we ran into a very heavy snowstorm and became hopelessly lost. F/Sgt. Boyd wasn't the slightest bit concerned as he growled to me: 'Let's go down to ground level and see if we can find a railway line.' Sure enough, down at almost nought feet we found our line. Following it at only several feet above the track, we quite suddenly encountered Caledonia railway station. I vividly recall looking *up* and seeing the huge sign sitting on the platform [of the station] reading 'Caledonia.'"

A month after this initial letter, Bill Davies invited me to lunch and a tour through the Victorian building that housed the Royal Canadian Military Institute (RCMI) on University Avenue in Toronto. In the RCMI's plush carpeted and dimly lit library on the second floor, Davies offered the postscript to his encounter with F/Sgt. Boyd. He told me that despite getting lost in that November snowstorm, he had eventually received his observer's brevet (graduated) at Mount Hope and survived the war, completing his tour of operational flights mostly with Pathfinder Force (PFF). These were the special squadrons of bomber crews organized in August 1942 to fly at low altitude in advance of the main bomber stream to locate and mark with flares the bombing targets for each nighttime operation.

Davies pointed out a volume on the subject on the library shelf—*Path Finders at War*, by British aviation writer Chaz Bowyer. The author claimed PFF crews were "perhaps the most experienced and highly trained within the Royal Air Force" and that its members faced terrifying odds against completing a full tour. A dedication inside the RCMI volume, signed by the author himself, congratulated "Flight Lieutenant W.I. 'Bill' Davies, DFC, who survived forty-three operational sorties serving with No. 156 Squadron PFF, RAF, due to the keenness and discipline of his bomber crew, to whom he remains ever grateful." Noting the Distinguished Flying Cross award, I offered congratulations to Davies too. He modestly accepted it, but refused to be called a hero. He reserved that designation for the man who'd introduced him to the tools of survival in the air, his one-time flying instructor.

"Heroes, such as the unflappable F/Sgt. Boyd, deserve a huge pat on the back," Davies wrote to me finally. "I wonder where he is today?"

That was the spring of 1991. My book on the subject of BCATP instructors, *Behind the Glory*, was published in the fall of 1992. Out of the blue, the following April in 1993, I received a letter care of my publisher at the time. The letter explained that the writer had been browsing through a bookstore where he had come across *Behind the Glory*. As veterans often do, the man turned to the index to see if there might be any references that rang familiar. Being an air force vet trained in Canada, he first checked the index reference for his SFTS location, where he'd received his wings. Moving on to his first posting, an air navigation school, he found the reference to Mount Hope and could hardly believe his eyes.

"I read 'the pilot flying the Anson was Flight Sergeant Boyd.' That was me!" he wrote. As modest as his former student Bill Davies, Frank Boyd went on to write, "At the time, I did not consider we did anything particularly spectacular. We only did the job we were given and that was to give student navigators and bomb-aimers the best training possible and when they got lost (which was not infrequent), bring them back safely to base."

That's when Frank Boyd decided to buy the book. He subsequently came down with the flu, he wrote, and that gave him ample time to read the book and to plan his next "target—a trip to Caledonia," the place he and Davies had found below the snowstorm in November 1943. He said he couldn't recall the exact location of the railway station in the town, so he turned to the navigator in his automobile passenger seat, his wife, and the two set about looking for the spot. They found a train station that had effectively been out of service for a decade. When they stopped for a look, he remembered the passage in the book, about Bill Davies looking *up* to see the sign on the platform, which was no longer there.

"I was, and still am, amazed at my nerve and audacity," Boyd wrote. But he wanted to see the sign Davies had seen in 1943. "There are trees which are higher than the station roof. And there is a pylon partly obscuring the only indication that the station is at Caledonia, namely the word 'Caledonia' painted on one end of the building. I must assume that the trees have grown or maybe have been planted, and the pylon erected since 1943, or else I wouldn't be typing this letter to you."

Frank Boyd explained in his letter that he'd left Mount Hope in 1944 and got a posting to No. 5 Operational Training Unit at Boundary Bay and Abbotsford, British Columbia. There, as a captain, he learned to fly B-24 Liberators and was finally sent overseas to the Far East, where he participated in operations against the Japanese until VJ Day in August 1945. The sentiment in his letter seemed to deflect Bill Davies's effusive commendation.

"If I was able to impart anything to any of the students who had to fly with me, which was of benefit to them in their service later, then I believe, like many others, that we made our contribution to winning [the war], whether or not they took part in actual operations." He signed the letter "former F/Sgt. Boyd."

Thus, the second coincidental meeting between airmen Boyd and Davies had occurred in my post office box. The moment I finished reading Boyd's letter I raced to contact Davies. He too found it difficult to believe the coincidence. Fortunately, Boyd lived in Hamilton and so the RCMI in downtown Toronto, once again, provided a perfect location for a reunion of two. It was the first time the two men had seen each other in almost fifty years. Hugs, looks of astonishment, and tears flowed as the once exasperated navigation student Bill Davies met the former "unflappable" F/Sgt. Boyd. I stayed a short while as the men began to lunch, but made sure there was plenty of time and space in the institute's dining room for the two men to shed the years together. And just remember.

On a midsummer's afternoon in 1997, I drove from my home near Toronto to Almonte, an eastern Ontario town, population about 4,000. Known principally for its large nineteenth-century woollen mills and for being the birthplace of James Naismith, inventor of the game of basketball, Almonte owed its name to a rather odd piece of military history. In 1856, town fathers—made up mostly of Irish immigrants—chose to honour a Mexican general, Juan Almonte, for championing independence in the face of American aggression.

In keeping with that tradition of paying tribute to singular acts of bravery in uniform, following the Great War, Almonte civic officials had erected a monument near the centre of town in memory of Lt. Alexander George Rosamond, a native son killed at Courcelette, France, on September 15, 1918. The cenotaph was further inscribed "to the men of Almonte, volunteers who fell for freedom." Following the Second World War, the town had further inscribed the cenotaph with the names of those killed between 1939 and 1945. However, it had inexplicably delayed adding the dates 1950 to 1953 to recognize those killed during the Korean War. On this cloudy and blustery July day in 1997, the town was correcting that oversight. It was rededicating the Almonte cenotaph as a tribute to Korean War veterans who'd come from across Canada and the United States for the ceremony.

"It's only fifteen years ago that a Korean War inscription was added to the National War Memorial in Ottawa," an attending politician admitted. "Originally designated as a UN police action, events in Korea are now generally recognized as wartime."

Following the ninety-minute ceremony, the veterans—numbering several hundred—were dismissed by the parade commander and given a few hours' break through the midday until a similar rededication ceremony at Carleton Place, about ten kilometres away. I took the opportunity to spend time with two of the Korean War veterans who had attended the morning ceremony. Jacques Boire, who lived in a walk-up apartment complex at the other end of Almonte, invited me to join him and a comrade-in-arms from the Korean War.

Less than two weeks from celebrating his seventieth birthday, Jacques Boire, or Jimmy as he suggested everybody knew him, had experienced close contact with Canada's wartime history from an early age. Boire's father had studied engineering at McGill University in Montreal and, upon graduation in 1917, made his way into the Royal Flying Corps, but a crash during flight training resulted in severe head injuries and he died in 1934 when Jim was only six. Three uncles had also served in the Great War, and two cousins were Second World War veterans. As a result, in July 1950, when Prime Minister Louis St. Laurent announced that Canada would raise a special force for Korea, Boire felt he should sign up. He shook his head and chortled, however, at his memory of the creation of the special force and its then nebulous mandate.

"St. Laurent came on [CBC] radio and said he had decided to send a brigade to Korea," Boire said. "At the request of the United Nations, it was to be called a 'police action.' I remember a cartoon in a British Columbia newspaper showing Canadian soldiers giving parking tickets to Koreans."

Boire had enlisted in 1949 and earned his commission in the reserve army. The following year, as a lieutenant, he transferred to the Royal 22e Régiment, the Vandoos, in time to help organize the

2nd Battalion, which was to be trained at Valcartier, Quebec, by 1st Battalion veterans, then made up principally of men with Second World War experience. Among them was Boire's apartment guest that day in Almonte, Hal Merrithew. Two years older than Boire, Merrithew had served with the Royal Canadian Regiment during the Second World War. It was hot inside Boire's downtown apartment, so both men had shed their blue blazers and I couldn't see Merrithew's ribbons to determine where or when he had served. So I asked.

"I joined in January 1944," he told me, "but we were in action for about three weeks before the war ended, maybe four weeks."

Merrithew may have served only a few weeks at the front, but it included fighting in Italy in March of 1945, then a rapid trans-Mediterranean passage to the port of Marseilles, a trek across France to Belgium, then to a reorganization point at the Reichswald Forest in western Germany, back across the Deventer River into Holland in time for the liberation in May 1945, and eventually to the North Sea port of Ijmuiden, where his battalion finished the war by disarming 25,000 Germans garrisoned in that town alone.

Post-war, as a civilian, Merrithew explained that he had studied at a business college. In the late 1940s, an accountant's wages weren't bad—$84 a month versus $79 the army was offering—but the army paycheque included clothing, food, and accommodation. Consequently, he re-enlisted, this time in the service corps, and became an instructor at Camp Borden in 1950 about the time the Korean War broke out. Even though some trainees at Borden were older and had veteran status, they soon noticed Corporal Merrithew's ribbons and respected his Second World War experience in Italy and Holland. They obeyed his drill orders on the parade square.

Except that as it turned out, parade work was the wrong kind of training for Korea. Even Merrithew admitted it was improper preparation. Given twenty-five men to supervise, however, Cpl. Merrithew put his charges through old-fashioned basic training the old-fashioned way—twelve hours a day, doing right turns or about-faces non-stop and then repeating the process the following day—to

Merrithew's satisfaction. For the veterans it was intended to restore the discipline they'd learned between 1939 and 1945; for the real recruits, basic training reduced everything to command and respond, so that if the order was "charge," everybody charged at the same time at the same speed and in the same direction, Merrithew said.

Boire came across his apartment kitchen with beers for the three of us. "I think it's the roboticizing of human beings," he chimed in. When he arrived at Valcartier to train members of the 2nd Battalion of the Vandoos in August 1950, basic training was the same sort of thing. He called it "the clock system." One hour he taught them map reading. The next hour it was parade drill. The next it was first aid, then a final hour practising on weapons. Then repeat all of it. Next day, it was the same routine, with the same hours dedicated to the same lessons with exactly the same instructors, because, Boire emphasized, "in infantry we have to order men to do what is against their nature, something that may cause death. Infantry must react regardless of danger or fear. It's the source of discipline."

"As it turned out," Merrithew interrupted, "Korea wasn't that kind of war. The First World War was not a 'charge' type of thing even when going over the top. It was basically defence. Korea was basically defence. The Second World War was 'charge' and not defence. But how did you know what Korea was going to be until you arrived there?"

The war had begun in June 1950 when a series of skirmishes across the 38th parallel border exploded into an all-out offensive by North Korean troops toward Seoul, the South Korean capital. That summer signatories to the United Nations charter, including Canada, responded to a Security Council resolution to repel the attack and to restore the border and international peace. The UN called it "a war of containment." But by the end of July, the North Korean advance had boxed three American and five South Korean divisions into the southeastern corner of the country near the port of Pusan. In September 1950, a lightning strike by U.S. forces behind North Korean lines at Inch'on triggered a hasty North Korean withdrawal and retreat back across the 38th parallel. And in what he called "a war for rollback," Gen. Douglas MacArthur ordered the advance of American troops to North Korea's very border with China, the Yalu River, which brought the Communist Chinese armies into the war. Momentum of fighting shifted rapidly southward again until April 1951, when Canadian troops moved into the line at Kap'yong, just above the 38th parallel, where they helped to halt a second North Korean invasion of the south. From that point, with MacArthur removed from the picture, UN Command desired "a war of stabilization." A year after its opening salvos, the Korean War front had returned virtually to where it began.

At that point, Hal Merrithew was still several months from receiving a commission (his lieutenancy) and his eventual posting to Korea in 1952. However, the status of the war was not high on his priority list. Gaining the confidence of the men in his command was more important. During that summer of 1951, as the Communists and the UN initiated the first peace talks at Panmunjom near the 38th parallel, Merrithew tried to build his collection of trainees into a cohesive platoon. Since he'd worked with most of them for months through basic training, he described a growing knowledge of his platoon's strengths and weaknesses, of its personalities. Before his men went into the front line, Lt. Merrithew understood which of his men could credibly lead and which would loyally follow.

"You get some devil-may-care guys, absolutely zero fear," he said. "You get other men who are afraid, but you can depend on them because they'll always do their job. The third type is cautious, hangs back on actions. . . . So you have to build your platoon with the fearless, the meek, and the cautious."

I had no idea commanding men could be so scientific. I had no idea this Korean War veteran would witness his science put to the test so seriously. Merrithew explained that as soon as his platoon of new recruits arrived from Canada, it was augmented by men partway through their overseas tours—Royal 22e soldiers with months of front-line experience in Korea, men willing to do the job, but not eager to take unnecessary risks. Merrithew didn't concern himself with that. The platoon's first assignment, it turned out, was minefield repair. In front of each UN defensive position of trenches, bunkers, dugouts on top and on the flanks of Hill 355, for example, Canadian troops maintained a zone of land mines. Around the minefield, pioneers (minefield specialists) had erected barbed-wire fences both as a barrier to enemy patrols and a warning to friendly patrols. Because Hill 355 had become such a vital vantage point in a war of attrition, it attracted plenty of incoming enemy artillery shells and mortars; consequently, pioneers frequently had to repair the minefield and its perimeters at night. This challenge turned out to be a watershed assignment for both the newly arrived lieutenant and his philosophy of command.

My interview with the two veterans in that Almonte apartment now took Hal Merrithew to the core of his Korean War memories. I needed to know how soldiers repaired barbed-wire fences around live mines, *in the dark*. Merrithew explained that each repair patrol began long before it entered the corridor that led into no man's land to the enemy side of the defensive Canadian minefield. Each soldier prepared lengths of new barbed wire—each strand four feet long, each with a loop on either end. Merrithew said he organized his patrol in two-man teams—a good leader and a good follower in each pair. Then when the patrol went to the outer reaches of the minefield barrier, a man finding a break would thread the broken strand through the end of the repair strand. He would hand the other end of the repair strand to his partner, who in turn would find the other broken strand, thread it through the eye at the other end of the repair strand, draw it tight, and wrap it back on itself to close the gap. Meanwhile, those men not repairing wire worked with a sergeant in the platoon manning a defensive position on the hill in case the patrol came under attack.

"All this was done without talking and in darkness where no one could see. You got to the point that you could do the repair almost as quickly as you could walk," Merrithew said. "You didn't have to give orders. If there was a bit of moonlight you could see that it was working. I just walked up and down the whole line keeping control of the operation. Knowing the men was why it worked so smoothly."

Merrithew added one other important ingredient to his regimen. The patrols went out into no man's land on average four times per week. Once every rotation—when every platoon member had taken his turn repairing wire or at the defensive position—the lieutenant took a turn at each as well. That way, Merrithew deduced, each soldier knew his commanding officer would not demand of his troops anything that he would not demand of himself. Each function of each night's operation was, as far as Merrithew could determine, understood by all men in his platoon—every man knew every other man's job. And each operation was balanced—the same complement of personalities existed among the wire repair team as among the hill defenders. Merrithew sensed that if anything unexpected happened, the strong would lead the meek through whatever the night action threw at them.

"Once you get into an operation," Jim Boire agreed, "it's often not the rank structure, but the natural leaders that take over."

It occurred to me that during the course of my interview with the two men, I had not asked them one of my pat questions: "When were you most afraid?" Merrithew had a pat answer: "If anyone said they went to war and weren't afraid, there's something wrong with them. You're always afraid, but you keep that fear under control. You have a job to do and you go do it."

During Merrithew's tour of duty in 1952, the peace negotiations seemed interminable and fruitless. Fighting in most sectors along the 38th parallel devolved from frontal attacks characteristic of the first year of the war, to skirmishes initiated from well-established trenches and live-in bunkers. The front-line routine of the war included duty at a listening outpost in no man's land or sending out small night patrols designed to reconnoitre what the other side was up to or to capture prisoners to yield similar information. Consequently, those Canadian troops assigned to listening-post duty—manning outposts in no man's land as an early warning device—ran the greatest risk of being overrun, killed, or captured by enemy patrols. Sitting and listening alone in the dark far from friendly lines, while vital, proved among the most fearful assignments.

Once again, Merrithew came up with a strategy to ease his men's fears. He turned to one of the most lethal and (according to the Geneva Convention) illegal types of land mines—the so-called bounding Betsys.

"I took two or three of these things," Merrithew said. "I placed them about fifty yards in front of every listening post and I hooked a piece of telephone cable to them. By pulling on the wire, a sentry could set off his own little artillery barrage out in front of his listening post along most of the logical approaches to our lines. . . . This made the troops feel much better about the listening posts. And we never lost another man as prisoner of war after that."

All his ingenuity had one significant drawback. Since these devices were illegal, and since Merrithew, his battalion commander, and the companies sending troops to the listening posts were the only ones who knew about them, when the Vandoos had to vacate the position (to be replaced by other UN troops), so did the improvised artillery. Removing bounding Betsys, however, proved more tricky than setting them. Often it meant crawling about on hands and knees feeling the way to the mines, disarming them with a safety pin, and excavating them from the ground, again at night. To add to the challenge, the night the Royal 22e Régiment was due to leave the front line, a light snow had fallen, so any physical landmarks to make the ground recognizable had disappeared under a blanket of snow. Even so, Merrithew managed crawl to the mine locations and disarm the explosives successfully at all outposts except one. Despite three attempts he couldn't locate the final outpost mines. He told his colonel, as the Vandoos left that morning, he would stay behind and disarm the last mine after sun-up.

"I went out at daylight," Merrithew recalled with horror, "and I found that I had crawled right over top of one of the mines. There were my prints in the snow—my hands and knees. I hadn't found the mine during the night, but I had actually straddled it without knowing it. I wasn't the least bit afraid out there doing that at night, but knowing how close I had come to death, then I became afraid. I actually became weak with fear."

He stopped the interview momentarily to regain his composure. I let his vulnerability pass. I changed the subject. We had much more to talk about, but clearly, we had tripped over more than the thought of that unexploded mine beneath the snow. Only later in the afternoon, at a community-sponsored reception, did I learn what had actually crossed Hal Merrithew's mind during our interview. Through the afternoon, as I watched the veterans do a second parade at the Carleton Place cenotaph acknowledging Korean War sacrifice, Jim Boire spurred my curiosity. As I said, I had not seen the collection of medals above the left breast pocket of Merrithew's blazer. Had I seen them, I would have noticed the blue and white ribbon from which hung a silver cross with Imperial Crowns at each tip and the Royal Cypher at the centre—signifying meritorious service by an officer in battle.

"You know he won the Military Cross in Korea, don't you," Boire said to me that afternoon. "You should ask him about it. It's quite a story."

I thought I had heard Hal Merrithew's death-defying story—growing weak at the thought of straddling an unexploded bounding Betsy that morning in the snow in front of Hill 355. He had hinted at it when he talked about training his platoon. He had introduced it when he described the work of minefield repair. He had given me a taste of coping with fear when he recalled sowing mines around outposts to ease anxious sentries. But what the veteran lieutenant had not given me in our first interview was the story of October 8, 1952. When I approached him again, pointed to the M.C. among his medals, and asked if he would share the story behind it, he led me to a picnic table a fair distance from the main community reception. We were well out of earshot when we finally sat down for him to recount that autumn night in Korea forty-five years before.

"I was in the command post. I was checking out an area for minefield repairs," Merrithew began. "As I explained to you this afternoon, I had my repair group all ready to go out. I was standing there when the colonel got a call from one of the forward companies. One of his [Canadian] standing patrols was returning and . . . had inadvertently walked into a [Canadian] minefield. A five-man patrol had gone through the fence. It was after dark and the colonel asked what we could do."

As quickly as any reflex in his body, Merrithew said he knew exactly where the minefield was and that he would lead a rescue party to retrieve the patrolmen who had mistakenly entered it. Moments later, the lieutenant had cancelled the night's wire repair operation. Then, with equal directness, he selected two men from his platoon to assist him in the rescue. Cpl. J.P. Roland Pearce, or J.P. as he was known, was twenty; he was average height and weight, shy, and soft-spoken—one of those meek types, Merrithew explained—but with plenty of explosives experience from his days inside the mines near his home in Sudbury, Ontario. The second man, L/Cpl. Dion, was heavier, taller, and more talkative than Pearce—one of those eager-to-volunteer types in Merrithew's command. These were the personalities and attributes he sensed he needed in such an emergency. Suddenly, the mind's-eye image of his two patrolmen overcame Merrithew. He stopped speaking, on the verge of tears.

"What could you see?" I asked trying to help him through the story.

"Nothing. I couldn't even see the ground," he said. "I stopped at the friendly side of the minefield. And I heard the moaning and crying [of the wounded men in the minefield]." Still fighting back his emotions, Merrithew described leading the protective party of six and the rescue team—Corporals Pearce and Dion—through the known gap in the minefield into no man's land to begin the rescue. In spite of the darkness and the massive nature of the minefield (defending as much as a kilometre or two of Canadian positions), Merrithew said he knew exactly where to enter the minefield. He said he talked his two corporals through the rescue in whispers. They reached the first mine and Merrithew—taking a few minutes to insert a safety pin before moving on—disabled it. They reached the location of the second mine, and Merrithew directed Pearce to find it and disable it. It took a little longer because Pearce tried to locate it with a metal detector and earphones, but there was so much metal debris in the ground from years of shelling that Pearce had to resort to probing the damp earth with his bayonet. Presently, he found the bounding Betsy, inserted the safety pin, and whispered back to Merrithew, "Disarmed." Then the lieutenant encountered the first casualty.

"He was dead," he said. "But you can't just grab a casualty, pick him up, and bring him out. You must search all around him to make sure he's not in contact or close to another mine. Otherwise you'd jeopardize the whole operation. We searched all around and found there were no other mines close by. And Cpl. Pearce and Cpl. Dion carried him out of the minefield. I told the stretcher bearer he was definitely dead . . . and moved him away where he couldn't be seen by the protective patrol. Nothing is worse to a man than to see a dead man, because he thinks 'That could be me.'"

To make an already tense situation more so, a member of the protective party told Merrithew he thought he heard movement out in no man's land. Possibly a Chinese patrol. The lieutenant radioed back to the command post asking for friendly artillery fire and machine-gun bursts over their heads to disguise their location and activity. As shells began exploding and tracers raked the lower slope beyond the Canadian pioneers, Merrithew sent Pearce and Dion back into the minefield to continue the rescue. They found a wounded patrolman; using the same precautions as before, they consoled him and brought him out safely. The third casualty they found was a dead patrolman. The fourth Dion and Pearce brought out alive, but he died of wounds within an hour. The fifth and final member of the ill-fated patrol, Pte. Albert Leclerc, lay farthest into the minefield. Cpl. Pearce needed more time than any of the others, Merrithew said, to bring him to safety. He paused.

"How long had the rescue taken?" I asked.

"About an hour and a half," Merrithew said. "But the job wasn't done. We had to re-arm the minefield. Put the mines back where they belonged. Put detonators back on them. It wasn't easy. I had never seen such a dark night in all my life. I couldn't even see the ground. Everything had to be done by feel. And I had two good men." He began to break down, unable to complete the thought. And I wondered out loud that maybe they had not survived the war, that Dion and Pearce had become casualties too.

"No," Merrithew said, trying to recover his composure. "They both got the M.M., the Military Medal. But the last time I ever saw them was about June of '53."

"What happened?" I asked.

"Well, they both got out of the army. And I stayed in. I just never saw them again."

I suddenly realized why this skilled and decorated veteran was so despondent. It wasn't because memories of the dead and wounded from that errant patrol haunted him, though they couldn't have been easy to forget. It had nothing to do with any fears of entering that live minefield on the darkest night he could ever remember in his life. No. The reason for his temporary breakdown was simply because the two young men with whom he had shared such a nerve-racking mission that night in Korea, the two men in whom he had such confidence for their skill and the balance of their personalities in carrying out that minefield rescue, had disappeared so suddenly and impersonally from his command. From his life.

"This past summer," Merrithew finally continued, "I went through Sudbury, Cpl. Pearce's home. I phoned every Pearce in the telephone book. But I couldn't find him. I suppose I should have done it forty years ago, but I didn't."

It was a story I had heard repeatedly from the scores of Korean War veterans I'd met in the 1990s. Very few of them received the heroes' welcomes that those returning in 1918 or 1945 did. No ticker-tape parades. No brass bands. No civic receptions. No passionate kisses in the middle of downtown streets—the way nurse Edith Shain and sailor Carl Muscarello had in that famous VJ Day photograph in New York City. No continuing friendships. By the time most Korean War veterans returned to cities and towns across Canada—as Hal Merrithew eventually did to the family farm on the Saint John River in New Brunswick—there was no finality or closure to the experience. I suggested to him that maybe it wasn't his fault for not trying to track down Pearce sooner. Maybe it was part of the legacy of the

Korean War, I said, "a war that never really ended, but just faded away."

"It did. It faded away," he repeated. "And friendships did too. Friends I had during the Second World War, I've been in contact with them ever since. But those men from Korea, I don't know. I can't explain it."

"When and how was the award presented?" I asked finally.

"It was awarded in March [1953]," he said, getting emotional again. "Got the Military Cross. I didn't expect anything. I didn't think I deserved any more than others. I can remember one of the young lads that night, said in very broken English, 'Sir, I know you'll save me.'" And he apologized repeatedly that he had cried in the interview. I thanked him for being so honest and thorough in his story. I appreciated how exposed he'd felt in telling me. We slowly walked back to the reception. I thanked Merrithew's Almonte buddy, Jim Boire, for the conversation that day and for the tip he'd given me to ask Merrithew about the M.C. I made sure I had their phone numbers and addresses for future reference and said my goodbyes to both men.

Exactly one week later, I met Jean-Paul Roland Pearce, the very same corporal who'd shared that rescue operation with Hal Merrithew in October 1952. It was the day before another dedication event, at which nearly 2,000 people would gather, this time, at a cemetery near Brampton, Ontario. The next day—Sunday, July 27, 1997—would mark the forty-fourth anniversary of the day the two sides in the Korean War agreed, not to end the war, but to cease hostilities. This anniversary and this event would bring many more dignitaries, more wreaths, another bugler to play "The Last Post" and "Reveille," more speeches, much pomp and circumstance. But as memorials go, this one would hold greater significance for Korean War vets in Canada than just about any other. It would be the inaugural unveiling of the Wall of Remembrance, a national monument conceived, financed, designed, and built by the Korean War veterans themselves. But that would come on Sunday. I had arrived on Saturday at an area sports complex, in search of veterans of the Royal 22e Régiment who had served in Korea. That's when someone pointed out Merrithew's courageous corporal.

"Are you Roland Pearce of the Vandoos?" I asked him.

"Yes," he said. "Joined in February 1951 in Toronto. Honourably discharged in 1953 . . . went back to the [INCO] mine in Sudbury. Stayed thirty-five years and retired in '89." He spoke English fluently, in short clipped sentences with a French accent.

"But you served as a corporal in Korea and got the Military Medal for a rescue in October 1952," I said, confirming I had the right man.

"That's right. Got a letter to go to Ottawa. I was allowed to take two guests—my mother and my fiancée. They put us up in a room and [we] went to the Governor General the next day. Vincent Massey presented it to me. Felt good . . . proud."

I couldn't believe the coincidence of this encounter. All I could think about was my visit with veteran Hal Merrithew the previous week. I kept seeing Merrithew's distraught face, hearing his sobs of frustration at never having had the chance to visit with Pearce or Dion to reflect on the dramatic minefield rescue they had experienced in Korea all those years ago. Nevertheless, I restrained my urge to blurt out that his former platoon commander wanted desperately to reconnect with him. First I wanted to hear Pearce's recollection of the minefield rescue story without his knowing I had Merrithew's account. Pearce talked initially about his family of four sisters and three brothers—one was wounded in Italy during the Second World War, another earned a Mentioned in Dispatches citation during the liberation of Normandy, and a third joined him enlisting with the Royal 22e Régiment and the special force bound for Korea in 1951. He described training at Valcartier, Quebec, a rough crossing of the Pacific in a troopship, and his arrival at the most contested front-line location in Korea, Hill 355.

"My sergeant took me to the trench and showed me a little dugout," he said. "'That's your home,' the sergeant said. And it was Christmas Day. . . . On the first night I began seeing things that weren't there. I saw something out there covered in snow. In my mind it was a Chink soldier crawling toward me. I stared at it and stared at it. The more I stared at it, the more it seemed like it was moving. But it wasn't. Next morning I got a close look at it and here was a stupid tree stump under the snow. Just your imagination."

"What did it mean to be a pioneer?" I asked.

"I worked with explosives, mines, and minefields," he said. "We laid mines with engineers. Sometimes we used to go with an infantry patrol to make sure they got through the minefield. I almost always worked at night."

Though the wartime technology and experiences were nearly a half-century old, Pearce recalled every detail. He pointed out the difference between anti-personnel mines—with a casing around the explosive and a prong with a trip wire that set it off—and anti-tank mines—large and round with enough explosive inside to break a tank's caterpillar track when it set off the mine. But the worst, he said, were the jumping mines, "with three little prongs and just barely covered with ground; if you stepped on one, you started a plunger which kicked the mine into the air before it exploded; that way it got more men."

This naturally led me to ask about the rescue in October 1952. He remembered the distress call that Merrithew received at the command post. He recalled accepting the assignment, like Dion, the moment his lieutenant approached the platoon for volunteers. En route to the minefield that night, he too had difficulty with the moaning of the wounded and dying men he heard. He knew how mines were sown into those minefields, every five or ten yards, and he had seen the damage they could inflict when Chinese Communist soldiers unwittingly entered the protective minefields and triggered bounding Betsys. He knew, he said, because when enemy patrols did set off the mines, it was his responsibility to retrieve the bodies and reset the mines. And even though every Canadian minefield had lists and precise diagrams of its contents, there was always the chance the records were incomplete.

"It was a pattern, eh," Pearce said. "Whoever laid the mines down might not care. You were never sure. It made you nervous and scared if you made the wrong move."

Because of my recent interview with Merrithew, the names of the rescued Canadian patrolmen were still fresh in my mind. I had also since found the official account reported by war correspondent Bill Boss. The Canadian Press reporter had focused on Cpl. Pearce's "cool nerves" and "deft work on his hands and knees" as the reason for the operation's success. In particular, Boss noted the rescue of Pte. Albert Leclerc, the patrolman who walked farthest into the field before someone triggered a bounding mine. When Pearce reached Leclerc, Boss reported, the man "froze where he fell, [keeping] one leg a few inches off the ground for an hour." I asked Pearce what had happened during that fifth and final rescue.

"There was a mine underneath him," Pearce said. "When I got to him, I talked to him, said it would be okay. I don't know how he did it, but he kept his leg in the air until I found the mine, defused it, removed it and then raised him up to follow me out. But there was no way he was going to walk and he panicked. So I put him over my shoulder and carried him out."

As in my conversation with Merrithew and Boire the week before, I asked Pearce about the fear factor. Pearce said he was more distracted by the friendly fire of machine guns and artillery shells streaking out into the darkness of no man's land. Working in total darkness, his eyes got used to the absence of light. He feared being blinded by the exploding shells down the slope of Hill 355. He strained to remain in tune with his other senses—hearing and touch—to guide him to the wounded patrolmen and the buried mines. After midnight, when the rescue mission and reactivating of the mines were complete, he tried to sleep. But in his mind he kept revisiting the minefield, the dead patrolmen, and the wounded ones he'd retrieved. And he thought about his rescue mates, Dion and Merrithew.

"I liked Merrithew," Pearce said finally. "He was a gentleman officer. He never tried to be the boss. Most of the men [in the platoon] were pure French, spoke no English. Merrithew spoke both. I used to go and sit and talk with him in English because he was often alone."

It seemed the perfect moment to tell Roland Pearce about the coincidence of our meeting. I explained that I had spent the previous

Saturday in Carleton Place, seated across a table from Lt. Merrithew. I said that now I had heard the 1952 rescue story twice in precisely the same sequence, his description nearly word for word the same as Merrithew's. He shrugged my amazement off as if to say, "Why would it be any different?" But I insisted that he speak to his former platoon commander as soon as possible. In fact, I took Pearce to a phone booth in the sports complex, used my credit card to phone Merrithew in Calabogie, Ontario, and announced to him on the phone that I had just met the Cpl. Pearce he'd described to me last weekend. And I handed the phone to Pearce. Much as I wanted to, I didn't eavesdrop on their conversation. When I saw Pearce the next day at the opening of the Wall of Remembrance in the Brampton cemetery, I asked how their chat had gone. He smiled and said they'd agreed to get together finally. Indeed, they met—for their reunion of two—during the Korea Veterans Association national convention at Ottawa in 2000.

On the sixth of June in 1969, I finished the last newscast of an overnight radio shift. It was just after 5 a.m. Those few listeners awake in Lindsay, Ontario, that Friday morning heard my report on the major stories of the day—a Mexican airliner crash, the countdown to the launch of Apollo 11 and plans for the first moonwalk, Richard Nixon announcing the withdrawal of 25,000 troops from Vietnam, Joe Namath quitting football, and observance of the twenty-fifth anniversary of D-Day.

Within minutes of my sign-off, there was a knock on the radio station front door. As I was alone in the building at that hour, I answered the door myself. Standing in the bright sunshine, saluting me, was a middle-aged man in full military uniform. He greeted me curtly, but politely.

"The Canadians have landed on Juno Beach," he announced to me.

Clearly, the events of June 6, 1944, had so affected the man, he probably relived that moment every year. Out of respect, I listened and said nothing. From the ribbons and medals on his chest I recognized he truly was a Second World War veteran and could well have dashed onto the beaches of Normandy a quarter century earlier. I'm sorry now that I didn't invite him into the radio station to recount his wartime experiences into a tape recorder. I wasn't—in my first year on the air—as inventive or as confident a broadcaster as I later learned to be, or else I might have led my unexpected veteran guest to an on-air microphone to tell my modest morning audience that day about his wartime experience. But I did not.

The encounter did, however, whet my appetite for veterans' stories, in particular, stories from those who'd witnessed or indeed participated in seminal Canadian moments, such as the wartime invasion of France. From then on, whenever I met other D-Day veterans, I always made time for them. I never tired of their landing stories from June 6, 1944. Every time I discovered another one, I remembered my unrequited moment with that unknown soldier at the front door of the Lindsay radio station and made an extra effort to meet him and listen to his recollections. That's why, in December 2002, when I heard about a D-Day glider pilot named Fred Sampson, I didn't waste any time contacting him and requesting an interview.

My first reaction to the veteran I met at his Port Hope, Ontario, apartment that chilly December day was to wonder how he'd become a pilot at all. He stood six-foot-five inches tall, barely able to make it under the doorway lintels in his apartment; I couldn't imagine him fitting into a wartime cockpit of any description. But with that first twinkle in his eye—a signal to any journalist that an interviewee has a library of juicy memories to offer—Fred Sampson launched into a classic Second World War enlisting tale. In December 1940, Sammy (as he was known) had made full use of his physical attributes to enlist underage.

"I couldn't get into the RAF, my first choice, because you had to have your birth certificate and I had to falsify my age," Sampson said. "So I went to an army recruiting place in Worthing, West Sussex.... I was tall, so I looked older than 17.... The recruiting officer asked my date of birth. So I said, 'May 16, 1923,' and he said, 'You're too young.' I said, 'How old do you have to be?' He told me eighteen.

So I walked around the block and came back in and said, 'I made a mistake. I was born in 1922.' He said, 'Okay.' And I joined the army."

Service in the Royal Sussex Regiment was fine for a time, but since Sampson's father had served with the Royal Flying Corps in the Great War, flying was Fred's real objective. In 1942, he learned that the British Army needed recruits for its Glider Pilot Regiment. He quickly applied and arrived for basic training at historic Salisbury Plain, "with Stonehenge for a backyard," in the south of England. The training proved rigorous (every order had to be carried out in double-quick time); the instruction was comprehensive (recruits learned engineering, gunnery, mortars, and parachute jumping); and the discipline bordered on anal (everybody slept in tents, but had to have a crease in his trousers the moment he got up in the morning). This was the Glider Pilot Regiment's method of weeding out the weak and ultimately creating "the total soldier" to fulfill any role on the ground at the front line once the pilot had landed his glider. However, although his height had helped him get by the recruiting officer in 1940, it played against him during his first days at Salisbury Plain.

"The commander of the glider pilots was George Chatterton, a Napoleonic character," Sampson said. "When we were first inspected, I was a corporal. A buddy of mine was also a corporal, tall, but not as tall as me (the taller ones always go to the right when you stand in ranks). So Chatterton [announces], 'You're only allowed to be six-foot-three. You can't be taller because of cockpits.' Of course, I'm six-foot-five. And he's in front of my buddy and he says, 'How tall are you, corporal?' 'Six-three, sir,' he said. And I thought, 'You bastard. I've got nowhere to go because I'm taller.' So Chatterton got to me and said, 'How tall are you, corporal?' I said, 'Six-foot-two-and-a-half.' And he said, 'That's the tallest six-foot-two-and-a-half I've ever seen in my life.' Forever after that, even when I got my wings [graduated], whenever he saw me, 'Still six-foot-two-and-a-half, sergeant?' 'Yes sir!'"

Fred Sampson's height, although incidental to his life otherwise, continued to play a key role in his fate in uniform during the war.

It had initially boosted his entry to the army, then nearly got him washed out of the Glider Pilot Regiment, but once inside the cockpit of his Horsa glider on active duty, Sammy's long arms and legs, I discovered, helped to save his life and those of his military passengers during his first critical glider mission on D-Day.

Though gliders were a major component of the initial early morning landings on June 6, 1944—delivering the 6th British Airborne Division, the 82nd and 101st U.S. Airborne Divisions, and the 1st Canadian Parachute Battalion to secure strategic locations on the flanks of the invasion beaches—they also capped the day's action. The evening airborne operation, code-named "Mallard," launched more gliders full of paratroops and stores to reinforce all of the advanced airborne positions inland from the coast. Fifteen squadrons of fighter aircraft would escort the multi-engine tug planes (Stirlings and Halifaxes) as they towed gliders (Horsas and Hamilcars) over the Channel and released them to come down at landing zones on the Normandy farmland north of Caen.

During his pre-flight briefing at Keevil aerodrome in south-central England, Sampson said he and the rest of the glider crews had examined reconnaissance movies, survey maps, and models of the French landing zones. Among other things, aerial photography revealed a landing-zone feature that had given Sampson pause. As part of their invasion deterrent, the Germans had erected anti-glider poles, which the Allied airmen nicknamed "Rommel's asparagus." The glider pilots were told these wooden poles, about the height and width of telephone poles, filled many of the open fields north of Caen. They were also informed that the paratroops already on the ground D-Day morning would destroy them by the time the Operation Mallard gliders arrived in the evening. In the final briefing, just before the operation, Sampson met the pilot who would be tugging his Horsa to France. Sampson said he thought his name was Bob.

For the evening mission on June 6, Sampson explained, he would pilot his glider loaded with a six-pounder anti-tank gun, a padre, his jeep and trailer, a signals officer, and five troops to a controlled crash landing in France. His four-and-a-half-ton Horsa fully loaded weighed eight and a half tons. Fred itemized his carry-on equipment for me: five francs (so-called "escape" money), a silk map sewn inside his uniform, a state-of-the-art Swiss watch, an American carbine, a rucksack with survival gear and grenades and, though it was against the Geneva Convention, a fixed-blade commando knife strapped to his thigh.

H-Hour for Operation Mallard takeoff was 7 o'clock. When it was their turn, Sampson's tug plane, a Stirling, taxied to the centre of the runway. With the one-inch-thick hemp tow line (containing an intercom for cockpit-to-cockpit communication) already attached to Sampson's Horsa, the tow plane accelerated down the runway. A green light at the end of the runway signalled that the tow line was taut and the glider was actually in-tow. Before long, the tow plane and Sampson's glider had climbed to join the rest of the armada for the trip to Normandy. It would be daylight until well after the operation was complete, two hours later.

The formation crossed the Channel three abreast and about 500 feet apart. The pairings of tugs and gliders levelled off at 3,000 feet travelling at about 165 miles per hour. Sampson recalled the weather was clear and winds calm. Closer to the invasion beaches, the formation dropped to under 1,000 feet. Minutes after crossing the coastline, at about 800 feet, Sampson spotted his landing zone and prepared to disconnect his Horsa from the tow line. Sampson remembered calling out on the intercom, "Cheerio," to his tug pilot, Bob, which elicited a "Good luck, Sammy," just before he released the glider for its descent to the landing zone.

Sampson drifted slightly below the tug plane and looked down to plan his descent to the landing zone. In the instant he looked away, however, the sky ahead of him suddenly filled with an unexpected obstacle: the first of the Stirling's payload, twenty-six steel containers, was falling and the containers' parachutes were opening directly in Sampson's glide path. Apparently, the tug plane's bomb-aimer, anxious to complete the next phase of the mission, had opened the Stirling's bomb-bay doors and released all of the forty-gallon canisters. Sampson had no choice but to dive and bank away from this deadly obstruction. In seconds, however, his Horsa glider had dropped to less than 200 feet above the landing zone. Then Sampson saw them: Rommel's asparagus dead ahead.

"Beautifully lined up like German soldiers," Sampson remembered. "So I thought, 'I've got to go. I'll line up and put the fuselage [of the glider] between the lines of poles. I'm going to lose my wings, no doubt about it, but keep my speed and keep going.' Suddenly, I see along this beautiful line of poles, there's one out of place, right in the middle of my path. I remember thinking, 'Who the fuck put that one there?' And I burst out laughing realizing what I'd just said to myself. My second pilot thought I'd gone off my head. I figured the poles were so well lined up, if I go forty-five degrees, they'll be lined up with an opening between them too."

Rapidly altering the direction of an engine-less aircraft is difficult at the best of times. But fully loaded, with 17,000 pounds of dead weight behind him, virtually no altitude at his disposal, and with conditions demanding a perfect turn with pinpoint accuracy between obstacles that could dash his wooden glider to smithereens in seconds, Flight Sergeant Sampson needed something more in his pocket than French francs and a commando knife.

As we sat in his apartment, Fred Sampson became more animated with each step of the story. By the time he reached its climax over Rommel's asparagus, he was standing up in the middle of his living room re-enacting his emergency manoeuvres in the cockpit of the Horsa. I realized here was one moment in his military career when his six-foot-five stature proved a blessing. With all the strength he could muster, but with the added leverage and extension of his non-regulation long arms and legs, Fred said he nearly stood on his rudder pedals and yanked on the control column in front of him to redirect the Horsa forty-five degrees to the right and into a new gap between the rows of poles. Then, with the wings of the glider disintegrating, he said he turned to his brakes to try to bring the fuselage of the Horsa to a full and safe stop.

"When we touched down, we were going eighty miles an hour," Sampson concluded. "With differential braking, I managed to keep the fuselage straight. The wings were just shorn right off. Miraculously, nobody was hurt. When we finally stopped, we dropped the tail off right away and unloaded the jeep, the trailer, the anti-tank gun, and troops. The men were all congratulating me. 'Marvellous landing,' they said. 'Any landing is marvellous under those circumstances,' I said."

With his passengers disembarked and on their way to their own land objectives, Fred Sampson's only remaining job was to retreat on foot to the beach, find a landing craft bound for England, and return to his glider station as quickly as possible. Forty-eight hours after he'd crash-landed in Normandy, Sampson was reunited with his tug pilot back at Keevil station in Salisbury Plain. Since the tug pilot was an RCAF officer, F/Sgt. Sampson was not allowed to share a drink with him in the officers' mess. Despite the near miss when the Stirling's bomb-aimer decided to drop the fuel canisters prematurely, however, Sampson thanked his tug pilot, Bob, for delivering his glider to the landing zone. As a token of his gratitude, Sampson took the fixed-blade commando knife still strapped to his leg and gave it to the RCAF airman. Sampson went on to a regimental commission, additional glider operations (including Market-Garden, flying the British Airborne over the Rhein River bridge at Arnhem, the "bridge too far" operation), and finally a posting to India and Burma until the United States dropped atomic bombs on Japan in August 1945.

He never saw Bob again.

That's because Bob wasn't really Bob at all. After my lengthy conversation with Fred Sampson, I felt compelled to find his tug pilot, if he was still alive. It took a few weeks, but I learned that his real name was Walter Schierer. I managed to trace the veteran RCAF pilot to Vancouver. When we spoke on the phone, I asked him to clear up the mistaken identity issue; why did Fred know him as Bob, when he was actually Walter?

No, Schierer said, Bob wasn't a nickname. He had used it to falsify his records. Just like Fred Sampson, Schierer needed help to wiggle his way into the services. Born and raised on a mixed farm outside Ponoka, Alberta, Walter had finished high school in the mid-1930s, travelled with his family in the United States for a while, worked his way up from baker to assistant chef at a hospital back home, and in 1940 decided to volunteer for the army before the army conscripted him. In truth, he really wanted to join the air force. The problem he faced, however, was how to get out of the army. Easy enough, he calculated.

"I knew a guy in Ponoka who had the qualifications," Schierer told me. "I mean, he had Grade 12 and I even knew his mother's name before she got married. So I sat down and wrote this letter to the department of education and the department of vital statistics. Could I get a copy of *my* birth certificate? Sure enough they sent me the stuff for Robert Holmes. Holmes was a good friend of mine, blind as a bat. So there'd be no way he'd ever get into the service. So I just joined [the air force] under an assumed name."

Walter Schierer became Leading Aircraftman Bob Holmes and went through the entire British Commonwealth Air Training Plan in Canada using his assumed name, until he graduated and received his wings in October 1942. That's when Flying Officer Bob Holmes's conscience got the better of him. He confessed to his commanding officer and legally changed his identity back to Walter Schierer before going overseas that winter. Throughout 1943, Schierer built up his flying hours doing operational training at stations around the United Kingdom. He was finally sent to a Heavy Conversion Unit and learned to fly the four-engine Stirling bomber, which turned out to be the best powered aircraft for tugging Horsa gliders. Beginning in February 1944, F/O Schierer flew more tugging exercises than just about anything else, sometimes three lifts a day. It was clear, in addition to the frequent supply drops he made that winter and spring, that towing gliders would become his primary role as the invasion plan evolved. For D-Day, Schierer was teamed up with Sampson, but since most of Schierer's RCAF mates still knew him as Bob, that's what Fred called him.

This story seemed more attractive than I ever could have imagined. There are few moments in the researching and writing of history as delicious as having two eyewitnesses to the same event.

Often I had enjoyed the opportunity of interviewing two men from the same regiment who recalled a specific military engagement. Occasionally, I found veterans from the same squadron, tank troop, warship, or medical unit offering similar but rarely exactly the same impressions. Generally, when I needed additional verification for the details of battles or sections of battles, however, I would turn to official war diaries (assembled and published by the military unit itself) as a cross-reference to the veterans' anecdotes. But because, as one veteran once told me, "war is the six feet in front and on either side you," finding two witnesses to corroborate the details of a precise event I've found is nearly impossible.

Consequently, when I realized I had two pilots who were literally tied together for Operation Mallard on D-Day evening, I wondered whether I could reunite them, in effect put them in the same room to retell their experiences side by side. I presented the proposal to Walter, who had the economic means and free time to fly across the country from Vancouver to Toronto. He was also eager to rendezvous with his glider pilot partner, Fred. The date was set. Walter purchased the airline ticket and flew to Pearson International in late February 2003. I met him at the airport, drove him to Fred's apartment in Port Hope, and reacquainted a man who'd lied about his name with a man who'd lied about his age—both in 1940—to get into the services.

Again, the moment of first contact at Fred's apartment door after so many years was powerful and tearful. It didn't take long for Walter to feel comfortable at Fred's apartment. Bachelor veterans have simple tastes and keep only the belongings they really need close by. Fred's den, for example, much like Walter's, was full of history books, war documentaries, some framed photographs, and a few mementos. Once he had given his guest the tour, Fred took his favourite chair in the den and invited Walter to a second. I rolled the audio tape and steadily moved the two veterans to June 6, 1944. I learned, among other things, that Operation Mallard (the mission the two shared) was actually Schierer's second sortie of D-Day. Just after 1 o'clock in the early morning of June 6, he and his five-man crew had flown their

"J for Jig" Stirling to a drop zone near Caen in the British Airborne sector. In the dark, they had safely dropped twenty British paratroopers and at about dawn were returning to their station at Keevil aerodrome in south-central England.

"I was coming back when the Americans were going in," he said. "They were dropping gliders in Cherbourg when I turned for England. And their stream still hadn't cleared the English coast when I arrived back in England. . . . It was the greatest armada I'd ever seen.

"We'd just got back from dropping the paratroopers. We'd had a couple of hours' sleep and then I'm back at the station again to be briefed on the glider tug operation. I was dropped off at my aircraft and happened to say to the guy that's bombing up [loading the aircraft with its payload], 'What're you putting up there?' He said, 'I wouldn't want to be flying *this* one. The guy has twenty-six canisters of gasoline.'"

That's how Fred Sampson first learned how dangerously close he'd come to buying it over Normandy. The canisters that appeared in his windscreen, moments after disconnecting from Schierer's tow plane, each contained forty gallons of gas. On the ground they would offer a re-supply of fuel for the British Airborne at the end of Day One of the invasion. In the air they nearly brought down Sampson's Horsa. Schierer had no explanation as to why his bomb-aimer released the canisters so quickly. He said he remembered cutting back on the Stirling's power after the glider release to allow the bomb-aimer to complete his job that day. Schierer said he didn't realize how quickly the canister drop had happened.

"Oh, it was quick," Fred interjected. "I said, 'Cheerio.' I heard, 'Good luck, Sammy,' come back, and I suddenly see the containers coming at me. Jesus Christ, the chutes developed quickly."

"He was supposed to wait a minute or so," Schierer said.

"I think he was a bit jittery. We all were," Sampson added.

Schierer nodded in agreement, but then pointed out that the rest of his trip, like Sampson's, was no picnic either. Following the notorious gas canister drop, Schierer maintained his 800 feet of altitude and then manoeuvred his Stirling just to the right of his wing commander to fly in formation for the trip back to England. Their flight path toward the Channel took them across the coastal village of Lion-sur-Mer, in fact, directly over the steeple of the community cathedral. Sensing that his wing commander hadn't left enough room for both aircraft to pass comfortably to the left of the church spire, Schierer veered to the right of it.

"The Germans had a gunner up there," Schierer said. "He couldn't fire at the other planes because the church building was in the way. So when I came to the right side, did he ever go after me. He had 1-mm cannon. Thank God for Seedhouse, my gunner. He could see the guy shooting at us because of the tracer bullets and he was giving me directions. 'Go down. Right up. Left down,' he's screaming to keep us away from the bullets. But we did get hit down the port side.

"We got out of there, but the guy behind me, you'd think he'd seen what was happening and would fly somewhere else. But he just came stooging along and the guy in the steeple shot him down. He must've killed the pilot, because the plane gradually rolled over, left wing down, and went straight into the sea. Everyone was lost."

Nor were Schierer's troubles over once he reached the Channel. Several of the remaining Stirlings in the squadron saw Schierer take the cannon shots in the engine and moved in around him for protection as he made his way back across the Channel. He seemed to be struggling to keep the aircraft straight and level, but figured it better to bail out over friendly territory than to ditch in the sea. Schierer managed to fly directly northbound for the British coast and straight home to Keevil. Only when he throttled back on his final approach did the stricken Hercules engine not respond. He shut it down and landed on three engines.

"When we got down and looked, there were one hundred and forty-two bullet holes in the plane," Schierer said. "The anti-aircraft shells had blown three cylinders (of fourteen) right off the top of the engine and it still ran all the way home. I flew twenty-two missions . . . and it's only when I have time to think that I realize how scared we were."

Walter Schierer and I both turned to Fred Sampson as if to ask, does that compare with the crash landing among Rommel's asparagus? Was he afraid he wouldn't make it down between the poles in that Normandy field? In fact, of the 240 glider pilots on Operation Mallard that evening, thirty-nine were killed during the landings or attempting to make their way back to the beaches. Still, the RAF planners considered the operation "singularly successful" because ninety-five per cent of the gliders reached their landing zones. Fred said he recalled his sleepless nights inside the security wire at Keevil station before the D-Day mission.

"The reason I didn't sleep any of those nights," he said, "I wondered if, on the mission, I was going to be a coward."

Our three-way conversation continued through most of that February morning. For a break, we ventured out on that winter's day to a main street restaurant in Port Hope. We shared a lunch and more stories of their lives since the war. The two veterans laughed over hijinks experienced with other aircrew, who survived full tours—upwards of forty and fifty missions. They lamented over the seemingly endless list of others who didn't come back. The end of my part in the Schierer-Sampson reunion was approaching. The two men had planned several more days of reminiscing together.

Before I left, Walter Schierer had one more loose end to tie up. Back at Fred's apartment he retrieved a wrapped package from his suitcase, a gift in return for the hospitality of his one-time glider pilot partner. Fred Sampson unwrapped the gift quickly. There were a few more tears. Walter was returning it to its rightful owner, Fred's commando knife, the one he'd given his tug pilot in gratitude for a successful D-Day operation, fifty-nine years earlier.*

---

* I visited Walter Schierer in Vancouver in the spring of 2004 when his remembrances of D-Day were published in my book *Juno*. Fred Sampson joined me that same spring for a trip to Normandy in tribute to the sixtieth anniversary observances of D-Day in France. Walter—the tug pilot—died after a battle with leukemia and pneumonia, on February 2, 2005. Just weeks later, on March 12, 2005, Fred—the glider pilot—died of respiratory complications and pneumonia.

D-Day veteran Fred Barnard and I have often been reunited since our chance meeting in that queue at the bank in 2003. When I launched my book about D-Day at an event in the town where he and I live, Fred attended. When I pointed him out in the audience and asked that he be acknowledged, he said he first felt embarrassed, but eventually proud of his, and his brother Donald's, service in Europe. Each year when June 6 comes along, I make sure I buy him a beer at the local Legion and at least once during that meeting, I say "Thank you." In 2007, we came together again thanks to none other than President Jacques Chirac. In his annual announcement of military awards, the French president informed Fred Barnard by letter that the French Republic was naming him "Chevalier de l'ordre national de la Légion d'Honneur."

"Why me?" Barnard asked.

"For the exemplary and outstanding behaviour you demonstrated during the fierce battles of the liberation of France and Europe," Chirac's letter went on. "By awarding you such a high distinction, France wants to honour a great Canadian soldier who fought for freedom. This is an achievement you can be proud of."

The presentation of the medal took place at the Moss Park Armoury in Toronto on March 28, 2007. I attended and watched as Fred Barnard and five other Canadian veterans—Barney Danson, Jim McCullough, Art Boon, T.J. Bennett, and William Hale—received the Legion of Honour from French ambassador Daniel Jouanneau. At the reception following the presentations, the ambassador's wife approached Fred and congratulated him. She explained that she wasn't alive when Canadians liberated her country, but she had learned what they did. She kissed him on both cheeks and thanked him for the gift of her freedom.

Taking a glass of imported Calvados, the potent liquor that grateful French citizens had shared with their liberators in 1944, Fred Barnard toasted another evening of incredible memories. Later in the spring of 2007, I got together with the Legion of Honour winner and I presented him a picture of his brother Don Barnard's gravesite, just up from Juno Beach where he'd been killed on D-Day. I had travelled to Normandy, placed a Canadian flag at the base of Don's headstone in the Beny-sur-Mer war cemetery, and photographed it for Fred. I thought how far our friendship had come since meeting by coincidence in that bank queue in 2003.

9

"NO ARMOUR AGAINST FATE"

FATE—or destiny or kismet or chance or fortune or luck—isn't known for dealing impartially with all mortals. It is perhaps just as true in peacetime as in wartime, but in wartime the stakes are higher. In nearly thirty years of interviews and correspondence with veterans, I've listened to scores of near-death war stories. Of course, as a journalist and historian I expect them. I even encourage them. But without exception whenever they come, I find myself as unsettled by hearing them (and seeing them in my mind's eye) as the veteran retelling them. Each tale inevitably ends with the storyteller shrugging off his own survival as accidental, the luck of the draw—or just fate.

In 1994, I was in Ottawa, sitting in the basement family room of a former Royal Canadian Navy petty officer. During several hours of conversation, Terry Manuel offered his own accounts of the Battle of the Atlantic, which he characterized as "the longest and most deadly of all [Second World War] battles." I learned that the most deadly for him occurred during the early spring morning when his navy minesweeper, HMCS *Esquimalt*, was sunk by a single U-boat torpedo amidships. The Bangor-class sweeper sank in just four minutes, drowning twenty-seven of Manuel's crew mates. The next seven hours of exposure to the icy Atlantic elements killed another eighteen men. Manuel, one of twenty-six survivors picked up by sister sweeper HMCS *Sarnia*, remarked on the irony of it all: sunk just fifty kilometres from Halifax harbour, on April 16, 1945, three weeks short of VE Day, the end of the war. The lifelong mariner said he could never express adequately his good fortune nor "the full horror of the suffering, the discipline, unselfishness and bravery shown . . . that unforgettable day in the water."

When I met Newfoundlander Hubert Thistle, in 1993, he frankly considered nearly all of his years since 1944 as gravy. Just twenty when he came ashore in Normandy as a wireless radio operator inside a Sherbrooke Fusiliers tank on D-Day, Thistle described his first day in France as uneventful. June 7 proved fairly routine too, until about noon, when his column of Fusiliers' recce tanks supporting North Nova Scotia infantry entered the village of Authie. There, German 88-mm guns found their mark, disabling Thistle's tank. He managed to escape the burning armoured vehicle but was taken prisoner by members of the 12th SS Panzer Division, whose ranks included crack troops of the Hitlerjugend, under the command of Col. Kurt Meyer. At Abbaye d'Ardenne, the fanatical Hitler youth soldiers stripped Thistle and a hundred other Canadian POWs of their watches, cigarettes, and papers and began executing their captives. They shot twenty-three Canadians that day.

"They took us into this barn, five of us, and lined us up. We were next," Thistle explained in 1993. "They had a sniper in front of us, ready to go. We shook hands, you know, like it was the end, when in came some high-ranking [German] officer and stopped him. . . . Just a split second and another five would be among the dead."

Veteran Tony Burns told me he remembered the night he died. It happened in the same hospital—Basingstoke, the neurological and plastic surgery hospital in Hampshire, England—where, in 1942, he had trained to become an operating room assistant (ORA). As an ORA trainee, he familiarized himself with the instruments of his wartime trade—aneurysm needles, forceps, drills, scissors, retractors, saws, scalp clips, traction tongs, suction tubing, and anesthetic gases. Then, fully qualified, ORA Burns landed on Juno Beach with No. 1 Canadian Mobile Neuro-Surgical Unit (CMNSU) shortly after D-Day. The CMNSU's specialty was administering first aid to soldiers with head wounds. In its first month ashore in Normandy, the CMNSU handled more than two hundred cases. Then, on August 23, Burns became the unit's first casualty. About noon, the trailer in which the surgeons and ORAs worked came under attack. An explosion outside capsized an instrument sterilizer full of hot water on Pte. Burns, scalding him across his back and arms. His medical colleagues immediately anesthetized him to treat his burns. They feared infection might set in, so they transferred him back to Basingstoke.

"I fell into a deep coma," he told me at his home in Halifax in 2003. "I remember my eyes were closed. I wasn't able to move a muscle. But I could hear every word being said. I could feel the chaplain near me giving me the last rites."

When he finally woke up, he found himself in a room full of wounded, each bandaged from head to toe. He was in the burns ward where every day the nursing staff wheeled patients to bathe in a tub of warm saline water. Though his scalded skin began to heal, the daily rhythm of soaking and bandaging proved excruciating. He felt guilty complaining in a ward with men more severely wounded than he was, but he told me the pain drove him crazy.

"One day, after several months of pain, I couldn't take it any more," he said. "So I took the rosary my father gave me, covered my head with a blanket, and died."

Apparently, it wasn't his time. Burns awoke fifty hours later surrounded by many of the doctors and nurses who had trained him, including his commanding officer. Major William Keith of the CMNSU gave Tony Burns a reason to live. Keith told him the unit would one day need him back on duty. Indeed, when Burns recrossed the Channel and caught up with his comrades in Ghent, Belgium, Dr. Keith was there to greet him; not only did Burns get his old job back, there was an added surprise.

"Dr. Keith threw a greatcoat over my shoulders to keep me warm," Burns said. "The coat had two pips [lieutenant stripes] on it. I started to take it off, but Dr. Keith smiled and said they were my pips as long as I was with the unit. A battlefield promotion, I guess."

On June 6, 1944, Bob Cameron was supposed to be seated in Convocation Hall about to receive his Honours B.A. degree from the University of Toronto. Instead, that morning he had come ashore at Juno Beach in the driver's seat of a Royal Canadian Corps of Signals jeep. With his two signals crew—Cpl. Leslie "Buck" Grittner and Cpl. John Tolstad—Lt. Cameron hit the shore of Nan sector just after 8:30 a.m. and began stringing communication wire from there to the advance division headquarters inland of the village of Bernières-sur-Mer. On one of his trips up from the beach, Cameron described giving a lift to war correspondents Ralph Allen and Ross Munro, and when the German counterattack began he remembered sharing his slit trench outside HQ with Munro. Cameron, aged eighty-four, relived all this—and accounts of a few close calls—from the comfort and safety of a favourite armchair at his Thornhill, Ontario, home in 2003. Within two months of D-Day, it turned out, his two loyal corporals were dead and so too almost Bob Cameron, the result of so-called friendly fire incidents. On August 8, two twelve-plane groups of U.S. Eighth Air Force B-17s accidentally bombed Canadian and Polish positions near Caen. Allied casualties amounted to sixty-five killed, including Tolstad and Grittner.

As Cameron remembered it, his own close shave occurred a week later, during the battle at Falaise, where Allied forces had nearly encircled the retreating German Fifth Panzer and Seventh Armies. Then serving as a brigade signals officer, Cameron said that the Canadians were advancing in conjunction with a 1st Polish Armoured Division as Allied forces attempted to cut off tens of thousands of German troops retreating through the Falaise gap. He recalled the Poles and Canadians positioned at a starting line, sitting out in the open countryside on August 14, 1944. As his group prepared to advance along the Falaise Road that afternoon, Cameron suddenly looked up to see Royal Air Force bombers flying low overhead, he thought, to provide air support for the attack. The Lancasters flew so low, Cameron said he saw the open bomb doors in the planes' bellies, even the faces of some of the crewmen inside the aircraft.

"The leading plane began to drop its load right on top of us. . . . It chewed us up beyond belief," Cameron said. "I ran out and spread a bright green recognition panel on the ground. Then I lay down in the centre of it with an Aldis signal lamp [pointed up at the bombers] spelling out 'F.R.I.E.N.D.S.' in Morse code."

He got no response. The RAF bombs kept falling on Canadian and Polish infantry and armoured troops, Cameron said, until the pilot of an Allied single-engine spotter aircraft finally flew up among the inbound bombers to wave them off.

"Hell, the Lancs were at least thirty times bigger than the spotter plane," Cameron told me. "Whoever that pilot was, he deserves a medal."

Not surprisingly, no medals were forthcoming. All told, Bomber Command in England had sent 417 Lancasters, 352 Halifaxes, and 42 Mosquitoes to strike six targets that afternoon outside Falaise. They dropped 3,723 tons of bombs short of their targets. Two aircraft were lost—one shot down by Allied anti-aircraft. The next day, an official army tally of the day's Canadian losses showed 65 dead, 241 wounded, and 91 missing (most of them more likely killed). The Polish forces sustained 42 killed and 51 missing. Air Chief Marshal Arthur Harris ordered an investigation. Two Pathfinder Force crews were reposted to ordinary crew duties; squadron and flight commanders involved in the incident were ordered to give up their commands, and all implicated crews received marks on their records ensuring they not serve on any similar close-to-front-line operations in future. Miraculously, Bob Cameron survived and wrote home to reassure his wife shortly afterward:

"Darling. Most of the time we need all the help we can get, but . . . who needs friends like this?" Cameron wrote, then recalling the earlier loss of his two corporals, he added, "[First] 3rd Div. advanced HQ was plastered by 700 U.S. B-17s by mistake [on August 8]. Major-General [R.F.L.] Keller was badly wounded and both my D-Day buddies—Buck Grittner and John Tolstad were killed. Once again [at Falaise] it could have been me. . . . It can't be luck. I really must be blessed."

Listening to such stories, I recalled the lines of the sixteenth-century dramatist James Shirley, who wrote:

> The glories of our blood and state
> Are shadows, not substantial things;
> There is no armour against fate;
> Death lays his icy hand on kings.

From my very first encounters with veterans, dating back to my earliest broadcast interviews about D-Day in the late 1960s, I often kept the question of fate in my back pocket. Not until I sensed the moment was the right one did I pop the question about whether faith, good fortune, or the supernatural had anything to do with survival. Nor have I ever asked any but more elderly, longer out-of-uniform veterans such things. Inevitably, many more years of life experience tended to add spice to their concluding remarks about the quirks of survival.

Veterans' overseas diaries between 1914 and 1918 credited letters from home, a comrade's lifesaving hand, that notorious tot of rum, and the grace of God for bringing them home safely from the Great War. Decorated Spitfire pilot Charley Fox never stopped wondering why, despite 222 operational flights (the equivalent of two full tours in 1944–45) he'd not been killed, constantly asking himself, "Why not me?" Gerry Emon served as a provost (military police) behind the lines in the Korean War. "God keep me from heroes," he always said. "They draw fire." His guiding principle generally worked, until the December day he was riding in the passenger seat of a truck travelling behind the front lines and a booby-trap bomb exploded in the glove compartment. The force that threw him through the passenger door and into a nearby creek-bed shattered his shoulders; lacerated his face, hands, and stomach; and nearly severed his legs. Quick work by doctors at an advanced dressing station saved his life and two years of orthopedic and plastic surgery at Sunnybrook Hospital in Toronto eventually put him back on his feet. His near-death experience had occurred a long way from the fighting, far from any risk-takers on the battlefield, and the only heroes he probably ever encountered were the surgeons at that advanced dressing station.

More than half a century later, another veteran of another war—Canada's first combat mission since the Korean War—sat at my kitchen table in Uxbridge, Ontario. Brian Decaire was a solidly built young man, just twenty-six. Hair cropped short. His face showed some strain, some nervousness, but he looked directly back at me as I asked him—partway through the interview—about the wounds he'd sustained in Afghanistan.

"Well, the Blackhawk chopper lands at base," he began.

"The base at Kandahar?" I asked.

"At Kandahar. Yeah, we're in the medical area, where all the medical tents are. So me and Brett [Perry] we're just sitting in the one tent. . . . The C.O., Lt. Col. Pat Stogran, and a padre came and sat with us. I know they wanted to comfort us, but I really didn't want to listen. . . . I'd rather have had a good buddy there, you know."

Decaire, I learned, would almost rather be with a buddy—not necessarily even an officer in the same military unit—than anybody, maybe even his family. And certainly not in an interview on tape talking about himself. That winter, when I contacted him through his aunt, who lived in my community, it took a few tries before he agreed to meet with me one evening at my house. He admitted he wasn't used to doing interviews with the media. It seemed very foreign to him, he said. And since being wounded in Afghanistan two years before, his experience with journalists had not been positive. "When I hear reporters get things wrong, it pisses me off," he told me. That's why, when he arrived, Brian Decaire—formerly a corporal in the

3rd Battalion, Princess Patricia's Canadian Light Infantry serving in Afghanistan—brought with him a pad of handwritten notes, a journal, something from which he could read prepared answers to questions he expected. He referred to it, for example, when I asked him about his shrapnel wounds.

"My hand was bleeding. . . . The swelling was so massive, they couldn't get a good assessment," he said, then he read from his journal. "One of the more traumatic memories in the hospital . . . is this doctor. 'Tell me the worst-case scenario for me,' [I said]. He said, 'Worst-case scenario, you'd have to lose your hand.' 'If every single thing were to go wrong, if I were to get infection, if nothing were to go right, I'd lose my hand.' Lose my hand? Fuck. I want to be a SAR Tech [search and rescue technician]. I'm still thinking about SAR Tech. Lose my fucking hand? It was a shock to hear that."

Earlier that morning—April 17, 2002—Decaire and nine other members of his Canadian Battle Group were conducting a live-fire drill in an area known as Tarnak Farm about five kilometres from the Canadian base at Kandahar. During a simulated ground attack by members of No. 3 Platoon of the 3rd Battalion of PPCLI, an American F-16 pilot flying through the airspace overhead mistook them for insurgents and dropped a 500-pound laser-guided bomb on their position. Four Canadians were killed and eight were wounded, including Brian Decaire.

Cpl. Decaire had witnessed and survived the much publicized "friendly fire" incident.

During my interview with him, I looked at Decaire's right hand, the one that shrapnel had penetrated. I told him it didn't look damaged at all. He said it wasn't. I digested his comment about wanting to become a search and rescue technician, but wasn't clear how it connected to his experience in Afghanistan. Nevertheless I sensed that nothing from his tour overseas in the war on terror had changed those intentions. He shook his head and reiterated, "Nothing."

Initially, I had some difficulty considering this man a veteran. Remember, I have interviewed thousands of vets—almost all from

Canadian wartime campaigns of fifty, sixty, and eighty years ago. That is to say, most of the veterans I have questioned were soldiers before women ran for political office or served in front-line military roles, before the widespread use of antibiotics, and before satellite and Internet technology. The veteran seated at my kitchen table was born at Portage la Prairie, Manitoba, in 1977. Although he was aware of Canadian military history and proud of it, much of his knowledge of it had come from many of the sources I had explored: accounts and analysis in books, images from documentary film, and anecdotes related by elderly former combatants. Still, I had to keep reminding myself, by definition—service in a war zone—this man, who was the same age as my own daughters, was a veteran.

Although not exactly a military brat, Brian Decaire had come from that environment. His father had served in the military and therefore moved about the country, but when Brian was born, Gary Decaire took a building inspector's position with the government and settled his family in St. Vital, a suburb of Winnipeg. As a youngster, very little grabbed Brian's attention, he said, until his mother gave him a copy of Robert Mason Lee's *Death and Deliverance*, about a team of search and rescue specialists who tracked down and saved the victims of a Hercules transport crash on Ellesmere Island in 1991. At the recruiting office in Winnipeg, an officer told him he'd have to work on his fitness level and serve three or four years in the military before getting a chance to join the search and rescue service. Decaire signed up October 1, 1997. He'd just turned twenty.

At St. Jean, Quebec, he received basic training. He thought the conditions and routine there resembled a prison. Up at 5 a.m., making beds, polishing boots, running in cadence, and impressing the master corporal who yelled at everybody. He endured countless inspections, drills, field exercises, and hours of PT—physical training. After two months he moved on to sixteen weeks at battle school in Wainwright, Alberta, where the rhythm didn't change, just the content. In the first four weeks, it was parades and push-ups, but after that, recruits were organized into platoons and sections with section commanders who became their infanteer instructors in the 3rd Battalion of the PPCLI. It sounded pretty dehumanizing, I commented to him, the way Hollywood depicted the Marines or the Airborne.

"Geez, Hollywood makes things look a lot more fantastic than they are," he said. "It was hard. I got homesick, that's for sure. I'd just turned twenty."

"Was there hazing?" I asked.

"No," he said quickly. He seemed to take the question almost as if I were insulting his regiment. "We were all in the same boat. Who's going to initiate you?"

Whether there was hazing or not didn't really matter to me. But what did emerge from the question was something I had seen among veterans of the World Wars and Korea. Because the trainees were all in the same boat, as Decaire said, they connected. The bond might simply have been recruits commiserating. It might have been young men, cut off from the comforts of home, developing a community of the powerless against a hierarchy of the powerful, their instructors. I'd seen this most important spark of collegiality or military camaraderie before. I'd had it described to me by veterans of trench warfare training at Shorncliffe in England in 1916, by sprog airmen posted to Canada in the British Commonwealth Air Training Plan in the 1940s, and by volunteers in Canada's Special Force, training for Korea at Fort Lewis in the state of Washington in 1950. Whatever the spark, Decaire explained that the training experience initiated friendships that helped him get through the grind of repetitive exercises and putdowns by irate instructors. He met Aaron Bygrove the first day of basic training, Shane Brennan at battle school, and Brett Perry later during mortar platoon training. Bygrove served in pioneer platoon, Brennan in a rifle company, and Perry shared duties with Decaire operating an 84-mm rocket launcher; they all became among Decaire's closest friends. All eventually served with the 3rd Battalion of the PPCLI in Afghanistan in 2002.

Whether the friendships began simply because the recruits all shared the common experience of enduring basic training and battle school, or whether the bond became the common denominator during overseas operations, they proved a personal bulwark for Decaire. His fellow privates or corporals—very often his section or platoon mates—in the 3rd Battalion of PPCLI became more than best buddies. Decaire considered them companions and confidants on course, after hours, and during his postings—in 1998 to the Canadian Forces Base in Edmonton, then with the NATO mission to Bosnia in 2000, then (following the September 11, 2001, terrorist attacks) to Afghanistan. The route to Kandahar seemed a whirlwind. First the National Defence announcement came, followed by more intense training at Wainwright; then a U.S. military transport scooped up the 3rd Battalion and disgorged it at Kandahar airport in February 2002.

"Those first four weeks, it was like six hours on, six hours off doing security. Dusk to dawn, everyone was up . . . in the trenches. You were zombies," Decaire said. "Brett Perry was pretty much who I hung with, in the whole thing. We shared a tent. We were sleeping in our cots, still in our boots. We didn't even take our sleeping bags out, because we thought the attack was coming any moment. We did that for like the first week. A nightmare. Then it was 'Fuck this, I'm getting into the bag 'cause it's just so cold.'"

"How did you cope with the *real* threat?" I asked.

"One minute you're just sitting. Then, it's 'Okay, let's go!'. . . Me and Brett had to psych ourselves up all the time," he said. "I'll watch your back. You watch mine. Getting ready to do something, just killing. Kill or be killed. That's the mentality I had."

While perhaps this was an overreaction by a relative newcomer to the war zone, Decaire explained he and Perry could turn this kind of forced intensity on and off whenever and wherever the battalion operated that first winter. To balance the intensity, however, Decaire also admitted a predilection for precaution. His tendency to move more slowly or take extra care was perhaps a healthy counterbalance to Brett Perry's tendency for bravado. He related an incident during a mid-winter operation to a mountain in the middle of the desert, known as the Whale feature. Operating from U.S. attack helicopters, Decaire and the battalion rushed from landed choppers presumably to hunt down and kill al-Qaeda. At one point, he and Perry faced a hurried climb down through rugged terrain littered with unexploded "bomblets." Decaire took the descent slowly. Perry leapt more aggressively from rock to rock.

"Sure enough, a rock gives way and [Perry] does a couple of somersaults and lands on his ass," Decaire said. "His legs spread apart and there's a couple of bomblets right between his legs. All he says is 'How's my face? Do I have any scratches on my face?' How he looked was all he was worried about. I had a good chuckle out of it."

I let Decaire enjoy the amusement at the expense of his buddy's impulsiveness. But it occurred to me that Decaire's nature may have played a role in his survival in Afghanistan.

"How did your cautiousness serve you the night of the friendly fire incident?" I asked.

He hesitated a moment. As he had before, he didn't appear capable of offering an ad lib response. He looked down to the pages of his prepared notes and read, "This is definitely a day that's changed my life. I mean, people die tragic deaths every day, whether it's someone's son being killed by a drunk driver or an F-16 pilot with a 500-pound laser bomb. Both are just as tragic. . . . But this changed my life."

From that point on, Brian Decaire slowly, methodically—offering me every detail that maintained respect for his fallen platoon mates—took me through the events of that night in the Afghan desert. Revisiting the incident occasionally frightened him again. It angered him. It disgusted him. Once or twice it took him to the verge of tears. But having agreed to our meeting that winter night, he wasn't about to let me down.

From his notes he reiterated that April 17 was a routine day. Training was routine. As he had numerous times before, that day Decaire said he got up before sunrise to run. Running in the dark wasn't allowed; running in the heat of the day was impractical. So he and fellow corporal Ainsworth Dyer ran beside the Kandahar base runway. They had set out the course—placing a marker every hundred metres—and ran back and forth to accumulate the distance. Dyer was six-foot-five in height and weighed 240 pounds, but Decaire said that morning, like most, Dyer completed a ten-kilometre run in under forty minutes. After his run with Dyer, Decaire showered and shaved and, while waiting for the night's planned exercises, he did crossword puzzles.

Late in the afternoon members of "A" Company assembled at the embarkation point within Kandahar base. There, Decaire remembered his section commander, Sgt. Lorne Ford, telling his men to climb aboard the trucks. When his group got to the training site, Decaire said the sun had completely set and he could see the lights of the base twinkling five kilometres to the southeast. Tarnak Farm, he told me, had formerly served as one of Osama bin Laden's training facilities. Before 9/11, the massive complex had consisted of eighty mud buildings—barracks and practice sites for thousands of al-Qaeda fighters. After the September 11 attacks, American fighter jets had targeted the complex and bombed it to rubble. When the Taliban regime fell in Afghanistan, sending its holdouts to the hills, Canadian military leaders in the area asked a local governor if they could stage live-fire drills at Tarnak Farm and designated it a restricted operating zone.

Decaire took paper and pencil and drew me a map of the area. He apologized for the roughness of the artistry. But like the prepared notes, having a personally drawn map of the area in front of him seemed to refocus him on the job at hand—showing me the site of the incident and getting through his story. His diagram showed essentially open desert with the rubble of the former al-Qaeda barracks, including a circular mud hut troops called "the corral," offering the only discernable landmark. He also sketched in the hulks of a couple of tanks just north of the corral that, he said, exercise groups used as targets. On the perimeter of the attack zone, he sketched in what looked like roads but were actually narrow drainage ditches, or wadis, around the site's outer edges—one running east and west and another north and south. The intersection of these two wadis provided the training groups with an obvious starting point from which to launch attacks against imaginary enemy insurgents entrenched in the rubble or operating the tanks. Finally, he drew the administration area, located several hundred metres to the east of the live-fire zone. That's where the troop transport trucks, an ambulance, and the commanding officer's Iltis jeep assembled at the southeast edge of the training area, just as the skies over Tarnak Farm darkened with nightfall.

"Each of the sections would rotate through the range," Decaire recalled. "We had this scenario. . . . A rifle section with their weapons dead and a team, with a C-6 machine gun and a Karl Gustav 84-mm rocket launcher, were to travel up the wadi. . . . There's a couple of tank hulls about 400 metres downrange. We're to walk along the wadi to a figure eleven target [marking the beginning of the attack], find tanks and destroy them."

All evening long, Decaire explained, other sections of "A" Company of the PPCLI had worked through similar live-fire drills at Tarnak Farm. At about 9 p.m. all members of Decaire's group were clear with the scenario and 3 Section had begun moving up the wadi to take its turn.

With the exercise underway in Decaire's head, there at my kitchen table, he referred to the paper one more time to show me the configuration—right to left—of all ten men as they arranged themselves along the west wall of the wadi. Farthest up the wadi were Brett Perry and Decaire himself, manning the Karl Gustav rocket launcher. Next was M/Cpl. Stan Clark, directing the assault, and second-in-command Cpl. René Paquette armed with a C-9 machine gun. To their left were M/Cpl. Curtis Hollister, the weapons detachment commander, along with Pte. Nathan Smith, who loaded the C-6 machine gun, and Cpl. Ainsworth Dyer, who fired it. The quartermaster for "A" Company, Sgt. Marc Léger, had positioned himself slightly behind the C-6 gun in the wadi; he was there to ensure the exercise was conducted safely. Pte. Richard Green was adjacent to the C-6 position armed with a disposable anti-tank rocket that he was expected to fire to initiate the attack; he was also responsible for detonating a Claymore mine to signal the section's pullback some minutes later. And finally, watching the action as best he could in the dark, at the opposite end of the column from Perry and Decaire, was the section commander, Sgt. Lorne Ford.

"How long was the column of men?" I asked.

"From Ford to me was about twenty metres," he said.

"That close?"

"Yeah. It was pretty tight."

"Can you describe exactly what you were doing?"

And he gave the description to me, complete with the exact sequence and his approximation of the sounds he heard. He mentioned, as an aside, that he had taken the precaution of putting ear plugs in that night.

"I fired the first few rounds from the Karl Gustav, okay," he said. "Brett was loading for me 'cause it's a two-man operation. . . . After I fire the first few rounds, I gave it to Brett and I become the loader. So I loaded it for him and he got the first two rounds off, no problem. And the third round. Pfft. Pfft. Fire. Boom. I checked the back blast—'cause it's like a fireball behind you and it could really hurt guys if they're behind you—to make sure no one is there. . . .

"Right before I give him the ready [for the final shell to be fired]—I'm going to slap his back 'cause it's loud with guns firing—I hear this whistling sound. I said, 'What the fuck is that?' And I look toward the centre of the section and all I see is white. Intense white and intense heat just engulfs me. The only thing I can compare the whistling sound to is . . . when the anvil comes down on top of the coyote in the Bugs Bunny cartoon. I swear to God, that's exactly what it sounded like.

"I don't remember hearing an explosion. It definitely wasn't loud. It was the white and the heat that just . . . ahhhh . . . I felt like I got punched in the right side of my face. The shrapnel, I guess . . . and I was on my back. Could barely see anything 'cause I totally lost my night vision because it was so bright and it was so dark that night."

The laser-directed bomb from the U.S. F-16 had ploughed into the section and exploded exactly where Smith and Dyer lay firing their machine gun, just ten or fifteen metres from where Decaire and Perry crouched with their weapon. The initial explosion killed Green, Smith, and Léger outright. Dyer was mortally wounded and died moments afterward. Ford had a massive gash on his thigh and facial wounds. Hot shrapnel struck Hollister on the left side of his face. The concussion of the blast hit Paquette in the chest causing internal bleeding. Others from the section, including Clark and Perry, had less serious wounds. And two men, not in the section and a hundred metres away—Norm Link and Decaire's friend Shane Brennan—had been hit by flying debris. I learned these details from newspaper and public documents later. But with one of the survivors sitting in front of me, I felt I had to know as many of his feelings and reactions as he cared to share. When I asked him about his immediate response he spoke without his notes.

Decaire said he first wondered if he was still alive. He remembered his face felt sore, his right hand as if it were in a vise and on fire. He wondered whether his hand was still there or not. He tried to sit up to get his bearings and he recalled hearing the sound of a jet engine trailing off. Moments before, his world was alive with the sounds of firing weapons. Then, nothing. He expected to hear the sharp commands of his sergeant or 2IC rattling off directions—where to go, what to do—but instead he was struck by the momentary eerie silence. Then the first of horrible sounds of his wounded section mates. Whether an antidote or a result of the shock of the scene, Decaire's training appeared to kick in next.

"From the moment of impact it was only like thirty seconds," he said, "and I get up and start to make my way down the line. The first guy I came to was Paquette. When I saw him he was about halfway down," referring to his notes, "halfway down the hill lying on his left side. I made sure his ABCs were good."

"ABCs?" I asked.

"Airway, breathing, circulation. There was nothing else I could have done," he told me. "I may sound like I was calm, cool, and collected, but I'm sure I had a look in my eyes like a deer in the headlights. Everyone had that look in their eyes."

"Fear?" I asked.

"Can't describe it any better," he continued. "More like shock . . . it didn't make a difference or whatever. I just didn't want to stop and shut 'er down."

And with only a bit of a pause he added that he wanted me to hear about the rest of what he saw, but he didn't want it recorded. He described finding Léger's body, Smith dead next to him, and initially little or no sign at all of Green's body. His voice rose in emotion as he described the body of Dyer, with whom he'd gone through battle school. But he shook his head at how Hollister—positioned among the four who died—had managed to survive.

"See this," he said, pointing to his original diagram where Léger, Smith, Dyer, and Green were situated on the edge of the wadi. "Killed, killed, killed, killed, and Hollister right there. Right underneath [the bomb]. How he's alive. I think it's a miracle any of . . . I'm alive."

After a few moments, I asked him to repeat what he'd just said. Did he really think it was a miracle? He insisted that he just couldn't understand it, that it just didn't seem possible. He didn't seem to want the conversation to explore any spiritual aspects of his survival. So he returned to his diagram, to the physics of the event. He seemed to want to help explain to me why he'd survived. He reiterated things from his position on the wadi.

"I'm here. We're shooting down range. The bomb hit, I think on kind of an angle," he went on, poking the diagram with the pencil. "I don't know physics. It's a crazy science and force and power. I think this whole trench really fucked up the physics. If we were all here in the middle of the desert on a billiard table of sand with no cover, we probably would all be hamburger, but because of that one little valley [the wadi] I'm still here."

"Do you consider it fate?" I asked.

He paused a second. Then he shrugged. It seemed to trigger another incident that took place that day. He went back to his journal and read from his notes. He explained that before the live-fire drill at Tarnak Farm earlier that same morning, the company had conducted another training exercise—rehearsing how to load casualties aboard medical evacuation helicopters. He said he remembered that during the practice Cpl. Ainsworth Dyer was taking photographs in the chopper cockpit and of his platoon mates doing the exercise. He pointed out finally that Dyer had used a disposable camera.

Then Decaire left his notes for a second and stared off as if retrieving one last memory of the day. After the bombing, he said, he recalled sitting in that same chopper on the ground at Tarnak Farm in the middle of the night. The helicopter's engines were accelerating to transport him and the other wounded back to the base at Kandahar for additional medical attention. It was the first time he'd sat still since the beginning of the live-fire exercise. He said he was temporarily disoriented and couldn't remember from the noise and vibration of the chopper when it was actually airborne. The impact of the night's events suddenly caught up with him.

"I looked over my shoulder to see a medic checking one of the injured guys. They were all on stretchers. I thought about my family, the dead guys, and how close I'd come. That's when I broke down. . . ."

I had never really witnessed it before. Nor would I presume to have the medical expertise to recognize it, but I sensed that Brian Decaire was still coping with some elements of war zone post-traumatic stress. I had seen some tension in my interview subject, but anyone—civilian or military—not regularly exposed to media questioning might have felt equally nervous. His journal often became a means of collecting his thoughts or a momentary refuge if he felt he couldn't come up with an appropriate ad lib response. The images of the dead and wounded obviously bothered him. He periodically asked me to stop the tape recorder, not to protect himself, but to protect his fallen comrades. Once or twice his emotions took over his responses, particularly when Decaire assessed the role of the U.S. pilot in the bombing. That seemed an appropriate outlet for his anger at the unnecessary loss of his four platoon mates. And yet, as strong and as capable as I found this young veteran to be, I sensed he needed more time to sort out the Tarnak Farm incident. His body and mind had not completely healed the wounds of that night. Ultimately, I thanked him for revisiting a tough subject.

"I don't need psychologists," he said finally. "I've got good family, good friends."

Some months after my session with Brian Decaire, I tracked down the medic who had led the team on duty that night at the Tarnak Farm firing range. In the fall of 2004, Sgt. Bill Wilson happened to be on a course at Canadian Forces Base (CFB) Borden, not too far from Barrie, Ontario. We agreed to meet at his barracks room to talk about his military career and in particular the events of April 17, 2002. But for a series of coincidences, it turned out, Wilson would not have been serving in Afghanistan in 2002. But for those same happenstance events, I learned that Wilson's three-man medical unit may have made the difference for several of the PPCLI wounded that night.

"Normally, if it was just a platoon going out, I don't go out. I would send one of my guys," Wilson explained. "But if the whole company is going out, we all go out. That's why we were all there that night."

Not that this man ever considered shirking responsibility. Among the first things I learned from my conversation with Bill Wilson at Borden was his passion to do what his training had taught him. At every opportunity, whether facing an apparently insurmountable challenge or just routine orders, the thirty-seven-year-old medic appeared to leap into every aspect of his career wholeheartedly. Right from the beginning of his contact with the military, that natural or acquired commitment had motivated him through basic training at CFB Cornwallis, Nova Scotia; French language training at St. Jean, Quebec; study at Canadian Forces Medical Services School; and eventually his medical postings across Canada and during four different overseas tours of duty. He never said so in egotistical terms, but I also sensed he considered himself the best qualified person assigned to these specific medical postings. Nevertheless, it was that series of coincidental events, what some might call fate, that brought Sgt. Bill Wilson to Tarnak Farm on April 17, 2002.

As we began our conversation, in addition to telling me his birth date and the names of his parents and siblings, Wilson admitted to me outright that as a youngster he was an introvert and so to try to compensate for that he joined Katimavik. He said that he thrived on the experiences of the dollar-a-day youth volunteer program—living in a dormitory, cooking for others, learning French, and community building. Next, he tried a business administration course at a college in North Bay. When he realized that a desk job had little attraction for him, on a hunch he walked into a military recruiting centre. The recruiter assessed Wilson's test scores and questionnaire responses and told him he could sign up to become a military police officer, weapons technician, or medic.

"I said, 'Well, I want a job where I help people,'" Wilson explained. "So I took medic."

As he had hoped, the military changed him. Initially, it altered his fitness level and body shape; PT and the drill regimen increased his upper body musculature so much that by the time he left basic training at Cornwallis he had to have his uniform re-tailored. Much the way Katimavik had shown him how to contribute one's strengths to the greater good of the community, the military introduced him to teamwork, whether it was sharing responsibility for polishing boots and ironing uniforms or rotating duties at a military hospital. He seemed to relish all the work that being a lowly private sent his way. The tougher the challenge, the better. He served three years at the forces hospital in Cold Lake, Alberta, and concluded it was one of the best learning experiences of his new career. Not all the problems he faced were in hospital wards, however. In 1992, his older sister died suddenly, and although he had married and was looking forward to his first child, Wilson admitted his marriage was foundering. The same year he got a posting to the base at Petawawa, Ontario, in preparation for the Canadian military mission to Somalia.

Thinking that his strong belief in teamwork had helped get him through that tough year, I asked Wilson whom he turned to for strength.

"I think I'd become a very resilient person," he said. "I think I handle stress well. That's always been a given for me, handling stress. I do a lot of running, a lot of PT, a lot of exercising . . . to ease the tension and deal with the problems."

If he thought life's twists and turns at a military base on the Ottawa River were tough, they paled by comparison with his first tour of duty in Somalia in 1993. Wilson had to serve as a recording corporal when an American medic was mortally wounded in a land mine explosion. He had to transfer from ambulance to hospital a Canadian soldier struck by the negligent discharge of a barracks weapon. He was on duty the night that the beaten body of civilian Shidane Arone arrived at his medical station and coincidentally when the young soldier accused in Arone's death attempted to hang himself. In fact, the board of inquiry into the entire incident eventually questioned him for more than five hours. Wilson admitted he ran a lot to counterbalance the strain of the Somalia peacekeeping operation. When the mission ended, he considered never taking an overseas posting again.

"I think I had a bit of PTSD after [the mission] too. Bad dreams," he said.

"Was it ever attended to?" I asked.

"No," he said quite directly. "I just kind of pushed it aside and got on with my life. I mean, a month later I had a newborn [son] in my lap."

Not only was Wilson able to shift gears comfortably when his first overseas deployment ended, he said he even complained to the army's top psychiatrist. Wilson explained that the military had totally misunderstood how to treat PTSD or situational stress after traumatic events unfolded during his deployment in Somalia. He criticized the brass for sending colonels and sergeants major—soldiers of higher rank than those serving on the tour—to debrief the corporals and privates about dealing with the effects of stress and still carry on with the mission. Then, despite his own admitted trauma from the Somalia experience, he accepted yet another African assignment—a tour of duty to Rwanda, immediately after the tribal genocide there in 1994. Next, in 2000, he accepted a third overseas posting to serve in a Battalion Unit Medical Station with the peacekeeping mission to Bosnia. His superiors had promoted him to the rank of sergeant and had—in the field—given him the responsibility for running a unit medical station, including half a dozen medics and nearly a hundred other staff members.

"I enjoyed the role of responsibility," Wilson said. "That was a job learning responsibility. Independent duty [deciding] what to do if. . . . I love a challenge."

After Bosnia, Wilson took a posting to the Canadian Forces Base (CFB) Edmonton, where he eventually became the senior medic for the base's 1 Combat Engineer Regiment (CER). By that time, he was going through a divorce, which placed additional stress on his duties at 1 CER—where he and two other medics were responsible for the medical needs of 410 members of the regiment (in contrast, the 3rd Battalion of PPCLI, also stationed there, had thirteen medics for 460 troops). Then, following events on September 11, 2001, Canadian politicians decided to send troops to Afghanistan. Two sergeant medics other than Wilson were officially assigned to prepare for the deployment, so he rationalized, "Hot, desert, desolate. Been there. Done that," and went about his regular duties in Edmonton. Then one of the sergeants injured his back and Wilson got the call to replace him. It meant a fourth foreign posting for the thirty-five-year-old medic. In less than ten days, Sgt. Wilson had to deploy to Afghanistan—in charge of "A" Company's medical unit—meanwhile saying goodbye to his family again.

I asked him if having a family this time affected his decision to take the posting.

"I had kids, but they were with their mother. They were safe," he said. "I wasn't involved in a relationship at that time. So I thought I really don't have any ties."

"You mean, if there was a risk, if something happened to you, it wouldn't matter. Is that what you're saying?"

"A lot of people looked at me kind of strange," he said. "But knowing where I'd been, what I'd been doing, it was still the job for me. It was the lifestyle. So, I was like, 'Yeah, giddy-up. I'm ready.' When it comes right down to it, deployments are why I joined the military."

Not dreaded, but loved. Here was a eureka moment for me. During hundreds of interviews with veterans, particularly those remembering departure for their first-ever tour of duty overseas, I had noted any number of descriptive impressions: excitement, anticipation, nervousness, anxiety, worry, and bald-faced fear. Although I had heard some refer to their embarkation as the beginning of an adventure, something they felt they shouldn't miss, I couldn't remember anybody describing a deployment as something he craved. What made Wilson's admission even more compelling was that it had come on the eve of his fourth foreign tour in just over ten years. Granted, he also admitted he was struggling with marriage breakup, so leaving home may have presented a convenient escape. Still, his experiences in Somalia, Rwanda, and Bosnia had illustrated how ugly the conditions and nightmares could be. He'd admitted that they'd changed him. Nevertheless, for him a deployment to Afghanistan and the war against terror was a magnet, a lifestyle he preferred more than any other aspect of the military. But it turned out there was one more coincidence that put Bill Wilson at Tarnak Farm that April night in 2002.

"We were the first platoon to actually take R and R," he said. "You were living for the first couple of months through an intense ordeal, [then] you're in Dubai. Some guys went golfing, some went to the movies, and some just laid around on the beach. . . . I got my second wind."

After ninety-six hours in a world away from war, medic Wilson and members of No. 3 Platoon arrived back at Kandahar on April 16, in time to receive orders of the live-fire drill at Tarnak Farm the next night. Unlike other smaller exercises, because this training session involved an entire company of the PPCLI, it meant that Sgt. Wilson and his two subordinates—Cpl. Vic Speirs and Cpl. Jean de la Bourdonnaye (DLB for short)—all had to participate. The U.S. laser bomb exploded a few hundred metres from the medical unit's position in the admin area of Tarnak Farm. The back of their ambulance faced the blast area—Wilson inside the cab monitoring the radio, Speirs and de la Bourdonnaye standing behind the box of the vehicle. Wilson said he didn't see the explosion, but when the blast jolted him out of the ambulance cab he saw a massive cloud of black smoke rising over the firing range and the unmistakable sight of helmet scrim—the camouflage coating on the exterior of a soldier's helmet—burning on the ground. Within seconds, Speirs and Wilson had slung medical bags over their shoulders and were racing through the wadi toward the sound of men screaming in the darkness ahead of them. Wilson told de la Bourdonnaye to turn the ambulance around and drive it as close as he could to the blast site.

I'd used my next question hundreds of times, but in Wilson's case it never seemed more applicable. "What were you thinking as you ran?"

"I'm halfway down this gully and I'm thinking to myself, 'Medically, I'm in charge. I've got a role here, but I've got a different role.' . . . I have to provide whatever medical support I can to the injured. So triage became my first responsibility. Unfortunately, the other responsibility was to check the vitals of the dead—those who were in one piece—to make sure they were dead."

In the next minutes the medics found the bodies of Sgt. Léger, Cpl. Dyer, and Pte. Smith near the crater where the bomb had exploded. Initially, Green was nowhere to be found. Within ninety seconds of their arrival, Speirs and Wilson were providing advanced first aid and life-saving measures to Cpl. Paquette and M/Cpl. Hollister, both suffering principally from the concussion of the blast. Once de la Bourdonnaye had the ambulance in place, he found Sgt. Ford and began administering a tourniquet to his left leg. Wilson also supervised the efforts of Corporals Decaire and Perry—themselves suffering shrapnel injuries—as they administered what Wilson called "buddy first aid" to the remaining wounded.

It suddenly occurred to me that Wilson's medical team had found the bodies of the three dead Canadian troops and had accomplished life-saving first aid on several of the others in nighttime conditions. Initially homing in on the sounds of men crying for help, they would have had to rely on nearly superhuman eyesight to find the men of No. 3 Platoon and treat them in the darkness of the desert. When I questioned him about that during our interview in his barracks room at CFB Borden, Wilson pointed to a kind of miner's lamp sitting on the floor of his apartment. He turned it on to illustrate how powerful the lamp light was. And I complimented the Canadian Army for having such practical equipment on hand.

"No. We got them on our own," Wilson said. "DLB ordered three of them through his mum in Ottawa."

"You mean they weren't army issue?" I said in astonishment.

"You can buy them in most mountaineering stores. Forty-one dollars a piece. Great piece of kit. Vic didn't want one, so he had one of those key-chain flashlights. He had it in his mouth when he worked on Paquette. Me and DLB had these [miner's lamps] on our heads."

"You wore the lamp on your helmet or on your head?" I asked.

"Actually, I flew out of the ambulance so fast that I left my helmet, my rifle," Wilson said shaking his head. "I had my flak jacket (without plates in it), the lamp on my head and my [medical] bag on my back. In hindsight, worrying whether [the planes] might be coming back never even registered. I was so focused on the casualties.... My concern was to sort out this mess and get whoever is living out of there."

Once again, I realized I'd never listened to a military medic describe triage, advanced first aid or life-saving measures so soon after the deadly event. My own father had served as a medic in Gen. George S. Patton's U.S. Third Army, but he had never shared with me any of his first-aid exploits, not even the events of February 12, 1945, when (according to the citation my mother found in my dad's papers when he was near death in 2004) he saved four men. That face-to-face meeting with medic Bill Wilson at Borden, for me, felt like a casualty debriefing session, a post mortem, if you like. Moreover, at times, I imagined my own father explaining how he apparently entered the booby-trapped Campholz Woods in western Germany that winter day and by himself managed to evacuate to safety four wounded and disoriented stretcher bearers.

Later, Wilson talked about acclimatizing himself to the situation at Tarnak Farm. He described how he dealt with the four corpses and how he supervised the emergency first aid and categorized by priority the wounded men of No. 3 Platoon—"Pri 1" needing life-saving measures within an hour, "Pri 2" requiring the same within six hours, "Pri 3" walking wounded, and "Pri 4" as the dead. As he retraced his actions and reflected on them, I saw every other medic I've ever interviewed or researched, including liaison Tec 4 Sgt. Alex Barris, who'd been given the Bronze Star for his actions that day in western

Germany. And I sensed Bill Wilson and his corporal medics, like my father, had accomplished what they had because their training, their loyalty, and their body chemistry directed them that way. In my interview with him, Wilson called Cpl. Speirs "an adrenaline junkie," but I tend to think there was a lot of that natural drive in Wilson himself.

"I was pretty pumped up," he admitted. "I had adrenaline running through me too. . . . When you've never dealt with anything like that in your career . . . when you're called upon to respond and do your job as best you can, I was definitely elated to be able to perform the task. . . . I don't think I came down until we were back at Kandahar."

During the Blackhawk chopper drill that members of "A" Company had carried out earlier that day, those orchestrating the training drill emphasized the speed of the operation. In other words, delivering effective life-saving assistance to Pri 1 and Pri 2 wounded depended on rapid deployment of the chopper, equally rapid evacuation, and quick delivery to the operating theatre back at Kandahar airfield. According to Sgt. Wilson's notes and the board's records, the call for the Blackhawk medical evacuation came ten minutes after the explosion. It was on site twenty-seven minutes later, and after seventeen minutes on the ground it departed with five patients and had landed at Kandahar in fifty-four minutes. Officials later investigating the incident declared that response time well within the expected standard. Each of the three medics received the Deputy Chief of the Defence Staff Commendation (CDS).

When the media first ran stories of the so-called friendly fire incident, the community in which I live immediately went on the alert. Because it's a relatively small town, most of us knew that Jeff Peck, son of the former fire chief in Uxbridge, was serving as a lieutenant with "A" Company of Princess Patricia's Canadian Light Infantry in Afghanistan that spring. When we learned Jeff was all right, the details of the incident travelled around town like wildfire. I learned that Peck and his No. 2 Platoon had just completed their turn on the Tarnak Farm firing range earlier in the evening of April 17, so their training for the night was done. I also discovered that when the

U.S. laser-guided bomb crashed into members of the PPCLI's No. 3 Platoon along the north-south wadi, Peck sat with his company commander, Maj. Sean Hackett, on the hood of the Iltis jeep in the administration area about 200 metres from the explosion.

"It didn't blow me down. We were behind the Iltis," Peck explained to me later. "But there's a physics reason why we weren't blown down. . . . Lucky for us, the bomb hit inside the wadi, inside the ditch, so the shrapnel blew into the wadi. A bomb like that has a danger radius of 500 metres. If it had hit on the flat of the desert . . . it would have been a lot worse."

The same way Bill Wilson's training reflex spurred him to grab his medical pack and rush to the scene, Jeff Peck's response triggered a kind of mental Rolodex, something he called a threat analysis. Had a piece of Canadian weaponry malfunctioned on the range? Had somebody accidentally set off one of the Claymore mines? Was the Canadian exercise group under attack by a Taliban mortar? He admitted that a friendly-fire bomb didn't immediately enter his mind. In those first seconds after noise from the explosion gave way to an eerie silence, his first reflex was to account for his own men. As others in the admin area swore in disbelief, Peck dashed to the nearby troop transport trucks and shouted to his 2ICs to complete a head count of No. 2 Platoon members. His next job, he concluded, was to secure the perimeters of the casualty area and then, using glow sticks, mark key spots where wounded men (or, as it turned out, body parts) were located.

I approached Jeff Peck for an interview some months after I'd spoken to Brian Decaire in my kitchen. Peck was back in Canada and posted to Canadian Forces Joint Headquarters Kingston. He suggested there were many others more qualified to speak to me on the subject. After all, he had just been a witness to the incident, not a direct participant the way Decaire had been. However, I insisted and drove to Kingston. I was to learn from the young man who had been a neighbour in my town and who had grown up with my daughters that his service in the military would give him acknowledgement and satisfaction he craved in a career. I would also discover from him that operating in a war zone—even during a training exercise, such as the one at Tarnak Farm—left deep impressions not always as obvious as shrapnel penetrations or concussion wounds.

Not long after our interview began, I asked Jeff Peck about memories of the PPCLI men lost that night. He admitted that when the Tarnak Farm incident occurred he'd been serving with "A" Company only about a year, so his associations with the four soldiers were limited. He did have personal recollections of Marc Léger. Peck remembered a moment from the previous December, when the officers served a special Christmas dinner to the rank and file troops. During the meal, it was announced that Léger would receive a promotion from master corporal to sergeant. Peck said the reaction astounded him; he said he'd never heard such an ovation, Léger was liked by so many in the battalion. Then Peck recalled another memory of Léger. It turned out that the two men happened to be together on September 11, 2001.

"I was in Austria on a partnership for peace exercise, where a whole bunch of NATO countries train with aspiring NATO countries," Peck said. "I had a platoon consisting of American Marines, Moldavia officer cadets, Turkish soldiers, and Austrian soldiers. . . . During the three weeks of training 9/11 happened, and I remember walking into the barracks where we heard this attack was going on. Sgt. Léger made the comment, 'You know, we're in a completely different world now.' . . . Six months later he was dead."

There was something about being seventeen that affected Jeff Peck's decision to join the military. That year, 1997, one of his high school coaches enrolled him in a leadership camp run by the New Zealand army. The experience stuck with him. Jeff had also bonded with his grandfather, Jim Stephenson, a former RCAF rear gunner who was shot down in 1941 and spent the remainder of the war in a German POW camp. His granddad had joined the air force by lying about his age; he was seventeen. It was about that time Jeff also took an interest in a local gun club, where other veterans of the Second World War gathered occasionally to share stories. Their tales and trials registered on the impressionable teenager. He suddenly felt the military might help make something of his life, so he joined the reserves and later applied to study at Kingston's Royal Military College (RMC). It was no picnic. The first year he was failing a few of the subjects, getting no sleep, and bending under the stress of regimentation. Despite his slow start, by 1999 Peck had graduated because he said he'd learned to be goal oriented. He'd decided he would prove to his family, his peers, and himself that he could become an infantry officer in the Princess Patricia's.

"There's a memorial arch at RMC. It was built in the 1930s to commemorate the dead of the First World War. When we first arrived at RMC in the middle of the night—scared shitless—they walked us through that arch [knowing] the next time we'd be allowed to walk through it was upon graduation," Peck explained. "So I remember at graduation, we did our big parade, received our commissions [then] walked the kilometre down to the memorial and went through the arch. Symbolic and a lot of tradition. It was great. I'd done it."

That march under the arch marked a turning point. It became an emotional moment for his parents—his father realized his son was no longer a boy and his mother realized her son might now have to serve where he'd be in harm's way. For the young commissioned graduate, however, it meant finding a way of proving himself, not just as an administrator at an army desk, but as an active soldier. The year after RMC, he consented to a tour of duty in Bosnia as an officer handling civil and military co-operation—rebuilding infrastructure such as utilities, schools, and small businesses. It was a role somewhat stereotypical of Canada's peacekeeping legacy—using a very hands-on approach, immersing themselves in the community, and working in co-operation. And Peck was clearly proud of Canadian efforts to build trust in Bosnia.

"Why put a hundred men in a location?" Peck said. "You can have one reconnaissance vehicle that can see everything, but only takes two men to operate, so the rest of the hundred men can be doing things other than patrolling."

He alluded to what he knew of American initiatives, where U.S. troops arrived en masse, armed to the teeth, and then set up defensive works around compounds looking outward.

"There's a time and place for that," Peck said. "Bosnia in 2000 was not one of them."

But Afghanistan was different, I suggested to him, and all the rules changed, didn't they? I wanted the young officer to explain the warlike atmosphere he and his battalion found when they landed at Kandahar in 2002 as part of the NATO-led International Security Assistance Force (ISAF). It was, after all, Canada's first combat operation since Korea and that meant that rules of engagement became more robust. He confirmed that the rules "were in accordance with the law of armed conflict, meaning we have a known enemy and we can use up to and including deadly force against anyone." I wondered if that made the whole war on terror experience more intense, more unsettling, more like his grandfather Jim Stephenson's experience.

"It depended on the mission," Peck said. "On [one mission] we were told anyone on this mountain is enemy. There was no reason why they should be there. . . . But if we're going into a town, that's a whole different story. That's where you get into this rules of engagement, this escalation of force because you don't know. That's how Cpl. Jamie Murphy got killed, when a suicide bomber jumped on the Iltis and blew him up [in January 2004]. How do you know?"

"How did all this, this Afghanistan tour, affect you?" I asked.

"I'd like to say it has affected me for the best. I'd be lying if I said that," Peck said and he took a few seconds to give me his next thought. "It's been hard on my family. It's hurt my marriage . . ."

Immersion in an army on active service in a war zone, he said, changed him. It made him see the darker side of humankind. It took away much of his optimism about the world. It made him less patient with things, less patient with others. And even though he realized his experience in Afghanistan had put his relatives through a wringer, he didn't feel comfortable talking to them about it. He said it was common practice for the military to send troops coming out of a theatre of war through the island of Guam for several days of reintegration or decompression en route home. But when he returned to Canada, Peck said his patriarchal view of the family, in which a man remains strong, always able to cope, didn't allow him to show much emotion over the death of four PPCLI comrades. Not even to his wife. He admitted to being more selfish and unwilling to take on his wife's problems in addition to his own.

Toward the end of the interview, I asked him if the experience at Tarnak Farm made him less eager to take on another overseas posting.

"Again, I'd be lying if I said no." Again he paused as he thought about another impact of the Afghanistan mission on his life. "I've always wanted to have children, but I'm hesitant . . . because I still have some operational time where I'll be in a front-line unit. It might be hard for my family."

Just a month after his return from Afghanistan, Jeff Peck received a promotion to the rank of captain, due him after two years' service as a lieutenant. Six months after our conversation in the middle of 2004, he joined the Disaster Assistance Response Team of the Canadian Forces, providing clean water to victims of the tsunami in Sri Lanka. He and his wife decided to separate. He met a new partner and in the spring of 2009 the couple had their first child.

Since our paths crossed in our mutual hometown, Jeff Peck and I communicated periodically after our first interview. We rarely spoke about the friendly-fire incident again, until the summer of 2007. On July 4 of that year, PPCLI Capt. Matthew Dawe was killed—along with five other troops and an interpreter—by a roadside bomb in Afghanistan. His military superiors assigned Capt. Peck the job of assisting officer for Dawe's family. Although he didn't know Capt. Dawe personally, he had attended RMC with his brother James and served in Afghanistan with two other brothers, Peter and Phil. As assisting officer, one of Jeff's assignments was to travel with the Dawe family as a repatriation convoy took Matthew's body in a hearse from the tarmac at CFB Trenton, along 172 kilometres of Highway 401 and the Don Valley Parkway from the base to the coroner's office in Toronto. Following an autopsy, Dawe's body would be released to the family.

Though Peck didn't expect it, the assignment wrote the final chapter in his connection to the Afghanistan mission.

Since 2002, Peck had known about spontaneous assemblies of firefighters, police, veterans, and civilians paying homage to fallen Canadian troops along what later became officially "the Highway of Heroes." Not until he travelled with the convoy bringing Capt. Dawe's body to the forensic science centre in Toronto, however, did he witness one of these emotional outpourings first-hand. It moved him so greatly that he wrote an account for the local paper, asking me to offer editorial guidance. He didn't need my help.

"I can recall the exact moment I finally broke down following the Tarnak Farm friendly fire incident in April 2002," he began. "It wasn't when I saw, heard or smelled the effects of a 500-pound bomb on an unsuspecting and unprepared infantry company. Nor was it when I called my anxious parents. . . . Instead, about a month following the incident, I opened a care package from my mother and as always it included a two-week old *Toronto Star*. . . .

"It talked about how cars stopped on the side of the road, how people took off their hats, put their hands on their hearts, and gave a few seconds out of respect for these men. I'm not sure why . . . but I allowed myself—for that brief moment—a chance to grieve. . . ."

Peck's account from inside the limousines carrying the families—including Capt. Dawe's relatives—from Trenton to Toronto along the route proved the most compelling. He claimed that the speed of things had not allowed the families to grieve their loss. He said the families had been stuck in a feeling of disbelief that was suddenly shattered by the sight of the flag-draped casket being transferred from the transport aircraft to the hearse. But that was just the beginning.

"Nothing could have prepared me or the family for what we witnessed driving down the [Highway] 401 corridor that day. There was a police escort down the entire 401 and Don Valley Parkway. . . .

Every single overpass [there are 50 of them] was filled with people: firefighters, fire trucks, paramedics, veterans, boy scouts, even a contingent of bikers lining the route.... Initially, the family was shocked at this show of support. For the first time family members didn't feel as if they were alone. Their grief was being felt and shared by many Canadians.

"As we continued along the 401 and the crowds got larger, the mood inside the limousine shifted from grief to amazement and even to laughter.... Overwhelmed by the support, the family would give the thumbs up out the window.... At other times, something in the crowd triggered tears. For me, it was seeing veterans in wheelchairs struggling to stand and salute as we passed. In the limousines there was cheering and laughing and crying and remembering...."

Perhaps that trip along the repatriation route, the Highway of Heroes, gave Jeff Peck the closure he couldn't find among family members or comrades-in-arms immediately after April 17, 2002. Meantime, the friendly-fire incident altered Bill Wilson's life too. Since the age of thirteen, he had always bitten his nails; after that night at Tarnak Farm he stopped for good. Vic Speirs, his fellow medic that night, quit smoking permanently. And every year since, Wilson, Speirs, and their third colleague, Jean de la Bourdonnaye, have regularly assembled for a reunion of three in Edmonton to catch up, reflect, and reconnect. "It's our Remembrance Day," Wilson said. Surviving the Tarnak Farm bombing brought changes for Brian Decaire too. The summer after we talked, he began training to become a search and rescue tech. The next year, he and a fellow SAR tech parachuted from a Hercules aircraft in a blizzard to assist an aviator who'd crashed in the Northwest Territories; they received the Medal of Bravery from the Governor General at Rideau Hall for the successful rescue.

The stories the three Afghanistan veterans gave me in 2004 proved indelible. They weren't like the decimation at Dieppe or Hong Kong that elderly veterans had described to me. Their trials weren't as monumental as the Battle of the North Atlantic or Bomber Command's sorties to the Ruhr Valley. And while not as desperate or as costly as their own regiment's heroic stand at Kap'yong, to me their recollections of Tarnak Farm proved just as haunting. It took me some time to realize why.

In Jeff Peck's impatience back home, Bill Wilson's acknowledgement of adrenaline rush in action, and Brian Decaire's coping with the losses of April 17, I had witnessed something original. As a journalist and an author of history—often dealing with military events—I had always read war diaries, letters, and memoirs of eyewitnesses to relive the historical moment. As well, I had always interviewed those surviving witnesses a generation or two generations after the fact. My interview subjects were all elderly veterans. At scores of November 11 ceremonies, they had all recited the familiar lines: "They shall not grow old / As we who are left grow old. / Age shall not weary them / Nor the years condemn . . ." For better or worse, the years had allowed them the luxury of putting into context their wartime experiences in Europe, Asia, or Africa. A lifetime had passed since they had been given battledress to wear or orders to kill.

But in the case of these Afghanistan vets, all three were still in or close to active service. All three were remembering events the way friends and family recalled a recent car accident, a murder in the city, or last year's house fire. For the first time in my work with veterans' stories, I was viewing wartime events that were as vivid as yesterday, not a half century ago. More than that, through these three young men's recollections, for the first time, I could now see the near-death and coping experiences of every other veteran I'd ever met. Peck, Wilson, and Decaire had, for me, become a window to the trauma of their fathers' and grandfathers' wartime horrors. I'd never been closer to the anguish soldiers experience than through these three veterans' memories. Though young enough to be my children, they had shown me the face of war my father's generation must have known. Until now, I haven't thanked them enough for the gift of that insight.

10

KEEPERS OF THE FLAME

CHARLEY FOX'S DEATH seemed certain as many as a dozen times. That's the way of war. Strap a pilot into the cockpit of a military aircraft and that's a distinct possibility. Strap a student pilot into the second cockpit of a Harvard training airplane, give him control of that aircraft on an instruments-only takeoff, and the risk is exponential. It was the last day of November 1942 when Charley and his student, Ft. Sgt. Dwyer, accelerated the single-engine Harvard along the runway at the Dunnville, Ontario, service flight training school. Instructor Fox's hands were off the controls; trainee Dwyer's hands were on them, but he was under the hood (a canopy over his head so that he was taking off without visual reference, effectively blind). Moments into the takeoff attempt, Charley noted that their aircraft was veering to the left off the runway. On the intercom, he told Dwyer to correct it. The swing left continued. Now on frozen turf, the Harvard was nearly at flying speed, but its undercarriage was sticking to the snow and slush on the ground. Charley also spotted the airfield's outer perimeter fence dead ahead.

"I took full control," he said, "and jammed on full power. I bounced [the Harvard] over the fence, got up to about seventy-five feet and the right wing went down [stalled]. We went in with the right wing hitting first. It snapped off... and we're lying on our right side. I'm not hurt, but I'm turning off switches because I can hear gasoline dripping out of the ruptured fuel tank. Suddenly, there's this knock on my canopy.

"'Sir, sir, are you hurt?' said Dwyer from outside the aircraft. He'd managed to get through an escape hatch and he was immediately checking to see if I was all right."

The instructor and his trainee had survived a Harvard stall due to engine failure. What made the incident remarkable—and the story more spine-tingling as Charley related it to me—was that he would face a second airborne mechanical failure later that very same day. Told, after the first crash, that he should go to a hospital to be checked, Charley refused because he was expected to lead night-flying instruction at a neighbouring station in Welland, Ontario, later that evening. During one of those night flights—in a moonless, overcast sky, which made the black of the ground indistinguishable from the black of the sky—Charley told me that he and another student pilot put a Harvard into a loop.

"As we came over the top of the loop and the speed's building," he said, "we had a complete power failure [the engine stopped]. I was in a complete black vacuum and I'm suddenly not sure if I'm going up or coming down. That's I guess when experience takes over. I had to believe my instruments—needle, ball, and airspeed—and pulled it out of a dive and [got the engine running again] and got it flying straight and level. No moon, no stars in the sky. There wasn't a light on the ground. That woke me up."

I heard Charley tell those two sequential stories dozens of times as he and I travelled the country speaking to audiences. They always wanted to know every last detail about his courage facing those near misses. He didn't disappoint. But he never bragged about his quick thinking or heroic escapes. Instead, he would always explain that his thousands of hours of experience as an instructor in the British Commonwealth Air Training Plan had paid him an extraordinary dividend—how not to panic, but to rely on the basic flying skills as a means of survival. Even years later, in front of huge air-show audiences who clamoured for his tales of derring-do, he would make each incident seem more a parable about the importance of knowledge and experience than the defiance of death.

Charley never travelled without his personal collection of easels and cardboard panels bristling with maps, sketches, quotations, log entries, colour illustrations, and photographs from his own collection, many actually excerpted from the pages of his pilot's log books. One of the pictures Charley regularly displayed during his Torch Bearer sessions at schools, Remembrance banquets, history nights at the Royal Canadian Military Institute, and even one appearance he and I made at a shopping mall, always elicited sighs and queries. The photo showed the hulk of a Harvard trainer that had crashed right-side up in a wooded area near Bagotville, Quebec. That's where Charley had taken his operational training en route to his overseas posting on Spitfires in June 1943. What stood out in the snapshot pasted to one of Charley's panels was that the Harvard had no front end.

"That's when I had my mid-air collision," he told his audience. "I was leading a section of three Harvards. Three Hurricanes came along. One did a mock attack from below. The pilot in one must have blacked out, hit me, tore off my engine right to the fire wall. He spun in and was killed. . . . I opened the coop top, stood on the seat, and went over the side . . . and parachuted from 300 feet," barely enough altitude for his chute to open and cushion his descent. He later wrote in his log book beside that entry: "My guardian flew with me that day!"

Just as often, young audiences, business clubs, and veterans alike, wanted to hear about Charley's harrowing experiences as a Spitfire pilot. He always obliged, but never made himself the hero. In over a year of combat flying—during 234 sorties between D-Day and VE Day—he was in a Spitfire (or, as he said, "wearing a Spitfire") almost as often as he ate breakfast or changed his clothes. On his first sortie led by fighter ace Buzz Beurling—on February 15, 1944—a bumpy takeoff resulted in a tremor-filled flight aboard his Spitfire; he flew all the way to France and back with the tips of all four propeller blades sheared off. Five weeks later en route to gunnery practice in

Wales, his Spitfire's engine died on the final approach to the airfield; too low to bail out, he glided the Spit to a safe but, as he described it, "bags of twitch" landing. In July 1944, a trigger-happy Allied anti-aircraft gunner opened fire on his night flight of four Spitfires, but Charley managed to shepherd everybody down safely. A month after that, during a diving attack on a German tank, enemy anti-aircraft shells put a three-foot hole in Charley's Spitfire right behind the seat; he still landed the aircraft without incident. During Operation Market-Garden, the "bridge too far" operation in September 1944, Charley's log captured the drama of sorties in the cockpit of his Spitfire VZ-F.

"Germans tried to knock out Nijmegen [and] Arnhem bridges. Forty . . . sixty . . . ninety enemy aircraft against twelve of ours! Similar to Battle of Britain or Malta. A great big mix-up [dogfight]. Black crosses everywhere. When hit, I kept VZ-F rolling straight down. I thought 'This is it!' However, got control, two hands on joy stick. Chased by two F-190s [German fighter aircraft]. They finally gave up. Awkward landing in Le Culot, Belgium."

During the first full week of October, the fighters in his 412 Squadron had shot down thirty-one enemy fighter aircraft and scored seven more probable kills. Charley's log showed that—after only eight months on operations—he'd accumulated more than two hundred hours of combat flying time. But then, on October 6, 1944, in a sortie that very likely triggered plenty of nightmares, Charley suddenly found himself in an inexplicable dogfight, the one he described as "the toughest." En route home from a tangle with German fighters between Nijmegen and Arnhem, Charley had become separated from his wingman. His flight log described the astounding encounter:

"I looked behind to see a Spit catching up," he wrote. "Good. Wiggled my wings to wave greeting. I looked again and he was firing. I whipped my Spit straight up to give him a full view [of Allied insignia on the aircraft]. He circled and curved in firing again! It was a Spit with no markings. We had a real go then. No one got the advantage. We ended up flying head on. I got low on fuel so heading south I ducked under him and got back to base. . . ."

Then, rather than take credit for a superb exhibition of flying in front of his captivated audience (myself included), Charley concluded his story with one of his well-worn expressions: "Wouldn't you like to think it just was an accident, a misunderstanding," he said, "but we learned later it was a German pilot in a captured Spitfire."

Charley told me that a normal tour of duty for fighter pilots was about one hundred sorties or about two hundred hours in the air. By early 1945, his log totals illustrated the exceptional nature of his service—234 sweeps and 314.05 accumulated operational hours. His final combat entry on January 18, 1945, notes that he flew Spitfire VZ-F on a weather recce. Charley explained that if wing commanders had patchy weather information and couldn't decide whether to send up fighter aircraft in search of targets, they often called on him to fly to the target areas alone—as a kind of scout—then to return and report on cloud conditions, ceiling, turbulence, and of course, enemy activity. Charley's log noted one such sortie lasted an hour and three-quarters. Then, in a later note of explanation, he wrote:

"Another weather reconnaissance! [From] group headquarters to front lines down the Rhine. Ceiling about 300 feet. Nijmegen to Cologne, flew carefully. Weather crappy. Decided to [follow] highway west to Eindhoven. Still lousy. Do I land? What the heck? Took highway north to 's-Hertogenbosch—familiar territory. No problem. Above the trees. Watch high-rise buildings. Found railway. Going east. Curved left. White fields—was that water? There's my landmark—two high smokestacks. Pull up to circle and head south on 180 degrees. . . .

"Big bang. Big black puff. Friendly fire?! Pull into cloud. Canopy open. Propeller goes into full fine pitch. . . ."

Charley deduced that he had mistaken the smokestacks for those in an Allied-held area. In fact, he had strayed across the Rhine River over German-held territory, and an 88-mm, anti-aircraft battery north of the river had sighted his Spitfire and using proximity fuses had fired at his aircraft at about 12,000 feet. One of the German shells had exploded near the base of the Spit's propeller, piercing the plane's cowling and severing a hydraulic line. The broken line then began spewing oil back across his windscreen. Partly to evade the anti-aircraft, but also to reorient himself, Charley manoeuvred the Spitfire into a dive to a lower altitude. But because of all the hydraulic fluid now streaming across his windscreen, he was effectively flying blind. All he knew was that he was flying south away from enemy territory into a friendly zone in desperate search of an aerodrome.

"Can't see ahead. Weave back and forth. Still above 300 feet, looking for an airstrip. No dice!" his flight log's notes went on. "Down to ten gallons. Pick a field by big farm house. Attempt wheels up landing. . . ."

With hundreds of operational hours under his belt—in both friendly and hostile skies, aboard both training and combat aircraft, through both favourable and inclement weather—F/L Fox resorted to his instincts and his instruments. He couldn't find a working airstrip. He had perhaps a few minutes of fuel left in his tanks. So he gently reduced his speed and stalled the Spitfire metres above a farm field, allowing the crippled Spitfire to skid on its belly to an uneventful stop in the mud—a perfect, controlled crash landing. It was, it turned out, an inglorious end to a decorated fighter pilot's exceptional wartime career. Hitching a ride back to his air station at Heesch, in Holland, Charley was eight hours overdue. But safe and sound.

His commanding officer, Group Capt. Gordon McGregor, met him immediately and announced, "Fox, that's your last trip." His squadron leader, Dean Dover, echoed the same executive decision. "You're through," he said.

And later that night, Charley wrote his final entry for January 18, 1945: "Crash landed. Hit by flak. And how! . . . End of tour."

Even Charley sensed his time to quit had come. Soon after, word of his being awarded a second Distinguished Flying Cross came through. The citation said in part: "This officer has displayed exceptional courage and skill in pressing home his attacks against the enemy. . . . F/L Fox destroyed or damaged at least 64 enemy transports and since the invasion of Normandy has destroyed a total of 127 vehicles . . . displaying outstanding coolness and determination."

G/C McGregor then asked Charley, "Do you want to go to the palace [for the award ceremony]?"

"Nope," Charley said.

At twenty-five, Charles William Fox, who'd served King and country in an RCAF uniform for nearly five years, turned down the chance to meet George VI at Buckingham Palace for his very own award reception.

"I've been lucky," he told his C.O. "I'd better go home."

In one of many conversations I shared with Charley Fox about coming through the war in one piece, I asked him how he felt as he came home. Was there any sense of satisfaction in his honourable discharge? Was there any glory in being awarded the double DFC? Helping to win the war? Had he felt blessed surviving a full tour of duty? Or should he just chalk it up to good luck?

"You have this fatalistic view. If it's going to happen, it's going to happen," he said. "Some guys found it very awkward. Some had a fear of flying. Some had a fear of dying. They kept on. They'd come down after a flight wringing wet with fear. They kept pushing themselves to do it. . . .

"On my way over I had a premonition. I looked out the window of the train [en route to embarkation aboard a ship overseas]. I saw this sign on a barn. I wondered whether I would see it again. Somehow I felt that I *would* see it again. And sure enough, I did. . . . I'd have to say I was lucky. Whether God had a bigger plan, who's to know?"

In the years I came to know and befriend Charley Fox, I noted that he went to church regularly. Indeed, after the war when he and his wife, Helen, moved to London, he was baptized, taught Sunday school, and even assisted at church communion. I never got the sense, however, that he was a devoutly religious or spiritual man during his service in the air force. In wartime, I've learned, things were different. People in uniform attended church service out of respect for their comrades, as not to let the padre down, and I guess, to ensure every last detail was covered before entering the battlefield.

Charley dutifully attended those front-line services. Although I often saw Charley Fox animated and impassioned, I don't think I ever heard him swear. I learned, however, that on his last day alive, he did swear—not at anybody, not at any deity, not at his fate, but perhaps in a momentary outburst of frustration.

On October 18, 2008, members of his favourite volunteer organization—the Canadian Harvard Aircraft Association—wrapped up another monthly meeting in a portable at Tillsonburg, Ontario. It had been there, nearly twenty years before, where I had met the man on a CHAA fly-day resupplying the cash float at the volunteer coffee stand. As was the club's custom, after the meeting, many of the CHAA members drove a short distance south from the airstrip into Tillsonburg for brunch at a local café. On this particular Saturday, however, Charley never arrived. En route, his car entered an intersection and collided with another vehicle. My closest veteran friend—a man who, after the death of my own father, often called me "son"—died in that crash. He had come through a handful of training accidents in Canada as well as more than three hundred hours of aerial combat overseas and had survived daily sorties on which countless other air crew perished. He had been awarded two Distinguished Flying Crosses, put Erwin Rommel out of the war. He had outlived the war and all its scars, seen and unseen, only to die in a car crash in his eighty-eighth year. As much as I had prepared for it, during all those years I came to know and love the man, the phone call informing me that Charley Fox had died crushed me. I am still trying to recover.

Several days later, at the funeral home in Thamesford, Ontario, a woman approached Charley's daughter, Sue. The woman explained that she didn't know the family, but that she happened on the crash site shortly after the accident. She told Sue she saw that Charley was gravely injured and managed to crawl into the crumpled car to comfort him. "She shared . . . that he was not in any visible pain and surveyed the trees, sky, and other surroundings with a look of peace on his face." The woman said that a police officer arrived before the paramedics did. He cut the seat belt away from Charley because it had tightened in the crash. And Charley responded to the officer, addressing him as "Sir," as only he would seeing a person of authority close by. But the woman said that Charley apparently also swore out loud several times.

"Damn. Damn," he'd blurted out repeatedly.

My sense of Charley Fox was that he wasn't cursing at anybody for what had happened. That wasn't his nature. Perhaps he was angry that his life of just over eighty-eight years was nearly done, with so much left undone. That his experience as husband, father, grandfather, veteran, and friend to so many was now behind him. That his work as the veterans' crusader was finished. That his time to tell and retell stories of the heroism he'd witnessed—at air training stations in Canada, at aerodromes in Britain, in the skies over a liberated Europe—had passed. That his role as a torch bearer enlightening Canadians about service and sacrifice of several generations of his countrymen—from the Great War to Afghanistan—was ending. Someone else would have to keep that flame burning.

When I began this work—part memoir and part exploratory journey—Charley Fox and so many other men and women of the services were never far from me. I could and often did consult them on their experiences whenever I needed to verify details I was assembling for a newspaper column, a magazine feature, a radio or TV documentary, or a book. Other times I just took an hour or an afternoon to be with them. Just to visit. Those veterans became more than sources to me. They were my living link to times I wanted, no, needed to understand. They were a part of my life's work as a writer and of my life. Many of them became close friends. Such was the case with Stephen Bell, the Dieppe veteran; air training instructors Charlie Konvalinka, Dick Ross, and John Stene; Air Transport Auxiliary ferry pilot Marion Orr; Len Badowich, the Korean War prisoner of war; D-Day glider pilot Fred Sampson and his tow pilot Walter Schierer; Harry Pope, the veteran of the Italian liberation; and navy crewmen Terry Manuel and Scott Young, among many others. One by one, I watched time steal their health, erode their faculties. Repeatedly, like the wartime younger brother at home dreading the missing- or killed-in-action telegram from Ottawa, I've learned of their sudden passing and felt that living link break and those close friendships end.

I cannot lie and say that their deaths inspire or spur me on. The passing of men and women who've taken me into their confidence and given me the gift of their memories hurts as much as if they were my own father and mother. Perhaps the greater hurt, however, is knowing they're not around to set me straight on a fact or make a wartime event come to life with their personal recollections. It's tougher, too, realizing I can't be with them next November 11 to recite "For the Fallen" in tribute to their comrades who died too young. And it's frustrating to know they won't be coming to the college where I teach to give our Remembrance Day tribute a physical presence for my students and fellow faculty. The same as losing a close friend or an immediate family member, each time another of my close veteran friends dies, as a chronicler of events in Canada's wartime history I feel orphaned.

Still, I recognize it's the wisdom of wartime experience these veterans have shared with me that overshadows my loss. I sense that carrying on, keeping their stories alive is living up to my side of the bargain when they consented to be interviewed. Each visit with a veteran has taught me a dimension of service I did not know existed. All of my sessions with them have deepened my respect for their courage—whether rewarded with medals or not. And every conversation has helped me be better prepared for the next. My encounters and friendships with veterans have given me—perhaps more than any other historian in the country—a stronger sense of esprit de corps among comrades and enmity for an enemy, a better knowledge of hardship and resilience, a more vivid picture of fear and coping with fear, a clearer understanding of traumatic stress and its after-effects, and always an understanding of commitment over convenience. Every veteran's insight has taught me volumes about the nature of the Canadian citizen armies of the past century. It's a story I am obliged to tell and retell.

Since the 1970s, I have tried to go beyond that iconic veteran's image—the elderly, former warrior clad in beret, flannels, and a chest full of service medals—standing solemnly for two minutes of silence at the community cenotaph. I've encouraged those mostly mum veterans to start talking at schools, business banquets, Canadian Club luncheons, church picnics, and on radio and television . . . and not just once a year, on November 11. On one hand—wherever I've worked or had occasion to MC Remembrance Day observances—I have encouraged and insisted on that two-minute silence. Meanwhile, on the other hand, I've campaigned to break that stereotypical silence and have pushed veterans to give us the reasons we should remember and recognize them for giving the world a second chance. Sometimes, I took risks and broke the stereotype to make the point.

In the fall of 2001, teachers at the high school I attended back in the 60s, in east-end Toronto, invited me to join a November 11 ceremony at Agincourt Collegiate. They asked me to draw from my wartime research and writing to help about a thousand students gathered in the high school auditorium to visualize Canada's wartime contribution on D-Day. To enrich the event for the students, the school also invited Jan de Vries, a veteran of the 1st Canadian Parachute Battalion and one of 600 men who had leapt from transport aircraft with the British airborne just as the invasion to liberate Europe began.

"When we jumped into Normandy during the night [June 5–6, 1944]," de Vries told the students, "we were seven miles off course."

Then the seventy-seven-year-old greying and weathered veteran, with his paratrooper's wings crest and service medals pinned to his chest, gave the assembly some context. He informed the auditorium of students it was his outfit's job to seize key bridges and causeways inland from the French coast in order to halt or delay German occupying troops from counterattacking Allied troops landing on the Normandy beaches. De Vries then casually described the potential consequences of his military action.

"If you were captured by the German army, you became a prisoner of war," de Vries said. "If you were captured by the SS, you were shot."

When Jan finished his dramatic presentation to the Remembrance Day assembly that morning, it then fell to me to help the students understand its significance. I sensed that as vivid as Jan de Vries's recounting of the battalion's perilous jump into occupied France had been in 1944, he might as well have been describing the Battle of Hastings in 1066. For these modern teenaged students, D-Day probably seemed like ancient history. That's when I discarded my plan to read D-Day excerpts from my books.

"How do you connect your lives with this elderly veteran standing in front of you?" I asked rhetorically. "I'll tell you how." I then asked for someone to turn up the house lights in the auditorium. I left the lectern on stage and walked down among the seats where the teenagers sat somewhat stunned at my aggressive approach.

"Who here has an older brother or sister, say eighteen or twenty years old?" I asked.

Up went a number of hands in response.

"Tell me their names." And I got an "Andrew" from one boy, a "Carol" from another. From a teenaged girl, there was an older brother named Thomas and a David from another. I went on. "Are Andrew, Carol, Thomas, and David pretty smart?"

Everybody laughed out loud at the thought of their older brother or sister being considered intelligent.

"Are they pretty responsible?" I pursued as the laughter died down. "Have they ever had to make a tough decision—a life or death decision? Probably not. But the man you just met—Jan de Vries—he made a number of life and death decisions. And not at the age of seventy-seven, like he is today."

I went on to explain that Jan de Vries had been a teenager when he made the decision to enlist in 1943. He trained for war as a paratrooper, travelled with his battalion halfway around the world, and then jumped into the darkness over occupied France not knowing where he'd land and, if he were captured, whether he'd become a POW or be executed on the spot.

"Jan de Vries did all that when he was eighteen or nineteen, not as the elderly man you see today," I emphasized. And I reminded the students not to think of the typical image of the veterans they'd be seeing at the local cenotaph at 11 o'clock later that morning. "No, think of your older brother Andrew or sister Carol or Thomas or David, as the soldiers of yesterday. Could they have done what those D-Day veterans did? . . . Could you?"

In that instant, in front of those thousand high school students, I think the stereotype was broken. The connection was made between a modern generation of naïve, complacent young people and the generation of youths who'd faced a world war and the potentially fatal decisions it threw at them sixty years before. Suddenly, Jan de Vries, the aging, former D-Day paratrooper on the auditorium stage in front of them, wasn't ancient history any more. The students, at least on this day in that auditorium, saw much more than they were looking at.

In many ways, that awakening parallels the re-education veterans have given me. I once looked upon veterans the way those Agincourt Collegiate students did, to be respected once a year at the downtown cenotaph. But my research, my interview visits, my public speaking, my friendships with them, and my retelling their stories have helped show me otherwise. They've helped me break the silence and the stereotype of the Canadian veteran.

Gavin McDonald's off-handed decision to enlist in the Canadian Corps only after the new well in his Craik, Saskatchewan, farmyard was drilled that fall of 1915 illustrated to me just how duty-driven and innocent recruits could be.

With his accounts of life behind the walls of a Korean War POW camp, Len Badowich showed me that sometimes a soldier's greatest weapon against his enemy didn't consist of steel or lead, but of keeping his wits about him.

As rigidly as WREN Ronnie Egan seemed to adhere to the rules and regulations of the system while in the service, I learned that her pride and independence wouldn't allow her to accept the system's rightful compensation—a veteran's pension—without first experiencing a genuine need.

Dieppe veteran Stephen Bell's photographic memory catalogued every insult and insensitivity at the hands of his German captors, but during our long friendship he admitted that he somehow forgot to hate when one German civilian offered him sustenance and shelter in his moment of greatest need.

A proud member of the Canadian Film and Photo Unit, recording images of Canadians fighting their way across Europe, Chuck Ross showed me that as antiquated as the film he shot might become, what he saw through his viewfinder and otherwise remained indelibly etched in his brain as if it were yesterday.

Sniper Ted Zuber revealed to me both the unfeeling nature of his wartime profession and its personal emotional cost.

Because she never stopped searching for the story of her brother Bill's death in Korea until she found it, Hazel Regan confirmed to me that for every wartime statistic a story must be told.

The leader of a courageous rescue in Korea, Hal Merrithew showed me that losing touch with comrades-in-arms, those under his command, was more painful than the horror of the rescue they accomplished.

Garth Webb proved to me that the commitment his fellow volunteers exhibited liberating Europe, Asia, and North Africa in the Second World War still had the power to affect change a generation later.

My own father, Alex Barris, proved to me that as much as fathers and sons can share, they often cannot share the debilitating accounts of war. In turn, I also learned from D-Day infantryman Fred Barnard that while the ghosts of his longest day would always haunt him, to keep them closeted all his life would be worse still.

The veterans I met from the Afghanistan mission, at this writing still more than a year from its end, opened my eyes to many continuing truths about humankind and warfare. These young men threw themselves into their training and relied on it completely in crisis. They grew closer to their comrades in the line, sometimes closer than to members of their own families. And they were no more able to explain their feelings (or absence of feelings) than their fathers or grandfathers had been. In them, I saw a stark continuum of the veteran experience. In them, I saw fear, I saw trauma, I saw loss, at closer range than at anytime in my professional writing career. I witnessed war damage in men who could have been my sons. And it frightened me to the core to learn that as many as a quarter of these vets needed psychiatric assistance en route home to civilian life or further armed service.*

How many more veterans returning from campaigns in 1918, 1945, or 1953 never made it to such statisticians' lists? How many more of them have medical teams, politicians, reporters, historians, or sons and daughters ignored standing in the silence at the cenotaph on Remembrance Day?

Despite my efforts and the work of like-minded Canadians to preserve their reflections, the living archives of Canada's wartime experience are fast disappearing. Not just in my circle of veteran friends, but generally, the ranks of Second World War and Korean War veterans across the country dwindle more rapidly every year. Some say Second World War vets are now dying by the thousands each week, which erases that living link I've cultivated for more than thirty years. And though I've delivered eulogies for many of those mentioned here, offering my remembrances of Charley Fox proved to be the toughest of all.

The memorial took place on Friday, October 24, 2008, a week or so after he'd died in that car crash. As I walked to the podium at the church in east London that morning, I paused before reading my prepared remarks. I said that I felt awkward standing in front of the public at a London venue without my ever-present co-MC Charley Fox beside me. Charley had always joined me when we presented veterans' stories in that part of the country. This time, I said, I was going to have to try to do it on my own and hope that I performed up

---

* According to information released under the Access to Information Act, the *Toronto Star* reported "as of April 2008, 700 soldiers and Mounties, who had served on the Afghan front lines—19 per cent of all forces deployed—had qualified for medical release from the Canadian Forces or RCMP with 'pensionable psychiatric condition.'"

to his high standard. I chose to begin with a flashback to my own father's memorial. I pointed out, among the hundreds who attended Dad's memorial in 2004, that Charley Fox had shown up unannounced.

Why? Because, he said, "I wanted to be there for you."

I suggested that phrase, "I wanted to be there for you," might well have been Charley's life motto. I recounted many of the times this man had shown up ready to put himself to work in the service of others. He was there for his family, his commanders, his comrades, and his country. There, teaching student sprog pilots in Canada to serve and survive in the air war overseas. There, in Fighter Command to protect the D-Day landings while, beneath him, his brother Ted Fox came ashore with the artillery on Juno Beach. There, for his 126 Wing mates for nineteen months of combat across northwestern Europe. There, at the end of the war to return to civvy street and provide for his family. There, long after the war to speak out for his lost comrades and those veterans in need. There, as honorary colonel of 412 Squadron to tell the air force story for all who would listen. There, for the array of service groups that called on him constantly, and to which he always gave voluntarily without a second's hesitation. And there for me whenever I wanted to find and publish veterans' stories.

"Charley Fox didn't teach me to fly," I said at his memorial finally, "but he taught me that my reach should exceed my grasp. He didn't teach me how to survive a tailspin or an aerial dogfight. But he gave me the tools to become a passionate veterans' advocate. Charley Fox didn't show me how to maintain needle, ball, and airspeed in a cockpit. But he did guide me to becoming a better writer, and, I think, a better person. . . .

"I just hope I can say—for the rest of my life and out of respect for his memory—'Charley, I wanted to be there for you.'"

Notes

CHAPTER ONE – BEYOND REMEMBRANCE

page

1 earned two DFC medals: "The Distinguished Flying Cross and How It Was Won," unpublished life story of John Stene, courtesy Laurel Goodings, with permission from daughter Sheila Stene.

1 "I live nearby": interviews at bridge vigil for Canadian soldiers Michael Freeman, Gregory Kruse, and Gaetan Roberge, Wynford Drive bridge, Toronto, December 30, 2008.

2 "Highway of Heroes": term used by *Toronto Sun* columnist Joe Warmington, June 25, 2007; officially named by the Province of Ontario, August 24, 2007.

3 "I've never done before": Ted Barris comment to CFRB Radio reporter Cheryl Camack, Wynford Drive bridge, Toronto, December 30, 2008.

4 "the forgotten war": phrase often used to describe the Korean War, coined by author John Melady, *Korea: Canada's Forgotten War* (Toronto: Macmillan, 1983).

5 "They shall not grow old": Laurence Binyon, excerpted from "For the Fallen," written in 1914.

6 servicing the Lancasters: Len Read, Remembrance Day observance at Centennial College, East York, Ontario, November 11, 2000.

CHAPTER TWO – "TORCH BEARER"

page

10 "What did you do in the war, Dad?": conversations with Alex Barris, Agincourt, Ontario, June 1964.

13 "Barris Beat": newspaper column by Alex Barris at *Globe and Mail* 1948 to 1956 and *Toronto Telegram* 1956 to 1969, as well as CBC TV show 1956 to 1958.

14 "living room war": term coined by American novelist and essayist Michael J. Arlen, *The Living-Room War* (New York: Viking, 1969).

14 "military industrial complex": Dwight Eisenhower, speech to the nation on disarmament, 1961.

16 "Harvard in all the world": Charley Fox at CHAA fly-day, Tillsonburg, Ontario, November 4, 1990.

17 "the decisive factor": Winston Churchill quoted in "A Decisive Factor," *Aeroplane Monthly*, February 1989, p. 98.

19 "on paper yet": Charley Fox, correspondence, London, Ontario, July 16, 1990.

22 "Why my Andy": Charley Fox, interview, London, Ontario, May 9, 1991.

23 "Tec 4 Barris": wording of "Bronze Star citation given to Alex Barris," U.S. Army document.

24 fourth-highest combat award: Section II, 3-14, p. 41, United States Army Regulations, Army Regulation 600-8-22—Military Awards, Department of the Army, December 11, 2006.

CHAPTER THREE – "THEY JUST FADE AWAY"

page

27 "a damn for Kaiser Bill": poem recited at commencement of Byng Boys Club meeting, Saint John, New Brunswick, May 22, 2007.

28 "the Byng Boys": F.A. McKenzie, *Canada's Day of Glory* (Toronto: William Briggs, 1918), p. 89

29 "20,000 visiting Canadians": Ted Barris, speech to the Byng Boys Club, Saint John, New Brunswick, May 22, 2007.

30 "those fixed points": Queen Elizabeth speech, Vimy Memorial, France, April 9, 2007.

30 "walking ghosts": Jayne MacAulay, author's wife, commenting on the students' presence at Vimy, April 9, 2007.

31 only Canadian killed: J.L. Granatstein and Desmond Morton, *Canada and the Two World Wars* (Toronto: Key Porter, 2003), p. 146.

31 "carrying lighted torches": Ella Mae Bongard, *Nobody Ever Wins a War: The World War I Diaries of Ella Mae Bongard* (Ottawa: Janeric, 1997), p. 58.

31 "the granting of credit": George Rennison, *Letters from the Front, Being a Record of the Part Played by Officers of the Bank in the Great War 1914-1919* (Toronto: Canadian Bank of Commerce, 1920), Vol. 1, p. 305.

31 fourteen more days: "Two Weeks' Jail After Signing of Armistice," *Toronto Daily Star*, March 1919.

32 "a look at this": Jean Gordon, conversation in Saskatoon, Saskatchewan, May 17, 2004.

32 "in the direction of Mons": Gavin McDonald, "Gavin McDonald's Narratives," c. 1960s, courtesy Jean Gordon and Judy Wood, Saskatoon, Saskatchewan.

34 filling sandbags with the chalk: George Hambley, diaries, Manitoba Archives MG7 H11.

35 "something behind me": McDonald, op cit.

36 "armistice for twenty years": Ferdinand Foch, quoted in Peter Vansittart, *Voices from the Great War* (London: Jonathan Cape, 2003), p. 263.

37 "my first experience of war": Anne Pompili (née) Keijzer, TVOntario location shoot, Newmarket, Ontario, October 24, 1994.

38 "never forget that date": Bruce Evans, TVOntario location shoot, Newmarket, Ontario, October 24, 1994.

39 eventually Holland: Bruce Evans, interview, Toronto, January 4, 2003.

39 hidden thirty Jewish friends: Anne Pompili (née) Keijzer, "Family History," unpublished memoir, with permission, Toronto, October 2004.

41 "decisions they did": Danielle Trueman, Pickering College, Newmarket, Ontario, October 24, 1994.

42 eighteen times: Ted Barris, *Deadlock in Korea: Canadians at War 1950–1953* (Toronto: Macmillan, 1999), p. 258.

43 "killed at Dieppe": Len Badowich, interview, Petawawa, Ontario, May 2, 1997.

46 brother's name and papers: Jim Gunn, "A Sniper Disarmed," unpublished memoir, courtesy Korea Veterans Association of Canada.

47 "Chinese hit the hill": Jim Gunn, interview, Petawawa, Ontario, May 2, 1997.

49 "United Nations prisoners": *Treatment of British Prisoners of War in Korea* (London: H.M. Stationery Office, 1955).

49 "victims of the ruling classes": R. Bruce McIntyre, "The Forgotten Thirty-Three: An Examination of Canadian Prisoners of War of the Korean War" (thesis presented to the University of Waterloo), p. 55.

53 "of their captivity": Joe MacSween, "Lost Weight in Red Prison Camps, Freed Canadians Decline to Talk," Canadian Press, August 30, 1953.

55 500,000 young people: Dominion Institute web site www.thememoryproject.com.

CHAPTER FOUR – WHY THEY DON'T TALK

page

58 "at the gravesite": Lewis Buck interviewed by Pierre Berton, William Ready Division of Archives and Research Collections, McMaster University.

58 "screen [and] categorize": Terry Copp and Bill McAndrew, *Battle Exhaustion: Soldiers and Psychiatrists in the Canadian Army, 1939–1945* (Montreal and Kingston: McGill-Queen's University Press: 1990), p. 21.

59 "social misfit": Jim McKinny, interview, Saskatoon, August 4, 1997.

60 "You're twenty-one": Don Kerr, interview, Port Perry, Ontario, January 25, 2003.

61 tears welling up: Don Kerr, interview, Courseulles-sur-Mer, France, June 7, 2003.

61 "highlight of my life": Don Kerr, conversation following Menin Gate ceremony, June 10, 2009.

62 "ethical problems on him": Roméo Dallaire, interview, in Quebec City, June 26, 2002.

64 "who answered the call": Charlie Konvalinka, correspondence, Toronto, November 12, 1990.

66 "a bunch of cowards": Charlie Konvalinka, interviews, Toronto, December 5 and 10, 1990.

71 "freedom and peacetime": Ted Barris eulogy at Charlie Konvalinka funeral, Toronto, December 10, 2004.

72 "Ronnie the Bren Gun Girl": Barris, *Days of Victory: Canadians Remember 1939–1945* (Toronto: Thomas Allen, 2005), first photo section, p. 6.

72 "great-granddaughter": Lotta Dempsey's 1943 feature story, quoted in Jean Bruce, *Back the Attack! Canadian Women During the Second World War—at Home and Abroad* (Toronto: Macmillan Canada, 1985), p. 57.

73 "we were always navy": Ronnie Egan, interview, Uxbridge, Ontario, 1993.

75 65,000 . . . 55,000: Tony German, *The Sea Is at Our Gates: The History of the Canadian Navy* (Toronto: McClelland & Stewart, 1990), p. 197.

75 "No Sailors or Dogs Allowed": Roy Harbin, interview, Agincourt, Ontario, June 17, 1993.

76 led an inquiry: Mr. Justice Roy L. Kellock, "Half Million Words in V-E Riot Evidence," *Toronto Daily Star*, June 18, 1945.

79 "lucky that day": Bob Hesketh, interview (including Bill Lennox), Toronto, January 23, 1991.

CHAPTER FIVE – SETTING THE RECORD STRAIGHT

page

81 "guest of the Führer": Stephen Bell, interview, Uxbridge, Ontario, August 19, 2007.

82 "up there was daylight": Stephen Bell, interview, Uxbridge, Ontario, 1993.

84 the beaches of bodies: Terence Robertson, *The Shame and the Glory: Dieppe* (Toronto: McClelland and Stewart, 1962), p. 383.

84 3,367 of the nearly 5,000 Canadians: J.L. Granatstein and Desmond Morton, *Bloody Victory: Canadians and the D-Day Campaign, 1944* (Toronto: Lester & Orpen Dennys, 1984), p. 11.

86 "7 a.m. to 6 p.m. every day": Stephen Bell, application for pension to Veterans Affairs Canada, March 1992.

87 "ever tasted in my life": Stephen Bell, interviews, Uxbridge, Ontario, 2002–2004.

91 "a lot to be thankful for": Stephen Bell, interview, Uxbridge, Ontario, May 21, 1993.

92 "couldn't get him to land": Charley Fox, interview with Steve Benedict, CHCH TV, Hamilton, Ontario, June 1983.

94 "Graduation Lecture": from the papers of John Bryan Kelshall, with permission from Anneliese Kelshall, correspondence, May 5, 1991, San Fernando, Trinidad.

99 of their own history: "Speech to Allied Air Forces Reunion," October 2, 1993, Barris files.

99 "recognition it merited": Charlie Konvalinka, interview, Toronto, December 5, 1990.

99 "what we actually did": John Campsie, correspondence, Toronto, July 17, 1991.

103 "It was late afternoon": Charley Fox, interview, London, Ontario, May 9, 1991.

104 military aircraft involved: Randy Boswell, "Canadian Spitfire ace given credit for shooting Rommel," quotes author Michel Lavigne, *National Post*, April 27, 2004.

105 depictions of combat: John Keegan, "Foreword," in Ted Barris, *Juno: Canadians at D-Day, June 6, 1944* (Toronto: Thomas Allen, 2004), p. xv.

106 "fellow army photographers": Mary Lea Bell, interview, Gibsons, British Columbia, July 2003.

106 right-hand assistant: Chuck Ross, interview, Edmonton, July 27, 2003.

108 "weapons in the dark": Ken Ewart, interview, Fort Saskatchewan, Alberta, July 27, 2003.

109 "a complete scoop": Richard Malone, *A World in Flames 1944–45* (Toronto: Collins, 1984), p. 32.

109 true cinematographer: Ted Barris, "The shot seen around the world," *Globe and Mail*, June 4, 2004.

109 "McDougall hit the beaches": Ken Bell quoted in Robert Lansdale, "20 Seconds of History—The D-Day Photos," *The Photographic Historical Society of Canada* newsletter, Vol. 4-4, June 2004.

110 three different landing craft: John Eckersley quoted in Robert Lansdale, "20 Seconds of History—The D-Day Photos."

111 "assault craft were mine": Bill Poulis quoted in Robert Lansdale, "20 Seconds of History—The D-Day Photos."

111 "newsreels around the world": Brian O'Regan, Ottawa, letter to Carol Phillips, Lucknow, Ontario, August 13, 1992.

111 "we recorded history": Chuck Ross quoted in Jim Farrell, *Edmonton Journal*, November 11, 2003.

113 four cameramen and two drivers: Chuck Ross, telephone conversation, Edmonton, July 5, 2009.

115 "car was in the lead . . .": Chuck Ross, interview, Edmonton, May 15, 2004.

116 "always be yesterday": Chuck Ross, D-Day speech, Edmonton, June 6, 2004.

CHAPTER SIX – "PUT A HUMAN FACE ON WAR"

page

118 climbed to 5,000 feet: Marion Orr, quoted in Shirley Render, *No Place for a Lady: The Story of Canadian Women Pilots, 1928-1992* (Winnipeg: Portage & Main, 1992), p. 91.

118 "knock down": Scott Young, interview, Peterborough, Ontario, July 12, 1993.

119 "no instruments": "Brick Bradford survived a Spitfire flight deep into China," *Critical Moments: Profiles of Members of the Greater Vancouver Branch of the Aircrew Association* (Vancouver: Aircrew Association, 1989), pp. 297–98.

119 "up and quit on me": John Trull, interview, Mississauga, Ontario, June 20, 1991.

119 "most important aircraft": Jackie Rae, interview, Toronto, December 27, 1990.

123 "amenities for naval crews": Joseph Schull, *The Far Distant Ships: An Official Account of Canadian Naval Operations in the Second World War* (Ottawa: Queen's Printer, 1961), p. 111.

123 "Canada's armed conflicts": "It's Almost Too Late," report by Canadian Merchant Navy Association to the Standing Senate Committee on Veterans Affairs, 1991.

123 "forced labour": George S. MacDonnell, *This Soldier's Story, 1939–1945* (Nepean, Ontario: Hong Kong Veterans Commemorative Association, 2000), p. 108.

124 air force service: Bruce, *Back the Attack!* p. 75.

124 "treated as one": Shirley Mills (née Smith), with permission, letters home to Sarnia, Ontario, 1942–43.

125 "D-Day Dodgers": Lady Nancy Astor, first British woman Member of Parliament, implying that men of the British Eighth Army deliberately avoided service in the "real war" in France.

126 "could be a man": Ted Zuber, interviews, Petawawa, Ontario, and Seeley's Bay, Ontario, May and October, 1997.

132 "had been eliminated": John Keegan, *The Face of Battle* (New York: Penguin, 1978), p. 328.

137 "service in Korea": Herb Pitts, interviews, Etobicoke, Ontario, and CBC Radio, *Fresh Air*, Toronto, June and July 1997.

144 "we would meet someone": Hazel Regan, interview, Brampton, Ontario, July 27, 1997.

CHAPTER SEVEN – FRONT ROW SEAT TO HISTORY

page

148 "Europe is largely ignored": Canada Normandy Project brochure, 1997, p. i.

149 "donating to this cause": Garth Webb, interview on CBC Radio, *Fresh Air*, Toronto, 1997.

150 "Americans won the war": Lise Cooper, interview, Toronto, March 4, 2003.

150 $3 million for the centre: Barris, *Juno: Canadians at D-Day, June 6, 1944*, p. 265.

151 "the hell Normandy was": Garth Webb, interview, Toronto, March 4, 2003.

152 earth and brush: Wes Alkenbrack, unpublished memoirs, with permission, Napanee, Ontario, September 2003.

153 W.J. Dupuis: 14th Field Regiment Active Service War Diary, June 6/7, 1944, p.26.

156 Darryl F. Zanuck view of D-Day: *The Longest Day*, produced by Darryl F. Zanuck for 20th Century Fox, 1962.

157 abandoning those vessels: John Clark, interview during Normandy tour, June 2004.

158 invasion troops to shore: Wilf Pound, interview during Normandy tour, June 2004.

158 "a deuce and a half": Viola Boyd, interview during Normandy tour, June 2004.

159 "Carpiquet airport": David Boyd, correspondence, Ottawa, August 25, 2008.

161 "crash-land": Fred Sampson, talk with children at Memorial de Caen, France, June 2, 2004.

162 "a thunderous roar": Lorne Empey, interview during Normandy tour, June 2004.

162 "dropped our hook": "The Memoirs of William Lorne Empey," with permission, May 23, 2005.

163 "the city of Caen": Bill Novick, interview, Trouville-sur-Mer, France, June 3, 2004.

164 "this week's *Time* magazine": May 31, 2004 edition, pp. 38–39.

165 "what the hell do you think we are?": David Boyd, correspondence, August 25, 2008.

168 "angels of freedom": Anne Pompili (née) Keijzer, interview, Newmarket, Ontario, October 24, 1994.

170 "for our home": Mayor of Baarn, Holland, Barris diary, Silent March ceremony, May 4, 2005.

170 "important to my family": Harry Roos, conversation at Baarn Silent March ceremony, May 4, 2005.

172 "by at least two months": Martin Middlebrook and Chris Everitt, *The Bomber Command War Diaries: An Operational Reference Book, 1939–1945* (London: Penguin, 1985), pp. 422–23.

172 were lost: ibid., p. 595.

173 "hold each other so tightly": Paul Van Nest, conversation during Dutch Liberation Tour, May 2005.

174 "I originally registered": Jim Ronan, conversation during Dutch Liberation Tour, May 2005.

175 "affects those involved": Jim Ronan, correspondence, Kingston, Ontario, March 26, 2005.

176 "time to hold me once": Patricia Williams, interview, Amsterdam, Holland, May 11, 2005.

177 "picture in our living room": Patricia Williams, correspondence, Creston, California, June 13, 2005.

177 illegally assisted Dutch civilians: Les Robinson, interview, Nijmegen, Holland, May 7, 2005.

178 "the hunger winter": Ann Vos, remembrance during Dutch Liberation Tour, May 7, 2005.

178 "raid on the farm": Mac Traas, remembrance during Dutch Liberation Tour, May 4, 2005.

179 "like a king": Corne Bibo, interview, Rotterdam, Holland, May 8, 2005.

180 "my fallen comrade": Ron Charland quoted in correspondence from Lorne Empey and Dorothy Deluzio, Kingston, Ontario, May 17, 2005.

CHAPTER EIGHT – REUNION OF TWO

page

186 "going down the ramp": Fred Barnard, interview, Uxbridge, Ontario, July 20, 2003.

186 "to inform you": telegram to Janet Barnard from Minister of National Defence, Ottawa, June 17, 1944.

187 eight weeks: F.J. Hatch, *Aerodrome of Democracy: Canada and the British Commonwealth Air Training Plan, 1939–1945* (Ottawa: Directorate of History, Department of National Defence, 1983), p. 129.

187 900 hours: ibid., p. 171.

187 The BCATP was: Ted Barris, *Behind the Glory: Canada's Role in the Allied Air War* (Toronto: Thomas Allen, 2005), p. 306.

188 "biggest dressing down": Bill Davies, correspondence, Toronto, April 8, 1991.

189 "took off from base": Bill Davies, correspondence, Toronto, March 19, 1991.

190 "most experienced and highly trained": Chaz Bowyer, *Path Finders at War* (Shepperton, Surrey, U.K.: Ian Allan Ltd., 1977), p. 6.

191 "That was me!": Frank Boyd, correspondence, Hamilton, Ontario, April 8, 1993.

193 "a UN police action": Ian Murray, speech at cenotaph rededication ceremony, Almonte, Ontario, July 19, 1997.

193 "a cartoon": Jim Boire, interview, Almonte, Ontario, July 19, 1997.

194 "joined in January 1944": Haldene Merrithew, interview, Almonte, Ontario, July 19, 1997.

200 "in the command post": Haldene Merrithew, interview, Carleton Place, Ontario, July 19, 1997.

205 "joined in February 1951": Roland Pearce, interview, Brampton, Ontario, July 27, 1997.

207 cool nerves: Bill Boss, "Walked Through Field of Mines to Lead His Comrades to Safety," Canadian Press, October 24, 1952.

209 "couldn't get into the RAF": Fred Sampson, interview, Port Hope, Ontario, December 30, 2002.

211 inland from the coast: Hilary St. George Saunders and Denis Richards, *Royal Air Force, 1939-1945*, Vol. III, *The Fight Is Won* (London: Her Majesty's Stationery Office, 1954), pp. 113–14.

215 "had the qualifications": Walter Schierer, interview, Port Hope, Ontario, February 19, 2003.

216 "six feet of war": George Griffiths, interview, Petawawa, Ontario, May 4, 1997.

219 back to the beaches: Ellis Plaice, *Red Berets '44*, published by The Illustrated London News, 1994, p. 98.

219 "singularly successful": Saunders and Richards, *Royal Air Force*, p. 114.

220 "exemplary and outstanding behaviour": Charles McGregor, quoting Chirac letter in "French Legion of Honour Presentations," *The Rifleman*, Queen's Own Rifles of Canada newsletter, April 2007.

CHAPTER NINE – "NO ARMOUR AGAINST FATE"

page

223 "deadly of all battles": Terry Manuel, interview, Gloucester, Ontario, June 1994.

224 watches, cigarettes, and papers: Ian J. Campbell, *Murder at the Abbaye: The Story of Twenty Canadian Soldiers Murdered at the Abbaye d'Ardenne* (Ottawa: Golden Dog Press, 1996), p. 106

224 "We were next": Hubert Thistle, interview, Toronto, August 24, 1993.

225 "the last rites": Tony Burns, correspondence, Halifax, February 3, 2003.

226 "battlefield promotion, I guess." Tony Burns, interview, Halifax, May 24, 2004.

227 "in Morse code": Bob Cameron, interview, Thornhill, Ontario, May 24, 2003.

227 the day's Canadian losses: Col. C.P. Stacey, *The Canadian Army, 1939–1945: An Official Historical Summary* (Ottawa: CND/King's Printer), p. 243.

228 "Why not me?": Charley Fox, interview, London, Ontario, May 9, 1991.

228 "They draw fire": Gerry Emon, interview, Almonte, Ontario, July 18, 1997.

229 "chopper lands at base": Brian Decaire, interview, Uxbridge, Ontario, March 17, 2004.

235 restricted operating zone: Michael Friscolanti, *Friendly Fire: The Untold Story of the U.S. Bombing That Killed Four Canadian Soldiers in Afghanistan* (Toronto: Wiley, 2005), p. 31.

241 "all there that night": Bill Wilson, interview, Borden, Ontario, November 23, 2004.

248 notes and the board's records: "Medical Response," PowerPoint presentation by Sgt. Bill Wilson, with permission, September 4, 2004.

249 "a lot worse.": Jeff Peck, interview, Kingston, Ontario, August 9, 2004.

253 roadside bomb in Afghanistan: Daniel Girard and Rosie Dimanno, "Capt. Dawe's sad fate," *Toronto Star*, July 5, 2007.

254 an account for the local paper: Jeff Peck, "Grief and laughter along the Highway of Heroes," with permission, first published by the *Uxbridge Cosmos*, July 26, 2007.

CHAPTER TEN – KEEPERS OF THE FLAME

page

257 "I took full control": Charley Fox, interview, London, Ontario, May 9, 1991.

259 "my guardian flew with me": Charley Fox pilot's log book, with permission, June 1, 1943.

259 ace Buzz Beurling: ibid., February 15, 1944.

260 "bags of twitch": ibid., March 31, 1944.

260 "bridge too far": ibid., September 27, 1944.

260 "Spit catching up": ibid., October 6, 1944.

261 "another weather reconnaissance": ibid., January 18, 1945.

262 "Fox, that's your last trip": Charley Fox quoting G/C Gordon McGregor, in interview with Steve Benedict, CHCH TV, Hamilton, Ontario, June 1983.

263 "fatalistic view": Charley Fox, interview, London, Ontario, May 9, 1991.

264 crushed me: Ila Fallowfield, member of Canadian Harvard Aircraft Association, phone call to the author, October 18, 2008.

264 "peace on his face": Sue Fox, correspondence, Thamesford, Ontario, June 30, 2009.

267 "seven miles off course": Jan de Vries, Remembrance Day speech at Agincourt Collegiate Institute, Agincourt, Ontario, November 11, 2001.

268 "I'll tell you how": Ted Barris's notes from Agincourt talk, November 11, 2001.

272 "I wanted to be there for you": Ted Barris eulogy for Charley Fox, London, Ontario, October 24, 2008.

Photograph Credits

FIRST SECTION

page

1 Charley Fox with Spitfires then and now—courtesy Fox family; "Attack on Rommel"—courtesy the artist Lance Russwurm

2 I.D. card, medic Barris, Bronze Star citation—author's collection

3 Byng Boys—courtesy Foster's Photography; Gavin McDonald—courtesy Jean Gordon and Judy Wood; Vimy students—author's collection

4 Bruce Evans—courtesy Evans; Anne (Keijzer) Pompili portrait and Pickering College tulip planting—courtesy Pompili

5 POWS in Red Cross truck, *Toronto Star* photographer Jim Lynch—courtesy Jim Lynch Jr.; Charlie Konvalinka—courtesy Dave Konvalinka; Bournemouth Personnel Reception Centre, DND PMR 72-459

6 Ronnie Egan—courtesy Egan; sailor on street—DND Justice Kellock collection; Bob Hesketh—courtesy Stella Hesketh; Don Kerr—courtesty Kerr

7 Dieppe prisoners—DND 1139 LO4; Stephen Bell as POW—courtesy Bell; Stephen Bell and author—author's collection

8 Bill Grant and film stills—courtesy the Ken Bell collection; CFPU group shot—courtesy Chuck Ross

SECOND SECTION

page

1 Jackie Rae— ; Ted Zuber—courtesy Zuber; "Reverse Slope" painting—Ted Zuber CWM 19890328-011, Beaverbrook Collection of War Art, copyright Canadian War Museum

2 Herb Pitts—courtesy Pitts; The Regans—courtesy Dick Loek; Garth Webb and artillery crew—courtesy Mary Lea Bell; Webb inset—author's collection

3 Wilf Pound and Lorne Empey, vets at Juno Beach Centre—author's collection

4 Fred and Don Barnard portraits and Legion of Honour reception—courtesy Fred Barnard; Jim Ronan—courtesy Ronan

5 Roland Pearce—courtesy Darlene Rachkowski (daughter); Hal Merrithew—courtesy Merrithew; Fred Sampson—courtesy Sampson; Walter Schierer—courtesy Schierer

6 Terry Manuel—courtesy Manuel; Tony Burns—courtesy Burns; Jan de Vries—courtesy de Vries

7 Afghanistan patrol and Tarnak Farm bombing site—courtesy Jeff Peck; Brian Decaire—courtesy Shelley Macbeth; Bill Wilson—courtesy Wilson

8 Highway of Heroes bridge—courtesy photographer Pete Fisher; Jeff Peck—courtesy Peck; Charley Fox and author—courtesy photographer Bruce MacRae

Index